SMASHING PUMPKINS

TALES OF A SCORCHED EARTH

by Amy Hanson

First edition published in 2004 by Helter Skelter Publishing
South Bank House, Black Prince Road, London SE1 7SJ
Copyright © 2004 Amy Hanson

Cover design by Chris Wilson@CWGD
Typesetting by Caroline Walker
Printed in Great Britain by CPI Bath

A CIP record for this book is available from the British Library

ISBN 1-900924-68-4

SMASHING PUMPKINS

TALES OF A SCORCHED EARTH

by Amy Hanson

Helter
Skelter
Publishing

CONTENTS

INTRODUCTION

Daedalus, fallen from King Minos' grace, was confined along with his son, Icarus, to the highest tower in the city. From that lofty prison, Icarus could only look out of the windows across the earth and out to the sea, but he could never reach close enough from this great height to grasp anything at all but air.

Daedalus planned their escape – and this was difficult, not only because the tower was so high, but also because Minos controlled all the roads of the land, the passages of the ocean and the lower regions of the air – and for a long time it looked nearly impossible that they would ever escape their prison. Icarus gazed out over the vista before him and dreamed, about the grass and fields and the salty brine of the sea which often wafted up to their keep on the breezes. But what he mostly dreamed about was freedom. Surely a day would come when he could test his thoughts, make reality of his dreams and take part in that which he could only hold at hand's length.

Daedalus, however, was a very smart man, able to reason, and even more artistic still. After careful study, he realized that Minos couldn't reach the skies where the birds soared, and so he set about fashioning wings for himself and Icarus. With feathers from birds that had come to their castle, and thread and warm wax for binding, Daedalus rendered a pair of wings for himself, then crafted an exquisite, smaller set for his beloved son. And Daedalus taught him to fly.

Icarus was bursting with the arrogance and glory of youth, and cast off his prison walls with glee. He swooped in air that was fresher than anything he'd smelled before, dived down to see the trees, their leafy tops and fruit hanging ripe, pregnant from the branches. He cavorted with terns and gulls over the ocean waters, watching as they swung down toward the waves to pluck fishy morsels for dinner. In a moment, the gift of these miraculous wings gave him the daring, the lifeblood, to do anything.

Icarus, though, was in a path of peril far greater than if Minos himself was charging forward with sword and death. The boy had been warned by his father not to fly too low, for the damp rising from the sea would clog his wings, nor to fly too high, where the heat from the sun would melt them.

The momentous day arrived and the pair launched themselves from the tower, and out over the fields, over the copse, and out over the water of the harbour. And as they soared, sunlight glinting on the arc of their wings, the tradesmen stopped to stare, and so did the farmers, and the ploughman and the sailors, at this vision of men who must surely be gods to fly like birds.

As they rose, Icarus, captivated by the sights below him, looked up briefly to see what was above. And, in that moment, all that was below fell away as he felt himself spellbound by the beauty, the radiance and the cocooning warmth of the glowing orb above him. With all thoughts out of his head, with this one intangible so nearly in reach, he ignored his father's words and soared up, up, up as if to touch the very heavens themselves.

It was a sight more beautiful than he'd ever seen. The sun warmed him as he rose, stunned him with its power, and as he swooped higher still, the rays that cut the blue skies became so hot as to scorch his robes, but he was too enraptured to reason. The searing forks in that rare air hove in juts of fire and melted the wax of his wings and they were torn, and Icarus was cast down into the sea. And Daedalus, looking for his son, caught sight of this body, tumbling and rolling without control from the firmament, only to be dashed on the surf below. Heartbroken, he flew down to the water, gathered his son's broken body and buried it beneath the waves, and called the land Icaria.

CHAPTER ONE
SORRY, YOUR PIZZA'S COLD

A great pioneer spirit, leading so that others may follow. Wheat fields and fallow ground, great swathes of land painted in water coloured words in the pages of the Great American Novel. That is the beginning to this story. Novelist Willa Cather captured the spirit of the early heartland, and so did Theodore Dreiser, except he pulled from the sordid affairs of the inner city. William Faulkner and F. Scott Fitzgerald furthered the heady tales of the disillusioned and the passionate, of the haves and have-nots in America. Ernest Hemingway took his people out of their homeland, out of their comfort zone, and put them on completely foreign soil to plumb the depths of the soul. Jack Kerouac brought the beat home, and then William Burroughs filled it with junk. And Raymond Carver taught us all about love.

Set to words, the rise and rot of this country, of the United States of America, unfolds in a rich tapestry – a cautionary tale, filled with sorrow, filled with triumph, filled with vainglorious alchemy. And somewhere in the middle of all those great things lies the truth. That small nugget, overlooked and often forlorn, that rich nut which is the crux of any history, pokes its tough husk through leaves of pages of all those great authors' books.

People's lives, too, can be a mirror and those tomes become a metaphor, for experience, for fortitude, for pushing hard against the grain to prise the very essence of life out of the lives we all lead. The Smashing Pumpkins are all of those things. They rose up in obscurity, peddling a sonic revolution that was just a whisper ahead of its time. They fought for their ideals and for their vision. They rose with raucous glory to place crowns upon their heads. And when those crowns turned to thorns they continued to fight the good fight regardless.

Translate their songs, those melodies and slashes of guitar feedback, and the band's rise and fall into words, and then put those words into the pages of a book, bound with the sweat and blood of their very being to create a story, a history, a mythology – a cautionary tale of the evolution of superstardom, of how the Smashing Pumpkins became their own Great American Novel.

It is the story of how the Smashing Pumpkins came to be, how they placed themselves in the middle of the highway that sped away from the parochial scene of their Chicago hometown, at precisely the same time as the American underground was stretching its limbs and flexing its muscles, and preparing to lift itself, *at last*, out of the countless weird hybrids that had plugged college radio stations for the past half-a-decade, and accepted a future that actually looked *into* the future, rather than at the gristly bones of the past.

It had been an awkward half-decade, after all; a span in which the promise of Punk and the compromise of New Wave were so swiftly co-opted by the MTV mainstream that the options for an alternative grew thinner and less palatable with every fresh turn. The one-chord noisemakers and the dissonant dissidents of the late 1980s, the Sonic Youths and Big Blacks and Swans, did not exist, after all, because they necessarily wanted to; they existed because they *had* to; because it was only by existing that they could stand aside from the crowds of cloying clones that played 'Simon Says' with the Cocteau Twins and the Smiths, and prove there was more to music than simply playing a tune.

There was no form to these ragged insurgents, no single solid shape into which their disparate brands of aural terrorism could be scooped to say, 'now, here is a scene.' Step back from the brutal iconoclasm that, by nature, each of these bands came to share, and it was leakage, not lineage, that lured, from every point of the American compass, the talents that would come to shape the decade that still lay ahead.

From the inner city sprawls of the Atlantic seaboard and the primordial rain forests of the Pacific Northwest, from the deserts of California and the vast, empty plains of the heartland, ideas and ideals slimed like snails' trails into the psyche, to merge with the ghosts of heroes past and the hopes of heroes to come, to create a landscape in which there were no heroes at all, just a porcupine mass of discontent that would tear down the plastic structure that was erected all around.

Jane's Addiction, the Red Hot Chili Peppers, the Pixies, REM, Soul Asylum, Mudhoney, Soundgarden, Ween…the barbarians poised at the gates of a breakthrough in 1989 were those that would indeed breakthrough before 1992, to sweep away the sweet sensations that had jerked to their industry puppet masters for a long, dry decade beforehand. And it was a sign of just how suddenly the walls caved in and the ceiling fell down that the pace-setting tastemakers of the establishment itself didn't even have a chance to slap a label on the uprising. No prettily-packaged Punks or pigeon-holed Power-Poppers, no gaggles of Goths nor flocks of seagulls – in posing an alternative to all of that, the only conceivable summary was just that, 'Alternative.' And, when you asked what it was an alternative to, the answer came back loud and clear. Everything. That was the universe that the Smashing Pumpkins dove into; that was the landscape that they themselves would disfigure.

With all the benefits of hindsight, it was inevitable that the Smashing

Pumpkins would burst into life at the moment they did, a collusion of talent and tension, a backlash of ego and eggshell emotions, as fragile as a newborn, yet resilient enough to ultimately assist in reshaping the entire musical climate of the early 1990s. Born of the ghosts of eras gone by, the morbid Goth, mordant Rock, and the intense palpitations of their Chicago hometown's own history, but nursed by the sweat of their own aspirations and devils, the Smashing Pumpkins forged a path that scythed straight through the marvellous backlash against MTV pap, soft Soul and softer Rock, edging the last hair-metal glam bands right off their hob-heeled boots, at the same time as holding the precocious packs of other period revolutionaries at studied arms length in their own right.

Chicago, located in the upper part of the Midwest, nestles at that dip of water where the vast palm of Lake Michigan reaches one finger into the United States. French Jesuit missionary Father Jacques Marquette and Canadian mapmaker Louis Jolliet were the first Europeans to cross the land that became Illinois in 1673 and, by 1818, the acreage they discovered, and in which so many others then settled, had been transformed from an American territory into an integral state. Chicago, the new land's principle enclave, grew likewise, from fort to plat, from township into a bustling city.

With a history that encompassed the rich tradition of the Indians who lived on the shores of the lake and the Jesuits who tried to convert them, the pioneers who wove west in search of fine land, fresh air and a new life, and the industrialists who brought Chicago into the new era, the city has always teemed with pluck and variety. The ancient forests and wild prairies were long ago gobbled up by subdivisions and strip malls, but still it's a tough breed of folk who weathered the great fire that nearly levelled the city in 1871, who fought through cholera and diphtheria epidemics, then bounced back through the devastating influenza epidemic as the roaring twenties rounded the bend.

Through snow, ice and the crippling heat of summer, through the gangster wars of Prohibition, and the brutal race riots that spanned the mid-1960s, Chicagoans grew with their city until it became a place that was thoroughly cosmopolitan, yet remained unsullied and unassuming through it all, still cracking the slow smile that only exists in the Midwest. The epitome of the staunch American get-up-and-go spirit from the moment it was founded, it is a place where blue-collar rubs shoulders with blue blood, and where both – no matter what their circumstance – are drenched in the icy spray that kicked off the lake during the bitter winters, and serenaded by horns from passing trade ships.

But the city represents more than that for, no matter how vast its history might be, its musical heritage is vaster still.

Chicago was originally all about the Blues. A true workingman's city, Chicago's musical roots first grew up in the spirit of freedom for newly emancipated slaves hiking up from the South along the well worn banks of the mighty Mississippi River. Settling in the northern metropolis was a tangible goal for anyone willing to give a good day's work for an honest day's pay. And, as the speakeasy and bootleg liquor underground supplanted the open supper clubs, Chicago found its natural coloration. Benny Goodman was born there, Louis Armstrong played there, and the grand Savoy Ballroom let everyone dance there. Later, as the music industry set about transforming art to artifice, those august bluesmen would be replaced by more homogenised sounds, and the surface of the streets became as smooth as any city in the union. But still it started with the Blues, and the underground has pulsed with them ever since.

All the great Blues legends gravitated to Chicago, to a city which was not simply insulated, but absolutely isolated from the rat race of New York and the craziness of Los Angeles, yet still lay on the highway that crosses the country, that allowed musicians to find their way. And it isn't too giant a step from the Blues that were the city's birthright, to the searing 60's and 70's rock'n'roll that blistered through sundry Smashing Pumpkins' earliest musical awareness.

The Rolling Stones recorded '(I Can't Get No) Satisfaction' at the legendary Chess Studios in 1965 and never lost their taste for the town. Cheap Trick were hometown heroes long before they became a national phenomenon, spearheading their schlock from Rockford, just to the northwest of Chicago and, when Steve Miller blew in to town before he became the Joker, he came for one thing. 'Muddy Waters was there, and Howling Wolf was there. And Junior Wells and Buddy Guy. It was like graduate school for music.'

Of course, Billy Corgan and the other Smashing Pumpkins wouldn't have remembered that – they were barely a glint in the eye when Miller paid his dues. But that tradition of working hard, putting in time and sweating through the clubs hadn't diminished in the slightest when the next generation opened their eyes and first inhaled the smells of spilled beer, stale smoke and electric dreams.

It was this history that seeped into the pores. It couldn't be helped – the blues man's riffs were pounded into the sidewalks, absorption by proximity to history. Those smells and so many attendant sensations spilled into the 1980s, as Chicago gave birth to bands like Naked Raygun and Ministry, Steve Albini's Big Black and KMFDM. But, though they slaughtered the Blues, they retained its tapestry, embroidered across the black-hearted glitter and sabre-toothed sex that they scattered across the city. Chess was supplanted by Wax Trax!, the Savoy Ballroom by the Cabaret Metro, and the Chicago house scene rose out of the ferment to tower for a moment before hop-scotching to the clubs in the east. And when Billy Corgan first decided to stand up and be counted, he absorbed all this with every fibre.

Born in Chicago on 17 March, 1967, William Patrick Corgan Jr was the son of airline flight attendant Martha, and William Sr, a jazz/blues guitarist who was on the road more often than he was off, gigging alongside future members of Windy City funkers Rufus, and the classical blues-rocking Chicago Transit Authority, before forming his own travelling combo.

Looking back from adulthood, Corgan recalled a childhood that was troubled, filled with the anxiety and disappointments that would ultimately send him into therapy around the time of the first two Smashing Pumpkins albums. Certainly it was a far cry from the sky-high apple pie and baseball diamond dream stereotype that informed the popular image of an American childhood. But it wasn't that unique in an era where the parents of a newly hatched and labelled Me Generation were more concerned with escaping from the cookie cutter lives of their own fifties-era incubation, than erecting solid foundations for those who came after them. Corgan's parents divorced when he was just out of toddler-hood and the boy was shuffled between family members, including his grandmother and great grandmother, before William Sr remarried and set about creating a new family, one that grew to include three brothers – Jesse, Andrew and Ricky.

Corgan and his step-mother, Penelope Anderson, got along well: in time, he came to 'consider her my own mother' and when, as he turned nine, William Sr and Anderson divorced, Corgan went to live with her, in nearby Carol Stream.

Despite the parental tangles, what always remained solidly in the background was his father's music. Corgan remembers that 'there were always people in and out of the house, musicians, and you know, subculture.' But, despite the cartwheeling circumstances that removed him from both of his parents, still he imbibed myriad lessons from his father – including an instinctive understanding of the ups and downside of the music business, the things to do and not to do, and all the to-ing and fro-ing that inevitably comes with the territory. And he rejected it, drawing back from the community of countless friends that seemed so essential to his father's way-of-life, and developing a fair bit of distrust along the way. Never trust anyone, never believe in anything they tell you. 'Only believe in yourself; don't ever put faith in anyone else, because they're just going to fuck with you, or hurt you, or disappoint you.'

These were words that Corgan lived by as a child, and they were words that he took with him to adulthood. At school he felt so removed from the other kids that it was almost natural to assume that he himself was 'a freak.' Later, of course, these same sensations played a major role in the friction that observers insisted so furiously between the members of the Smashing Pumpkins. A typical Type A – it's easier to depend on yourself, to do everything yourself, because then, if you should fly too close to the sun, if your wings should melt and you perceive yourself plummeting, there's no one to blame *but* yourself.

Impressions like these affect many people, creating life goals that aren't simply hard to achieve amid the overall uncertainty of life itself, but which also cement a vital need for control in all aspects of life, and a driving need for perfection that can quickly become as crippling as it is satisfying. But it wasn't Corgan's upbringing alone that cultivated that discontent; society, too, fostered it, from the moment an entire generation of kids was thrust into a world that was being reshaped every day, by politics, by parents, by an eternally shifting cultural landscape that lurched from ruthless selflessness to gluttonous selfishness at the drop of a hat.

His was the first generation so devilishly displaced by the modern era's penchant for divorce that its very soul was driven away from family at the same time as its heart became set on values; the first, too, to be inculcated by the Safety-Fascism of Political Correctness, a creed that has allowed an entire culture to spend so much time worrying what other people are doing (and saying and thinking), that it's forgotten how fucked up it is itself.

Passing through childhood while the United States struggled to make sense of the bloody and senseless battles fought in Vietnam and Cambodia, the children conceived and born in the shadows of a war not their own in the late 1960s hit their teens in time for the onset of American actor-cum-president Ronald Reagan's new discipline of yuppie MacDonald-omics, with all the economic upheavals that entailed. And then, as if that wasn't enough, they entered adolescence in the shadow of the most alarming nuclear showdown to shake the United States since the 1962 Cuban Missile Crisis. Emergency peeled off emergency, from the energy shortage that left the country gasping for breath, to the Iran Hostage Crisis that left its leaders starving for revenge, and onto the Soviet invasion of Afghanistan, in the days when that country was still treated like a poor, defenceless kitten – and that was just the warm up.

As boys-with-toys tensions mounted on every side, America's schoolchildren spent the first half of the 80s being herded into assemblies to watch the films shot when the Bombs were dropped on Hiroshima and Nagasaki in August 1945. With the images of kids their own age running through streets with the skin falling from their faces, and the network television pap of the nuclear war mini-series *The Day After* seared into growing brains, the implication was never 'if' but 'when.'

And as soon as you became reconciled to death by a thousand megatons, AIDS emerged to bring the end even closer to home. From crisis to crisis, the youth of the country ricocheted. It was no way to grow up and out in America. Nothing was safe, nothing was sure and nothing was all you could hope for. Or, once again, 'only believe in yourself; don't ever put faith in anyone else, because they're just going to fuck with you, or hurt you, or disappoint you.' Years later, in May 1999 the *Workers Online Review* would credit Corgan as summing up this 'post Cold War reality' with a line from the song 'Disarm' – 'the killer in me is the killer in you.'

Everyone had these same experiences, everybody searched for their own escape from reality. For Billy Corgan, a self-confessed loner who collected baseball cards, that escape loomed largest within the glammed- and tricked-out theatrics of 1970's rock and roll. From the pseudo Sat-antics of Black Sabbath to the vast symphonic plateaux of the Electric Light Orchestra, from Led Zeppelin to Van Halen and on, of course, to the parochial heroics of Cheap Trick, Corgan sucked it all in. At first, he later admitted, the connection was basic survival, a way of fitting in with the kids at Glenbard North High School, of 'being accepted, and escaping from this mortal, crumby existence.' Music was something he could talk about to make himself feel less lonely, it was something he could listen to, that took him out of himself for a moment.

That view shifted, however, shortly after his 15th birthday, on the day he spotted a guitar in a high-school friend's basement. It was a white Michael Schenker Flying-V guitar and, in a moment of clarity that rushed in on his soul with a velocity that would come to shape almost everything he did, he knew he wanted to play.

No matter that he couldn't hit a note; simply picking over the strings and laying the instrument across his body was a start. It wasn't long before he had an axe of his own, saving his cash then asking his Dad to pick him up a Sunburst finish Les Paul copy. In his own mind, he was already wielding the guitar like a god, like Schenker himself, teasing the girls and thrilling the boys with a phallic extension that spat chords like fire, winged fingers flying up and down the neck. Just playing sounds, making noise, crashing along to the riffs he picked up from Van Halen's first LP – 'the ultimate play-along album,' he calls it today. That was enough.

'I got the feeling that [my dad] didn't want me to play guitar,' Corgan told *Details* magazine. 'He told me later, he didn't think I'd have the dedication and perseverance.'

For most kids, taking up guitar was a teenage rite of passage. But for Corgan, it was the key to Valhalla. Those years spent watching his father play his way through the Midwestern rock scene kept replaying in his head, as he fell in love with the slash of strings, with the scream of feedback, with the universe of sounds that now lay at his very own fingertips – sensations he could still recall when he talked to *Guitar Player* in 1993, and chortled at the memory, 'standing in front of my Bassman stack and feeding back over Black Sabbath records...in key!'

Once he began to play, he found that learning came easy. He started catching live shows, sitting himself in line with the guitarist and watching every move. Occasional articles he wrote for Glenbard North High School's newspaper during his junior year echoed the attraction of guitars that did more than nail down riffs – a white-hot review for the latest Van Halen album, 1984's *1984*, and a spot-on prediction of the next wave of rock superstars: U2, REM and Metallica. But his tastes were never limited to the music that got him in with the jocks. As much as history informs us that Corgan was amped by Sabbath and Van Halen, he was also enthralled by the crop of post-Punk gothic bands that were filtering over from England; the Cure ranked high in his teenaged pantheon, and so did Bauhaus.

Best of them all, though, was New Order, who completed his Holy Trinity from the shattered remains of Joy Division, and who came to town in 1983, to find Corgan already scheming his next move. New Order bassist Peter Hook still remembers meeting the boy, earnestly tagging along to the restaurant with the Chicago show promoter, 'when he was fifteen and thinking of forming a band.' Hook had heard such pledges countless times, every time he met with fans. But something about this kid stuck in his mind with sufficient tenacity that, when the band was formed and making its own way, Hook remembered that meeting with near-paternal clarity.

Refining his style amid so many strong role models, Corgan's most powerful and tangible example remained his father, a man who'd lived the life of which Corgan was dreaming, and, once he realized his son was serious, offered sound advice every step of the way. 'One of the most genius things my dad ever told me was that I should never learn to play like anybody else,' recalled Corgan and suddenly, it was goodbye Eddie Van Halen, *au revoir* Bauhaus' Daniel Ash, and hello Billy Corgan, as he prepared to step away from the mirror in his bedroom and take his first steps out into Chicago.

As the 80s heaved around their own cleavage, only one name mattered on the local club scene – Wax Trax!. Founded in 1974 as a record store in Denver, Colorado, by partners Jim Nash and Dannie Flesher, Wax Trax! relocated to Chicago in 1978, taking over premises on North Lincoln Avenue, on the city's North Side. Nash and Flesher already had their own band, Strike Force, and were soon encouraging their customers to follow the same dream. By 1980, Wax Trax! had become a label, handling Strike Force's own debut EP before it began unleashing others; at the same time Wax Trax! itself was established as Chicago's premiere underground record store.

From there, events cascaded, as the label supplanted the store to become the United States' greatest, and some would argue only, outlet for the growing industrial electro movement. Chicago's pioneer spirit was at work again, as Wax Trax! wrote contracts with handshakes, brokered deals with words and fashioned the hot-house that grew household names out of Ministry, KMFDM and Front 242, as they in turn sprouted from the leather-clad, goth kids who were now too old for guitar heroics, but still too young to look beyond the city limits.

For Corgan, on the outside looking in, music became an all consuming passion, even overriding the traditional American birthright of a college education. 'I used music as an excuse not to go.' One day he went to visit friends at the University of Illinois. Arriving on the campus and wandering through halls and dorms he was suddenly stricken with dread by the realization that 'this is high school times ten... [and] I hated high school. I thought it was this weird biosphere of envy and meanness and jealousy.' Adding to his dislocation was his own appearance. The 'weird haircuts,' and the belief, as he puts it, that 'I was Mr Alternative. I thought, "I cannot handle this, there's no way".'

Instead he landed a job as a pizza delivery boy. 'I thought I'd take on the world,' he told *Live!* Magazine 'and, next thing you know, I was "sorry your pizza's cold Mr Johnson".'

Still he never lost sight of his muse. He was entranced – not necessarily by the music itself, but by the freedoms which it preached so garrulously. His first band, forming in early 1985, as Corgan bore down on his 18th birthday, intended taking those freedoms to the limit, its entire existence hinging, according to Corgan, around another piece of wisdom from his father, to create what he wanted, rather than sitting around and waiting for it to happen. Unfortunately, it didn't happen, but at least the Marked was a start. A lot of people don't even take their ambitions that far.

CHAPTER TWO
TIME HAS COME TODAY

Moody, clattering, gothic and grim, born to play what Corgan succinctly described as 'Hindu-influenced gloom,' the Marked took their name from the strawberry-red birthmarks that both Corgan and drummer Ron Roesing sported; Roesing recalled, "[Billy] was bragging to some girl about what a great guitar player he was. I was standing nearby and we kind of locked horns when he saw me. I have a birthmark on my face, which almost matches the birthmarks on Billy's wrists.'

Completed by bassist Dale Meiners, the trio threw themselves into action, writing songs, working up covers, rehearsing diligently, even recording their very first demos within a few months of getting together. But for all their enthusiasm, the Marked remained remarkably unable to land more than a handful of gigs outside their own rehearsal room. Too many other bands had already glutted the market, and too little about the Marked made them stand out from that crowd.

It was time for a holiday – the Marked marched down to St. Petersburg, Florida, for a little sun and surf, knowing that the city was neither a hot spot of rock'n'roll nor the first stop on any touring rock band's itinerary. Yet, that was what appealed about the place, both before they set out and after they arrived. Amid the swaying palms and sun-soaked beaches, the Marked sensed not only the traditional charms of such a grand getaway, but also the commercial possibilities of an under-whelmed arena – there were few other bands, but plenty of places to play. There was no local scene *per se*, but loads of kids who needed one. The only mistake that the band made was, they didn't ask themselves why that should be. They saw an opening and leaped into it, without wondering why the opening was there to begin with.

Trading vacation for relocation, the Marked bid farewell to Chicago and headed southeast to St Petersburg. Nine months later, they returned to Chicago. Florida was an absolute flop – there were reasons why no other bands had journeyed there before them; there were reasons why the band could stand on the beach at Fort De Soto Park and wonder why nobody else had fashionably big hair like theirs'. The fact that Fort De Soto is located in the south of Mullet Key should have been a tip off, though. Big goth hair has never rubbed comfortable shoulders with the short on top, long in the back styles that was so popular in the late 1980s, (and which one wishes was, but surely wasn't the inspiration for naming that particular land-section).

The fourth largest city in Florida was also a strong contender for the fourth largest black hole in 20th century culture, a metropolis whose most feted 'points of interest' included the first water reclamation plant ever built in the United States, and the tallest suspension bridge in the western hemisphere.

The Marked played no more than a couple of dozen live shows in the area, and they were little more than glorified rehearsals, as they ran through a clutch of songs that frequently outnumbered the audience that heard them. Corgan and Ron Roesing were writing new material furiously – a band that once prided itself on its taste in covers was soon performing no more than a handful, including a raw version of the Byrds' 'Eight Miles High,' and an even rawer take on Jimi Hendrix's 'Fire.' St Petersburg was reflected in a couple of numbers – Corgan composed 'Dali Holds The Hand Of God' after a visit to one of the city's more palatable attractions, a full-fledged Salvador Dali museum. 'I was a Dali fan,' Corgan acknowledged later, 'his work touched me. I think he was a genius and helped me to see the future. He was saturated by culture, and maybe that makes his work so pure, the same as it affects the purity of my work.' Songs that Corgan would return to in later years, 'Sun' among them, also existed in a rudimentary form. Few people, however, heard any of them, and fewer still cared.

Corgan himself, has dismissed these earliest stabs at musicianship with a good pinch of self-immolating humour and the warning that none of it was exactly earth-shattering. 'The band wasn't very good, but it was kind of the same idea behind the Pumpkins, that was loud music and quiet music, trying to put it all together. My signing wasn't very good and blah blah blah.'

The band were not wholly friendless during their months in St Petersburg. Local promoter Jonathan Morrill befriended the Marked early on – Corgan even stayed at his apartment for a time – and seemed intent on furthering their renown. Video footage of the lanky three piece, included in a short, soundless snippet in the Smashing Pumpkins' *Vieuphoria* video anthology, was actually shot by Morrill as part of a video documentary, the succinctly-titled *Video Marked*, that the band hoped would help promote them. In the event, only two copies were ever printed, a master and a back-up and, as the year wore on and the Marked remained unmarked by success, the allure of St Petersburg started to fade.

Returning to Chicago 'with [our] tail between [our] legs,' the band resumed its half-life of rehearsals and hopes. Corgan was living with his father now, and later claimed to have remained 'holed up in my room for about two years,' dishing out time via a handful of nothing jobs that paid enough to keep him in guitar strings and records, and dumb enough to let him keep his mind focused on his 'real' career. Turning himself inwards, he began to write; really write – for the first time honing his skill as a lyricist, putting feelings to rhythm and thought to tempo. And he didn't stop until he was ready to turn those thoughts towards a new sound, and a new era.

The Marked were still meeting up to rehearse, although the departure of Dale Meiners shortly after their return from Florida did nothing to advance their cause. Neither did Corgan's realisation that, when it came to making music, he was a lot more content when he reverted to type, back to his own first formative influences, but corralled by a stack of minimalist pop tones. It was with these icons worn firmly on his sleeve that he cast his eyes about for further musicians who shared a similar passion, and would delight in the pre-post-Punk-cum-Garage noise passion of rawking guitar solos. He found one in Japanese American guitarist James Iha.

Then a member of the local band called Snake Train, a confirmed punk rocker and a graphic arts student at Chicago's Loyola University, James Jonas Iha was born into the predominantly white, upper middle class Chicago suburb of Elk Grove on 26 March, 1968. Like Corgan, he grew up feeling like an outsider, struggling in the cliques and clashes of his Midwestern schools, where his heritage proved a hindrance in a neighbourhood filled with smiling, white middle-American faces.

With his earliest musical education shaped by his older brother Tom, a typical 1970's classic rock aficionado, Iha grew up listening to the only bands that meant anything to large portions of the populace – the Byrds, the Who, Black Sabbath.... That unsavoury education was shattered, however, when Punk and its offspring made their debut on the Chicago streets. All the same, the first gig he ever attended was a Metal festival in Alpine Valley Wisconsin. The 5 June 1982 show should have been even bigger. Rainbow, UFO and Riot were originally scheduled to have been joined by Iron Maiden. They pulled out, and Rainbow, too, curtailed their performance as the icy cold whipped guitarist Ritchie Blackmore offstage after no more than half an hour. They didn't even get a chance to play 'Man On The Silver Mountain' – an omission that so distressed the fourteen year old Iha that he still remembered the disappointment more than a decade later.

There were no such shenanigans at Iha's next gig as he forked over his allowance to catch Billy Idol, the bleached anglo-punk ball of snarl who rose from Roxy Club to Riches in under five years, and reinvigorated rock'n'roll even as Rock itself made paper-doll cut-outs from the angry broadsides of the New Wave.

Iha's musical loves shoved him out of the ball-park. In the early to mid 1980s, in the middle of the United States, you didn't actually need to be weird to be regarded as a pariah; you just needed people to think that you were. And by the time he reached high school, Iha acknowledged that he was well out of the popularity contest. He *was* the 'weird kid'; the one that the other kids avoided in the cafeteria and, when he did hang out with friends, they would all be asked the same question: 'Why are you hanging 'round him? He's weird'. 'I don't think I had a girlfriend the whole time I was there,' Iha reflected. But he did have his own inimitable style. 'I was wearing tie-dye shirts in 1983 when no one else wore them.'

By the time he turned fourteen, though he was certainly still a guitar-playing novice, Iha had formed his first band, the garage tinged Feds. Revelling in influences that reached from the New Wave inflections of the Pretenders and the Clash, to the wholesome Miss America-isms of the extremely youthful REM ('Radio Free Europe' was still hot on the racks), Iha compensated for what he describes as a fairly unremarkable academic career with some truly inspired riffing. And, over time, with fingers getting stronger and playing taking precedence, he found his skill level rising in leaps and bounds.

Another outlet lay in art and graphic design and, after he graduated from high school, Iha enrolled in Chicago's Loyola University, to take a degree in design and become a graduate in fine arts – his other courses included theology, psychology, and 'all these other things that didn't relate to art. But it was good.' Indeed, his ambitions were broad and noble, and they surely pleased his parents. But Iha was still driven by his musical desires and, when a mutual friend, Len, introduced him to Corgan, Iha's scholastic dreams began to drift out of his mind.

Corgan's early relationship with Iha was fractious; the pair misfired as often as they gelled, but there was a ying/yang attraction that both found difficult to resist. Ron Roesing, too, was impressed by the sense of shared destiny that, even this early, sparked between the pair and, in early 1987, the trio came together to record what Roesing describes as their first demo beneath a new band name that he and Corgan were toying with, the Smashing Pumpkins. 'It could have been any vegetable' Corgan reflected as he was asked for the umpteenth time what the significance of such nomenclatural gourd battering might be.

'We changed [our name] to The Smashing Pumpkins in '87,' Roesing recalled. 'There is a demo, the *Nothing Ever Changes* demo, which has James Iha, myself and Billy Corgan on it.' With Corgan gamely switching to bass while Iha stumbled through his own guitar chords, *Nothing Ever Changes* was recorded in the tiny home studio that Corgan Sr had set up, an ambitious effort that saw the trio lay down close to an hour's worth of material, ranging from completed songs ('The Vigil,' 'Breathe' and 'Heart And Cross' among them) and instrumental passages, to a handful of spoken-word selections that Corgan himself later dismissed as 'bad poetry.'

Despite the obvious enthusiasm that fed into *Nothing Ever Changes*, still the band was going nowhere, and Roesing slowly faded out, leaving Corgan and Iha alone to keep planning. A year shy of earning his degree, Iha quit Loyola around the same time as he and Corgan purchased a drum machine and decided that it was time to start working it all out in earnest.

Chicago musician Bob Nolan caught the two-man Smashing Pumpkins at one of the earliest shows they ever played, at Track, on the circuit of Polish drinking clubs that littered the inner city. They were, he shuddered, 'truly awful. I don't remember how I came to even be there, unless my own band was checking the place out before we played the next week, or something. I only remembered them because it was sometime around Halloween, and with a name like Smashing Pumpkins, what else could you expect? And because they had a drum machine that they hadn't quite figured out.'

'I think they played all original songs – there wasn't anything anyone recognised, anyway, and it was just this horrible noise, feedback and clicking, and the singer couldn't decide if he wanted to shout or bleat, so he did both. Nobody paid them any attention, and I don't remember staying for more than three or four songs. I couldn't believe it a year later, when I saw them again.... I couldn't believe they'd actually managed to survive that long."

They had survived because they were driven. Corgan and Iha worked doggedly through 1987, rehearsing, writing songs and gigging when they could. Back at dad's home studio, they made another demo tape, featuring 'Break,' 'Breathe', 'Sun' and 'Screaming,' and that helped land them a few more shows. But, by early 1988, it was becoming painfully apparent that the two guys and a drum machine routine wasn't going to propel them to the big time. It was time to complete the line-up – although they never expected to do so courtesy of the Dan Reed Network.

D'Arcy Wretzky was born on May Day, 1968, in South Haven, Michigan, one state over from Illinois. Growing up alongside sisters Tanya and Molly in a family where creativity was valued in all its manifestations, Wretzky not only listened to a wide variety of music but was encouraged to learn an instrument as well – in fact, she picked up two: oboe and 'classical violin for about nine or ten years,' as well as holding down a place in a local choir.

By the time she'd graduated from the disco days of grammar school to the cool neon of South Haven's LC Mohr High School in the early 1980s, Wretzky discovered for herself the morose joys of the post-punk nation, and her focus began to shift from her classical upbringing. She took up bass guitar, but her first band turned out to be an absolute non-event – according to her almost-hometown newspaper *The Flint Journal*, 'after graduation, she moved to France to join a band that had broken up by the time she got there'; she returned to the US and, by 1988, had moved to Chicago, with little more than her favourite teddy bear for company.

It was there, outside the Avalon nightclub, that she met Billy Corgan – when he barged into a conversation she was having with another friend, discussing the finer merits of the Dan Reed Network. One of the many late-1980's funk-rock-lite bands that dotted the American radio landscape, the Network had just scored a hit with the slightly slinky 'Ritual,' and Wretzky admitted that she rather liked the group. Corgan, on the other hand, considered them in somewhat less flattering light, and made certain his opinions were loudly voiced.

The meeting of the untried bassist and the dogged guitarist is now infamous in the annals of the Smashing Pumpkins' lore, a brittle highlight in the mythology that grew up around the band members as they came together. It's fascinating to consider how, in that mythology, so many seemingly insignificant incidents have so swollen out of proportion that they represent a virtual Bible for the Pumpkin faithful, regardless of how much import they might have for the Smashing Pumpkins themselves.

This meeting, of course, is one of the few that would prove of vital importance, both for the future of the Smashing Pumpkins' music, and that of the group's own internal dynamic. Corgan himself recalled the meeting for *Rolling Stone* in 1995. 'It's the symbolic genesis of our relationship. We see eye to eye, but never quite totally in sync. It just started like that.'

Wretzky agrees that she and Corgan were indeed having quite a heated conversation, as Corgan argued that it was apparent (at least to him) that Portland's Dan Reed Network had been put together by a record company and were, therefore, totally crap, while Wretzky simply countered that they weren't. To which Corgan snarled, he was a musician, and therefore he knew what he was talking about; only for Wretzky to announce that so was she, and therefore.... By the time the smoke settled and all the tangles were combed through, Wretzky had his phone number and promised to call the next day. And then, she said, 'my friends came and tore me away because we were about to come to blows. I wasn't as calm as it sounds.'

Neither had she settled by the time she arrived to meet her prospective new band mates. Corgan recalled, 'the first time she came over to my house, she was so nervous that she couldn't even play...But I thought she was nice and such an interesting person that....' He sent her home with a bunch of songs to learn, and tapes to listen to, and continued to put Wretzky through her, and his paces until she'd nailed every one. 'I listened to his tapes from [the Marked] and I really liked the music they were doing,' she remembered. 'I wanted to be doing it, too. I loved it.'

Clearly there was a spark, one that ignited Corgan and Iha's own strivings, and prompted them into more comprehensive action. As the three began to rehearse together, Wretzky's bass became the beat that supplanted the drum machine, to let the nascent Smashing Pumpkins rock and roll. There was only one minor difficulty. She was already a member of another local band, not only sharing a house with the rest of that group, but also waitressing for a business managed by the group's singer. For her, leaving the group wasn't simply a musical move, it would necessitate an absolute life change. For the next few months, till she figured out what to do, she had no alternative but to 'sneak out of the house to go to band practice with Billy.'

As the trio continued to gel, it quickly became apparent that Wretzky's personality was a strong one, and one to be reckoned with. Always willing to speak her mind, she has often been called the moral voice of the band, and it was her common-sense that helped deflect the rough edges that still sparked between Corgan and Iha – even as she prickled the band with a few edges of her own. Nevertheless, with Wretzky now officially on bass, and Iha on guitar, Corgan was free to do what he'd dreamed of since those days with the Flying-V, and release himself to become the Smashing Pumpkins' frontman – a whirling, manic dervish who handled his lead guitar melodies with the same passion as he spit out his vocals; singer and saint, god and muse – performer.

As a trio, still backed by that damnable drum machine, the Smashing Pumpkins made their official debut on 9 July, 1988, at the Chicago 21 club, a Polish bar located at the corner of Belmont and Austin avenues. Nearly a month later, on 10 August, they repeated the performance at the Avalon, in front of fifty curious onlookers paying $1 apiece for tickets. And, though the performance itself wasn't especially good, it did open the first door for the band, as Joe Shanahan, owner of the more prestigious Cabaret Metro, caught the Smashing Pumpkins' set and invited them to come and play his club. His only stipulation was they had to drop the drum machine first.

The Cabaret Metro, on 3730 North Clark, was among the crown jewels of the Chicago club scene. Built in 1926 as a Swedish Men's Club, the space metamorphosed into a theatre for stage plays. During the 70s, the theatre, like so many others across the country, became a popular gay bar and club before it was re-launched as a live music venue – the Cabaret Metro – in 1982.

With the Smart Bar downstairs for dancing, and the upstairs featuring one night of unsigned local bands every week, the venue alternated merrily between a myriad of big name acts that were passing through town, and up-and-coming local kiddies without deals. Even a lowly support slot at the Metro would push the Smashing Pumpkins up the local pecking order and, over the next couple of months, they chased every 'drummer available' lead they could find, until, at last, they were led to Jimmy Chamberlin.

Although Chamberlin had been gigging professionally for years, he had spent the summer and autumn of 1988 working with his brother, building custom-designed kick-ass houses, and helping out in a studio with his friend Dave Zukowski. It was Zukowski who put him in touch with Corgan, after hearing that the Smashing Pumpkins were 'looking for a drummer for one show at the Metro.'

One show suited Chamberlin. He'd been in the audience at their Avalon show and hadn't been impressed. Besides, he had sworn to himself that he was off the road for a while, to recover from years of touring the backwaters. After meeting with the Smashing Pumpkins, however, he had to admit that, at the back of his mind, there lurked one nagging doubt, a sense that the apparently mismatched trio of Corgan, Iha and Wretzky had *something* indefinable going for them. And, as they rehearsed in readiness for the looming Metro show, now set for 5 October, Chamberlin found that he was hooked.

Three years older than his band-mates – he was born in Joliet, Illinois, on 10 June 1964 – Jimmy Chamberlin grew up in the shadow of an older brother who himself was an accomplished young drummer, and a clarinet-playing father. Listening to records as a child, he studied the style of all the greats, from Blues to Swing and rock'n'roll, before setting his sights on Jazz. By the age of nine, Chamberlin had officially begun his formal musical education, taking lessons from the great Charlie Adams, himself a Chicago legend whose career had seen him study with the Minnesota Symphony's Marve Dahlgren, before forming his own band, Chameleon. Later, he relocated to Los Angeles, where he joined new age guru Yanni in a partnership that covered myriad albums and massive world tours. In the meantime, though, he passed his skill and tips on to Chamberlin, marvelling at a student who took his time at the kit very seriously, often drumming after school and 'sometimes play[ing] until 9:00.'

After Adams and Chamberlin parted ways, the boy moved on to a teacher who initiated him in Big Band era beats, before spending time with Soca and Samba. By the time he was in high school, Chamberlin had more formal education, and had been exposed to more music, than any of his peers. Indeed, while his musically-inclined classmates were content to simply bash and crash in the high-school band spirit, Chamberlin had graduated to an already functioning garage outfit, the Warrior Band, playing out in clubs on the weekend and pulling in a pay check. Screw school dances! By the time Chamberlin had been on the circuit for a couple of years he knew that 'music was something I was going to do for the rest of my life.'

Although he received an enormous amount of support from his family, there was still an emphasis placed on education, and Chamberlin put in a year-long stint at Northern Illinois University before permanently leaving academia behind for music – or, more specifically, polka. With the Warrior Band having fallen by the wayside, Chamberlin joined Eddie Carossa's Polka Party, an act that proudly appeared on local television, to the delight of the area's vast Polish community.

From there it was on to Razor's Edge, and it was while he was with that band that he played a gig with local heroes J.P. & The Cats. With horns, and vocals galore, that band – which numbered somewhere around ten musicians – played 'everything, from Jazz to "Wipeout." I was totally blown away.' Quitting Razor's Edge on the spot, Chamberlin joined the Cats full-time, remaining on board for the next three years until finally, he began to burn out. He left the band in early summer 1988 to recharge his batteries, but the task was completed a lot quicker than he expected. Barely six months into his semi-retirement, he was back in a band, adding his own unique flair to the Smashing Pumpkins' aspirations.

Indeed, it was Chamberlin's jazz-style drumming that so excited Corgan, long before he came to appreciate the foundation that it laid for his own music's development. Chamberlin was always, in his own words, 'a technique drummer,' eschewing click track drumming for the sound let loose by his own personality and style. For him, his playing was 'an emotional representation of somebody through music' – a precisely prescient echo of all that Corgan wanted to do through his lyrics, and a mirror that was about to refract the Smashing Pumpkins into a panorama of their own.

The Cabaret Metro gig itself passed off well; the Smashing Pumpkins were the first band on, opening up for October's Children and Love & Addiction, with a set that included 'She,' 'Under Your Spell' and the early-era crowd pleaser 'Spiteface,' which had been knocking around in one form or another since the Marked. Certainly Joe Shanahan was impressed enough to ask the band back at the end of November, by which time the Smashing Pumpkins, now confirmed as a solid quartet, had had time to work up an all-new live repertoire, that ended with what must have seemed a wholly self-fulfilling prophesy, a cover of the Chambers Brothers' 'Time Has Come Today.'

CHAPTER THREE
YOU AND ME AGAINST THE WORLD

With Chamberlin in and the drum machine out, the Smashing Pumpkins entered a new era in a confident, if still tentative style. Chamberlin remembers that 'the band came together very slowly. What we did is, we got together and said "let's give this a try because Billy's a good songwriter...we've all got a general direction...we all want to play our own music so let's see what's going on".'

Sequestered within their tiny practice space, with only a three-legged cat for company, Corgan would put his bandmates through their paces while 'ranting,' as Wretzky put it, about how the Smashing Pumpkins were set to become 'the biggest band on the planet, up there with the Stones and Led Zeppelin and the Beatles.'

Though the lead-up may have been slow, Corgan's vision was finally crystallizing – musically and, though he scarcely thought in such terms at the time, temperamentally, too. Almost from the get go, as people passed their rehearsal space or dropped by their dressing room, there bubbled a sense that all was not happy in the Smashing Pumpkins family: that argument, not ability, fuelled their chemistry, that dysfunction, not determination was all that held them together. But how dysfunctional were they really?

So much has been hinged on this question that it almost seems redundant to ask it. It makes for good copy, and that makes good news. But, look forward from the incarnation of the Smashing Pumpkins in 1988 through to the end of the 1990s – these four musicians stayed together, more or less, for nearly ten years, living in each other's company more often than not. How dysfunctional could they really be? Corgan himself coyly put the question to rest after hearing it one too many times, 'I don't see how a dysfunctional band could release eighty songs in five years.'

That tally of those songs would come in the future, of course; in the beginning, there was tension as the band rehearsed and hashed through riffs and lyrics, attempting to define their sound, and then place it in context of all that was happening around them. Their opening salvo, colliding goth spangle with glitterdust and a crash of classic rock guitar that cascaded out of bounds, was itself a fractious combination; one that only the deepest determination could pull of successfully, one that demanded the absolute attention of everybody involved. A straying thought during a band conversation, one misplaced idea in the heat of a rehearsal, and the entire process would break down not because the others hated it, but because the thought or idea did not belong, and the Smashing Pumpkins themselves were still learning to read each others' cues and ideas.

Musically, the group had already elected its icons, though few of their imprimaturs would show through just yet – in conversation, Billy Corgan's own eyes lit up the brightest at the mention of Bad Brains, the all-black Washington DC hardcore band whose training rose out of their jazz-fusion band background, whose mindset was shaped by their Rastafarian beliefs, and whose music was an unholy collision of social injustice and musical rebellion.

As with so many bands of their immediate musical ilk, Bad Brains were at their peak while Corgan was still at school – though they'd marched on through the remainder of the decade, and had just released a new live album. But the promise of their earliest recordings had never survived their first few singles, and, when Corgan thought of his own band's debt to Bad Brains, it was less their music than their promise, their savage refusal to be bound by Rock's rules, that he most breathlessly wanted to recapture.

It was the uniqueness of what the Smashing Pumpkins were trying to achieve that first brought them to local attention; that and the noisily twisted psychedelic pop'n'roll that kicked sand in the face of every local band who'd been paying their dues round the Chicago clubs for years. The Smashing Pumpkins themselves insisted that they were flying completely blind, without any firm sense of a future direction; Corgan declared, 'I'd always wanted to be in a rock band, but at the time when we started, I was afraid to play rock music because it wasn't very much in vogue.' He persevered out of stubbornness and a sense of grim self-belief – he was right, the rest were wrong, and the fact that he was going to make that point in the land of Wax Trax! and Thrill Kill Kult only amplified his determination to ensure he did it right.

The first opportunity to do that came completely out of the blue. On 16 November, the Smashing Pumpkins made their radio debut with a gig broadcast live by local WNUR; days later, out of Joe Shanahan's growing fascination with what the Smashing Pumpkins represented, they were offered an opportunity that, for a band whose profile was still barely a nose above sea-level, was little short of the gig of a lifetime – a sweet deal that wouldn't simply serve the Smashing Pumpkins the city on a platter, but would also open their eyes to the wider world, and give Corgan, at least, a mark on the barometer of where things were headed. It would also have repercussions that would, in part, force the Smashing Pumpkins to cast their eyes beyond the city limits a little more quickly than perhaps they had intended.

Playing their fourth ever gig as a true quartet, they opened for Los Angeles glam poppers Jane's Addiction on 23 November at the Cabaret Metro. It wasn't a gig they'd lobbied for – so far as they knew, the support for the show had been wrapped up weeks before. But something had gone wrong and when Shanahan called them there wasn't even enough time in which to get nervous.

It is impossible to overstate the importance of Shanahan's support, as Corgan told *Spiral Scratch*. 'Joe said "this is important, this is different," and the fact that he'd never done that before...and he runs the Metro, so not only does he see every band in Chicago, but he sees every band passing through. Every band touring, on the way up, plays the metro, and he's dealing with all this. It's a great club, a great room, there's all these people around, and he turns around for the first time and says "here's a band I really believe in".'

Now his belief was to be given its greatest test yet.

Jane's Addiction were a vital part of how Alternative music was shaping up at the end of the decade. With house music and Dee-Lite dance on the one side of the mainstream musical divide, and nice adult Rock on the other, the glammed out, punked up glitter of Perry Farrell's Jane's Addiction contradicted the title of their *Nothing's Shocking* LP completely, by suggesting that everything had the potential to be very shocking indeed, as Farrell set out to sublimate the centreline, using shock and roll to create controversy, to spark discussion, and to completely rearrange the way modern America thought about music.

Through the raining axis of strident guitars, and the screech of his own caterwauling tonsils, through the feathers and rimmed eyes of a ruined Los Angeles-after-dark, Farrell used his voice and his image – his *performance* – to create a post-modern art rock that rendered mere opinions utterly invalid. Whether you hated Jane's Addiction with every fibre of your soul, or worshipped the very ground Farrell trod on, there wasn't any question that his band was making an enormous impact – years later, as Billy Corgan reflected on the contemporary bands that helped to shape his view, Perry Farrell and Jane's Addiction certainly resonated. Indeed, Corgan would continue to reiterate that fervour, reflecting on the strides the Smashing Pumpkins would grow to take by categorizing their earliest days as 'a psychedelic Led Zeppelin/Jane's Addiction clone that couldn't write songs.' Harsh perhaps, but probably pretty astute at the time.

Prior to the Chicago gig, however, Corgan was only marginally aware of the band. He'd noticed their debut album, and had heard *Nothing's Shocking* but, even as Jane's maintained their commercial onslaught, Corgan felt perplexed by their success and disorientated by their sound. Farrell's style, he said, 'didn't hit me right...his voice was so whiny-weird.'

All that would change at the Metro. Hanging around to see Jane's Addiction's set in the flesh, Corgan was bowled away and, in one white hot flash, revised his opinion completely, seeing beyond the whine to the droll camp and sexy rock and soul, and into that somehow sickening whipsmart smarminess that so unnerved America's parents even as it sent their children shimmying into ecstasy. Farrell was the consummate showman and, through Corgan's newly opened eyes, Jane's Addiction were suddenly revealed as 'a culmination of sex, perversion, love and hate. For two songs you'd be mesmerized, and the next you'd think 'God, what a dick!'" And that might have been very true. But, for Corgan, both 'Bad Brains and Jane's Addiction set the tone for what we wanted to do live.'

Corgan took in the set, absorbed the band's visual impact, drank in their sonic assault and stored it all up to chew over later. And it made for a hearty meal. Revised and recast into the Smashing Pumpkins' own ethic, many of the very same qualities that Jane's unleashed during their own live shows would be dancing in the shadows when the Smashing Pumpkins commenced their decade-long series of tours. Interestingly, too, some of the very things that turned Corgan off and then onto Jane's Addiction, some of his strong feelings toward Farrell's onstage persona, would resurface during the Smashing Pumpkins' own tenure, as very similar words would be used by fans and fallow friends to describe Corgan's own live performance. But, let's make this very clear, the Smashing Pumpkins were not to be any hollow Jane's clone. Corgan had something else in mind entirely – something that circumstance would now force him to hasten.

For as long as the Smashing Pumpkins were trolling around the Chicago club scene, playing their songs and not making any waves, the glare of – as Corgan once called them – 'the boy's club of bands' who'd been grinding away at the outskirts for years, passed them by entirely. The Jane's Addiction gig, however, brought them screaming into prominence, recast them from fellow strugglers on the lowest rung of the ladder to snotty upstarts who'd done nothing to merit such glowing attention – such a peach of a gig. The Smashing Pumpkins had scarcely stepped out of their rehearsal room and already, they'd gone too far.

Corgan, of course, had nothing but disdain for the cacophony of whines and bitching that descended upon the band's head. The Jane's Addiction show was just one gig, in one city, and it would be forgotten tomorrow – if people shut up about it. But, if they didn't shut up: he'd milk their jealousy as thoroughly as he'd milked the applause of the audience that evening. His critics, he sniffed, were simply bands that wanted 'nothing more than to be popular in Chicago. It doesn't matter that they couldn't get arrested anywhere else. To me that's not success.' In 1992, he told *Spiral Scratch* magazine, 'y'know, I had a hundred people tell me "you'll never make it out of Chicago!"'

And besides, he explained elsewhere, plenty of unknown bands get good breaks. 'That doesn't necessarily mean that people will like them, does it?'

Later, Corgan would acknowledge that perhaps he did have a hand in fostering the acrimony that people perceived between the Smashing Pumpkins and the rest of the Chicago music community, that maybe there was some truth to the accusations of a bristly stand-offishness, and a demented drive to succeed. But he also pointed out that there had never come a time when the Smashing Pumpkins felt a part of the Chicago music scene, so why should they feel bad about being expelled from it? 'No one from the local community ever came and talked to us,' he reflected, 'and I was afraid to talk to anybody.' Besides, who was it that was doing most of the complaining? Bands that had been playing 'unsigned talent' nights at the beginning of the decade, and would still be playing them at the end, a tightly wound community who, Corgan disparaged, 'go way back to '83 or something. It's all so stupid and petty.'

Indeed it was, and Corgan had neither the time nor the inclination to throw himself into the fray. Neither did the rest of the Smashing Pumpkins. If Chicago thought they were too big for their boots, they'd simply find a different shoe shop – one whose tastes and range weren't so hog-tied by the morals of communal mediocrity. He'd never made any secret of his ambitions, after all – the Smashing Pumpkins wanted success, and they were going to go hell for leather to acquire it. And it didn't matter whether it was 'biggest rock god in the world' success, or simply a red-hot-rail out of Chicago, that would allow them to transform themselves into something that would endure across the country, in the underground market, in the mainstream, and in the brewing beginnings of the new Alternative scene.

In later years, of course, with that ambition fulfilled, Corgan would come to appreciate exactly what it was that kept so many bands tied to their home city's apron strings, the knowledge that gaining success necessitated losing many of the joys that had made it worth attaining in the first place, the sheer pleasure of getting up on stage and just letting rip, knowing that nothing was at stake.

That, of course, is a dichotomy that has played itself out since time immemorial, as a band rises from nothing to become something for everyone, and suddenly discovers, as Corgan reflected, that they are abruptly 'expected to deal with a lot of people, and people with very high standards.' Still, the initial goal readily (and regularly) overrides whatever downsides remain so far on the horizon as to be all-but unimaginable. In the beginning, it was thrill enough simply to get up on the stage, to tune up and play, to ensure that the music matched the mood within, and to have it resonate with everyone who paid the price of admission. And, for all the other failings that success might ultimately have created within the Smashing Pumpkins, that creed, in particular, would never slip out of sight.

From the first show at the Avalon to their last ever gig at the Metro, Corgan believed the most important thing was that the audience 'get it' – and, if they didn't – fuck them. If the Smashing Pumpkins' were playing well, the night was on fire. But, if they felt out of sync, then the shows could go screaming straight into the realms of absolute farce, with Corgan the manic ringmaster who made sure that it plumbed the necessary depths. He viewed each Smashing Pumpkins gig as his, and the band's own territory and, if they weren't in the mood to wow the audience, too fucking bad for the audience.

As far as Corgan was concerned, they could just leave and, when he looked back on that penchant for tearing a show to pieces, he realised not only was that actually 'a major breakthrough,' it was one of the little slices of Pumpkinhood that, again, forced the group outside of the everyday Chicago circuit. 'If [a gig's] bad, so what? Let it destroy itself, but make something of the moment.' That would become the band's phrase to live by.

Through the last months of 1988, in the backlash-framed wake of the Jane's Addiction show, the Smashing Pumpkins focused on getting further gigs under their belts, and earning enough cash to take the show onto a wider road. Gig after gig unrolled before the band's feet, as they lugged their equipment from club to club. No matter that, as their workload increased, so did the resentment against them. Bob Nolan spoke for many musicians when he snarled, 'the problem with the Smashing Pumpkins was, early on they landed a few good breaks, and they didn't let people forget it. But they didn't get gigs because people actually liked them. They got gigs because so many people were talking about how much they *didn't* like them. That was what was so funny about it in the end, the more people put down the Smashing Pumpkins, the more other people would go to see them, to find out what all the fuss was about. If you want to turn it around completely, it was the classic "local boy makes good" in reverse. They became the biggest band in Chicago by being the most disliked.'

Nolan admits that his opinions are maybe not the most objective; that no band can exist on bad vibes alone. But, even if a mere handful of outsiders elevated the Smashing Pumpkins to the status of pariahs, still the group themselves embraced that reputation, and used the hatred to advance their own cause, and heighten their own sense of purpose. You and me against the world.

CHAPTER FOUR
GOD BLESS OVERKILL

As the band's experience began to pile up, Corgan continued working to define himself as a writer. All that gigging, all that playing, all that living-breathing-eating the band was fuelling a creative burst that saw new songs enter the repertoire every time the group came together to rehearse. It had also, finally, dumped sufficient funds in the coffers that the quartet could afford to record a demo, and find out for itself what it was truly capable of.

Shortly before Christmas 1988, the Smashing Pumpkins booked themselves into the local Reel Time Studios with engineer Mark Ignoffo, for the first of what would be several open-ended sessions conducted over the next two years. This particular demo was not cut for purely selfish reasons, however. Chicago entrepreneur Barry Waterman's indie Halo Records label was planning a compilation LP of local talent for release the following year, *Light Into Dark*. The band had been invited to contribute. Waterman had been keeping tabs on the Smashing Pumpkins since early 1988, when his friends Tim and Marianne first mentioned them to him.

The label itself was named for a club hit scored by another of Waterman's projects – he was the manager of the band Ghost Swami, whose own talents would naturally be highlighted on the collection. So, too, would Gold September, the Poster Children, Seven Letters and the Price Of Priesthood.

Marianne worked with Wretzky at Dillinger's restaurant on Lincoln Avenue in Chicago, up the street from the Biograph Theater, where gunman John Dillinger met his bullet-riddled end in 1934. According to Waterman, '[Marianne] mentioned that maybe I could manage them...I replied with "well, maybe, but I can't just manage any old band – they have to be talented and we have to have a business relationship," or some such ridiculous drivel.' Drivel or not, Waterman and Wretzky did meet, and things flowed on from there. The Smashing Pumpkins' inclusion on *Light Into Dark* was the immediate consequence.

With so many bands represented and so many sounds to keep moving on the album, it was a challenge for Waterman to maintain a consistency as he stroked his baby into life. Both Poster Children and Ghost Swami recorded at the Chicago Recording Company with producer Iain Burgess, himself long established on the Midwest scene, producing primal punkoid noise for several of the region's heavy hitters (including Jawbox and the Didjits). He was also engineer for producer Steve Albini's Big Black debut album, 1987's *Atomizer*.

Seven Letters, meanwhile, was essentially a studio band produced by New Wave veteran Jeff Murphy, of the Shoes, and so on. Unlike the straightforward compilations that represented so many other city scenes of the day, where the focus would be on just one or two genres, *Light Into Dark* was a random sampling of all that Chicago's up and comers had to offer – indeed, its very title reflected the problems that confronted Waterman as he tried to groom the resultant tapes. He wound up linking them by mood alone – a light side, and a dark side. The Smashing Pumpkins would appear on both, with two songs drawn from their first Ignoffo session: 'My Dahlia' fell on the *Light* side; 'Sun,' with a nice oxymoronic twist, landed on the *Dark*. Corgan himself added to the group's burgeoning enigma of Pumpkinhood by refusing to allow his lyrics to be printed on the sleeve. Instead he offered up a German quote that translated as 'we all must bear much sorrow to enter God's kingdom.' Corgan would continue reluctant to publish his lyrics several years to come.

Light Into Dark was released with an official blow-out at Cabaret Metro on 17 March – coincidentally, Billy Corgan's birthday. Each of the five performing bands played a thirty minute set in front of a six hundred strong crowd that had braved both a freezing sleet storm and the drunken St. Patrick's Day revellers on the streets outside. A second release party followed in nearby Champaign-Urbana shortly after, taking over Trito's Uptown pizza place for a show headlined by the Poster Children, but with the Smashing Pumpkins at least turning in a fine enough showing that journalist Jim Sonnenberg, of the *Daily Illinois* newspaper, felt duty-bound to mention them. They also impressed WXRT DJ Johnny Mars sufficiently that he aired 'My Dahlia' on his *Big Beat* show. It was the first time the Smashing Pumpkins had ever been heard on commercial radio.

Light And Dark then returned the Smashing Pumpkins to the Chicago airwaves, as WZRD Radio broadcast an entire performance live – an album's worth of songs that included a reprisal of 'Sun' and a cover of Neil Young's 'Cinnamon Girl.' But it was with a particularly tusky version of 'Rhinoceros' that the Smashing Pumpkins truly excelled, one of the earliest-ever performances not only of the roaring guitar melody that Nirvana would soon be insisting smelled like teen spirit, but also a prescient marker of just where the Smashing Pumpkins themselves would be in a year's time.

Light Into Dark, however, was not progressing so gallantly. Although the buzz that surrounded its contributors had already garnered a fair amount of interest, and Waterman blanketed the area with advertising and promotion for both album and bands, financing for the record's launch remained tenuous and, though the album did make its way safely into local stores during the spring of 1989, hopes that it would serve as some sort of launch pad for the bands that took part were doomed to fall below expectations. No major labels came calling in search of its makers and Waterman himself ultimately conceded that the enterprise never did become the stepping stone he'd hoped it would be. Nevertheless, the project was 'a great idea, and I'm proud to have been able to have produced a great record and a small piece of history.' (After more than a decade out of print, Waterman's Halo records website finally reissued *Light Into Dark* on CD in 2002.)

Early 1989 also saw the Smashing Pumpkins back in Reel Time, again with Mark Ignoffo and Corgan producing, for their longest, and most productive session yet. Working through songs and drafts, the band rehearsed and recorded nearly twenty songs, many of which would be reworked for inclusion on *Gish* – early variants of 'Daydream,' 'Egg' and 'I Am One,' as well as two distinctly different versions of 'Honeyspider' and 'Rhinoceros' – one marked by a wicked Ignoffo organ solo, the other already remarkably close to the song's eventual incarnation on *Gish*. 'Bury Me,' 'Bye June,' 'Daughter,' 'Psychodelic' and 'Stars Fallin',' too, would appear on the Smashing Pumpkins' early cassette tape demos, and surface on various bootlegs much later on, with the latter appearing alternately as 'Stars Fall In' and 'Stars Falling.'

Although the band had already been selling home-made cassettes of songs at their early gigs, the *Moon* cassette, as they dubbed the end result, was a major step forward. Originally intended only as a demo reel for the band to use to snare a record deal, it was also pressed into service as the Smashing Pumpkins took their first steps at marketing and self promotion – no less than five hundred cassettes were manufactured, with costs cut down by the band members' patiently handwriting the nine song track listing.

It was a strong beginning, and indeed would lead to greater glories. Throughout the remainder of 1989 the Smashing Pumpkins gigged only infrequently. However they wrote and rehearsed constantly to ensure that every time they did step out in public they were even stronger and even more captivating than the time before. By the dawn of 1990, the group had decided that releasing their first single would be the logical next in the series of small steps that they were taking. They'd etched some good grooves, and now it was time to put them to even better use.

Culling two tracks, 'I Am One' and 'Not Worth Asking' from the Reel Time Studios sessions, the band took the tracks to local entrepreneur Mike "Potential" Po, and teamed up with him for a 45 through his own local indie label, Limited Potential – home, throughout its six year lifespan, to some of the Chicago area's most eye-catching bands: Screeching Weasels, Jim Ellison, the Poster Children and the Faith Dealers who had all linked with the label in the past, although, by the time the Smashing Pumpkins got in touch, Limited Potential was very much taking its first steps away from the fate that its name seemed to suggest. The recording studio where Po had hitherto been working had recently closed and he had decided to launch the label as a full-time occupation – in the past, it was as much a hobby as anything else.

Po lived in the same apartment building as Iha; which finally solved a mystery that had been haunting Po for some time – who on earth could be blaring Die Kruezen at all hours of the day. However, it was Poster Children manager Chris Corpora who, when Corgan first began talking about releasing a single, made the initial introduction.

The Smashing Pumpkins did not initially impress Po. He had received one of their early demos, and caught them again on *Light Into Dark*, and quickly wrote them off as little more than a 'quasi-jangly pseudo-psychedelic average kinda 1989 band.' With an uncanny echo of Billy Corgan's conversion to the Jane's Addiction cause, however, the group's live show knocked him out. A close friend, Amy, was organising that year's Loyola Radio Conference, and booked the Smashing Pumpkins into one of the shows. Po found himself 'tricked' into seeing them, and came away with all his past distaste wiped away, by the band itself, but most of all by Corgan.

Recalling the event on his mikepo.com website, he enthused, 'I'm mostly referring to his guitar playing. Now, don't ever accuse me of being any sort of fan of Yngwie Malmsteen-esque histrionics, or under any sort of impression that talent=star power – frankly, I can give a fuck about talent, as long as I'm entertained. But, still, it was the guitar playing. Instead of the self-indulgent psych twaddle I expected the then-paisley-adorned Smashing Pumpkins to sludge through, Billy came out and laced the admittedly psych/gloom-ridden set with his (by 1998, trademark) Brian May-interpreting-stolen-Aerosmith-licks HEAVY guitar playing. And I just didn't see it coming. I was taken aback, basically. Even better, he played with authority, without histrionics, in a way that essentially struck a nerve in me that was almost, um, scary.'

Looking back, Po recognised instinctively something that it took a lot of music critics several years to figure out – an understanding of what could be described, for want of a better term, as the international language of Rock, an awareness that critical acclaim, street smart hipness and platinum success are not the same thing as being a great band. Whether a group is scratching out primordial sludge from the riff-laden vat of early 1970's Blues Rock, or conducting chemistry experiments in some precocious art school rehearsal lab, great rock and roll music knows neither chronological nor charisma-laden boundaries. The Smashing Pumpkins were not hip, were not glib, and certainly did not dress for success. But inflamed by the righteous spirit that blazed within their breasts, they were as 'classic a rock band' as one could hope to encounter.

There was only one glimmer of contemporary awareness in their performance. A sharp jangle of guitars, a wistfulness in their drone and a certain fetching floweriness to their sleeves – the Paisley Underground was in full bloom at that time, and somebody had obviously been paying attention to it.

Although modern history has all but relegated the movement to a blink-and-you'll-miss-it sideline, the Paisley Underground served up a rich enough dish that it informed an entire crop of American youth. Named for the 1960's retro shirts and the unrelenting obscurity of the majority of its west coast practitioners, Paisley Underground was a backward-looking musical movement that flourished in the late 1980s. Occasionally looking forward through releases by the Rain Parade and Dream Syndicate, but for the most part content to offer up a whimsically psychedelic reflection of the more intense miasma that would soon be delivered by such British bands as My Bloody Valentine, Paisley's grasp on the late 1980s was tenacious enough for several bands subsequently to emerge as frontrunners in the grunge-and-thereabouts arena, initially dampening their feet (and furnishing their wardrobes) in the Paisley waters.

Po and the Smashing Pumpkins quickly came to an agreement and the initial pressing of 'I Am One,' just five hundred copies, was released in early summer 1990. Almost the entire pressing was passed on to Pravda, an indie-minded record store on Southport Avenue that often hosted live-in-store appearances – the Smashing Pumpkins included. It lay just a few steps away from the Cabaret Metro, and Po was staggered when he learned how fast the record was selling – ten copies in the first week, then twenty; by the end of the month, Pravda had shifted more than one hundred and fifty copies, and 'I Am One' was on its way to becoming the highest-selling local release the tiny shop had ever seen.

Quickly, Limited Potential pressed up another thousand copies and widened its distribution net. Soon, the same story was being told by shops as far afield as Madison, Milwaukee, Iowa City, places that the Smashing Pumpkins had never even played. Of course compared to the kind of figures the mainstream music industry flourished upon, such numbers were pitiful. But for a label of Limited Potential's size, and the Smashing Pumpkins' own status as virtual unknowns, it was akin to topping the chart.

But it was more than that. 'I Am One' was the song that provided the pivot point, the first opportunity for people outside the local scene to gain their first real taste of the Smashing Pumpkins. With Chamberlin's light drums – 'monster thunder tubs' as Mike Po describes them – keeping everything pinned down hard, those die-hard hipsters combing the indie record racks in search of the next big thing could not help but be titillated by Wretzky's eclectic bass and the dual guitar assault of Corgan and Iha, scything in and out of classic guitar solos with the ease that most people tie their shoes.

It was a marvellous, hideous, sexy single, and so unlike anything else that was rolling across the underground of the day; sleeker and lighter, sophisticated and subtle, immediately urgent and instant and resonant. From the moment stylus touched wax, with nuance of grace and a smattering of goth overtones, the Smashing Pumpkins sieved all their experiences through a rock machine and emerged with what one critic drooled was nothing less than 'an extension of everything that has gone before.'

Corgan's lyrics too, confessional and urgent, brutal and raw, untried and forceful, had a dynamism that had scarcely dared show its face in a decade, peeling back to the days when singers were not ashamed to speak of their own selves, rather than disguise their emotions beneath a cold, supine whine.

By 1990, however, the very term 'confessional writing' had long since been disgraced by the stream of so-called 'West Coast'-anchored songwriters who could think of nothing more fascinating than their own inner-child, although, seeking precedents for Corgan's lyrical notions swerves the listener sharply around those tormented troubadours, and into the more literary pastures that flourished in the United States during the 1950s; the half-crazed sacro-sanctimony that percolated out of the cultural and political witch-hunts of the age, and found voice in a group of poets that counted W.D. Snodgrass, Robert Lowell, Anne Sexton and Sylvia Plath among its ranks. Indeed, the entire confessional poetry genre stemmed from Snodgrass' seminal 'Heart's Needle,' the keynote poem of his 1959 Pulitzer Prize winning volume, and a verse that not only turned the direction in which contemporary poetry was moving, but also had direct influence on a generation of poets.

Most notable among them was Lowell, described by Sexton biographer Diane Wood Middlebrook as 'the most influential poet in Boston, perhaps in America, at the time.' In breaking the long-cherished taboo of using a first person voice as muse, Snodgrass changed the face of 20th century prose and poetry and, even as his own style moved markedly toward a more formal pitch and treatment, the seeds had been sown.

With the proliferation of the confessional voice in all artistic endeavours, it was finally acceptable to look deep within the sickest psyche to mine lyrical gold, a trend that bled effortlessly into the then-contemporary rock'n'folk arena, from the mid-decade impact of Bob Dylan and Leonard Cohen, through to John Lennon's purging embrace of Arthur Janov's primal scream therapy in the lead-up to his first solo album.

There, of course, the notion soured, as the 1970s bred a veritable glut of soft AOR miasmics, the Laura Nyros and James Taylors of the world singing out about their loves, lives and longings, and even Lou Reed's wild-siding coloured girls were soon going 'me-me-me me-me-me-me.' By the time the 1980s arrived to backlash against that, with cock-rock and arena-roll, and endless packets of coke to stoke up the smiles, even the leviathan overkill and synthi-snooze jingles with which the decade overflowed seemed somehow, sickeningly preferable to another night with a lovelorn saddo, weeping into his beard.

Corgan, on the vinyl of 'I Am One,' on the oxide tape of *Moon*, and in the swiftly-filling clubs that the Smashing Pumpkins stalked by night, stripped away all such ghastly memories; reminded the kids that it was, at last, alright to express their feelings again. For sure the wheel would turn once more, and a lot faster than anybody might have expected from their first exposure to the naked psychosis of the early 1990's Alternative pack. But Corgan himself neither defaced nor debased the cold, naked honesty of the emotions he addressed; he became known from the outset as a writer whose lyrics were bitter, biting and personal, and for whom song was more than simple therapy, it was a way to exorcise all those inner demons who taunted and tormented him.

Not sweet, but slivered, Corgan's lyrics amplified themselves into the band's own aesthetic, a birthright that he himself insisted had everything to do with them not being a 'rock mythology band,' at the same time as they fed off that mythology with every breath they took. A few years later, he explained, 'we're not so cute and hot and trendy, like Suede is, and like Led Zeppelin was...' so, he decided, 'if we can't be that, then let's be the opposite, which is reality times ten.'

How that translated to audiences, of course, was a matter of personal taste – meandering prose, pseudo-religious psychobabble, introspective leanings, dashboard confessional, all interpretations were valid, to be absorbed (or not) as the listener saw fit, but never to be ignored. Neither did his songs hang in isolation. Encased in hair and spit and fire, 'I Am One' brought the speaker into the realms of religious Trinitarian mythology, at the same time as inviting the listener, the other 'one' at the end of Corgan's lyrics, into the circle. But though it was whole, it was not complete, until 'Siva' delivered the response, to bring the ethereal bodily back to earth and thereby render it all organic. From something angelic to something slightly frightening, Corgan shifted, chameleon-like, through a world of his own imaginings, and other dreamers' realities. He speaks of inhaling, not living; of not giving, but unveiling. But unveiling what? That is a question for armchair psychiatrists alone. Corgan rarely discusses the meaning of his lyrics, because even he cannot know exactly what they mean to the individual listener. And that is how it should be.

Although Corgan's lyrics would occasionally fall by the wayside, it was the emotional drive behind the words that mattered most in the short term, and covered any stumbles that Corgan as lyricist made. What was clear, and startling, was that the same drive that would propel Corgan and the Smashing Pumpkins through much of the next decade was already well in place this early in their existence.

Yet the sense of brutal reality that permeated the best of these earliest songs was not only the personification of everything that Corgan's confessional lyrics embodied, it also became a tool with which the Smashing Pumpkins built multiple levels of perception, of image. It became their calling card, one of the identifying marks by which one would know that the band had ripped through town and spit it out behind them.

The record that ignited that rampage, 'I Am One,' was released just as the band launched into a summer's worth of Chicago-area gigs, a healthy handful of shows that saw them assume a near residency at both the Cabaret Metro and Avalon for the better part of May through August, opening for everyone from the Buzzcocks to That Petrol Emotion. That, in turn, was intended to prepare them for their first major journeys outside of Chicago, when September, 1990 served up shows in Wisconsin, Michigan, Minnesota and Iowa. It was the beginning of a way of life that would consume the majority of the Smashing Pumpkins' waking hours for close to a decade and, long before the clock rang down on 31 December, the Smashing Pumpkins knew that a door was swinging open before them. They had worked hard over the last eighteen months and it was time. The country was waiting, was rabidly eager for a change, and this was the band who would help encourage that shift.

They were launched.

CHAPTER FIVE
SMELLS LIKE RHINOCEROS, A LITTLE

Although the cocoon of hometown Chicago kept the Smashing Pumpkins warm, and was increasingly wrapping them in the arms of a rabidly faithful hometown crowd, the band's first shows outside the State were a rush. It was, for the Smashing Pumpkins, exciting to break the bonds of a city which was cosmopolitan and, at the same time, stifling. The taste of venues and spilled beer outside the Chicago city limits was exhilarating.

Indeed, as musically gestational as Chicago was, breeding and fostering a remarkably rich brew of sound, it also had its low points. Interviewed in 1991 by WXRT Radio, Corgan mourned that there simply wasn't enough competition to keep everyone's wits honed sharp, wishing that 'there were more places to play...more excitement. That's the drawback. At some point it's kind of a disappointment, because you go somewhere else and there's so much more excitement, and there's so much more genuine enthusiasm about music.'

One such hotbed of excitement and enthusiasm, as 1990 bled through the hour-glass, was Seattle, a long-jump across country to the northwest Pacific coast. There, a local music scene was flourishing both within its own geographical confines but, increasingly, further afield, their strivings amplified not only by a growing battalion of out-of-town, out-of-state and even out-of-country journalists, but also by the efforts of the local record label whose name, as much today as it was at the time, is synonymous with the 'Seattle sound': Sub Pop.

Founded and operated by Jonathan Poneman and Bruce Pavitt, Sub Pop had been around since the early 1980s, when it grew out of a fanzine of the same name. It edged into label-hood slowly, but its patience was swiftly to be rewarded as Sub Pop set about forging a cohesive spiritual identity that established it as one of the most imaginative, and certainly the feistiest, indie outfits around.

Swift deletion polices, limited edition coloured vinyl, picture sleeve releases and incredibly limited print runs raised the label's profile not only among record collectors, but also among connoisseurs of classy Indie Rock in general. It became a mark of honour to acquire a new Sub Pop release before your buddies; it was a major social coup to pick up one of the label's long-deleted near-oldies. And, when 1988 saw Sub Pop launch a Single of the Month Club, with a release by the then-unknown Nirvana, the pace grew even more frenzied.

Yet Sub Pop was never simply a train-spotters' club. Musically, too, Poneman and Pavitt appeared to have a finger firmly on the pulse beat of America's future longings: during the five years of operation that preceded the explosive outbreak that would place both Seattle and Sub Pop firmly on the musical map, almost every one of the acts that would contribute to that explosion passed through as one of the label's tastemakers: Green River, Soundgarden, Mudhoney, Tad, Nirvana....

The inclusion of many of these in the now-vastly profitable Single of the Month Club, inevitably added to their own cachet; and for every cynic who accused Sub Pop of operating nothing more than a well-devised marketing gimmick (an accusation that Sub Pop itself gladly acknowledged), there were others who truly believed that the label possessed a hot-line to the future – and one which had countless corresponding corridors that scouted out fresh meat from all over the country.

Sub Pop themselves had no name for the music they managed. But others were quick to fill that void. They called it Grunge, and Seattle really was its cradle, no matter where the Smashing Pumpkins – or any other band, for that matter – were set to fit into the equation.

With America's highest *per capita* suicide rate, and a mystifying penchant for long-running, and authority-eluding serial killers, the Pacific Northwest was an odd, oddly bred area of peaks and fog, of mottled night-time silence that could even scare the pants off Stephen King. You think rural Maine is weird? Try living in a city that seems to have been simply dropped between the mountains, which spends half the year almost physically cut off from the rest of the country, as the autumnal snows creep down from the peaks and the highways shut up for the season. Then the winter rain clouds arrive to shroud the environs, and the entire metropolis simply lays there, the ocean on one side, the mountains on the other, in the heart of the forests that seem older than time itself.

Neither was the city immune from the demons that stalked the countryside. By light, Seattle thrummed with energy. But, when the shops and offices closed for the day, the sidewalks themselves would roll up for the night. Passing through the downtown core, after a gig – or often, even on the way to a gig – one felt raw and exposed, even alone. You could have run free through New York's Times Square, dripping Rolex watches and diamonds, and you'd have felt more secure than when you walked up Second Ave. in between Pike and Pine.

Strip back the gauze of that heart of mysterious darkness, though, and a vibrant, vital, scene was revealed, churning out of sweaty nightclubs whose very names would one day ascend to immortality – no matter what the physical fate of the venues themselves. The Vogue, RKCNDY, the Off-Ramp, the OK Hotel, the Weathered Wall, the Central Tavern...you will search in vain for them all today, as the city's 21st century developers work to wipe out every last, lingering trace of its once glorious musical past. Step back fifteen years, however, and the clubs were pounding to a life force of its own. Again, journalists would quickly label it Grunge. But the bands themselves simply called it their own, for there truly was nothing else like it anywhere in America.

Neither was that mere supposition. They knew – they'd looked. Green River, the mid-80's progenitors of future icons Pearl Jam and Mudhoney – had travelled far and wide across the United States in search of any audience at all that might understand their energies, and wound up playing to the proverbial one-man-and-a-dog at New York City's CBGBs. Mother Love Bone thought they could camouflage their origins by relocating to LA and playing the traditional Metal card, but LA sussed them out and they were soon packed back to Seattle. Timeless hardcore, 70's Rock and 80's Glam all had their fans, of course, but no-one had ever tried mashing them together, and the 'Seattle sound' seemed determined to tell you why.

It's telling, really, how soft and scared the American market is. All but stillborn on the local media radar, Seattle needed to travel to the UK in search of succour. Of course, this was nothing new. From the Rolling Stones co-opting American Blues in the 1960s through the glam-packed assimilation of Andy Warhol's New York neuroses and on to the ravers who married Chicago Acid House to Rock and came out monsters, Britain was there first. And so it was as the 1980s folded up.

As Grunge was preparing to tsunami, but before anyone was cognizant enough to realise that there was a scene beginning to coalesce – a scene that was leapfrogging regionalism to break nationwide – the UK was hip to the foreshocks. However, even the bold pioneers of the British inkies were late to board the gravy train. Long before the first Sub Pop singles became clarion calls of the future, there were bands forming and disbanding up and down the Washington Coast, from Bellingham up north, to Seattle smack dab in the middle, and down Interstate 5 to the state capitol, Olympia. Jutting out coastward, grimy blue collar Aberdeen chucked up its own share of distortionists and, farther down the road into Oregon, the Portland scene just over the state line brought its own beasts to bear.

If you want to be archaeological about it Grunge can be traced back in time to the musical Adam and Eve of the Ducky Boys and Deranged Diction. With future Pearl Jam-ers Stone Gossard on the one hand and Jeff Ament on the other, these two groups birthed every Seattle grunge combo that would follow. From them came the revolting Mr. Epp, and then the infamous Green River with

Ament and future Mudhoney-ers Steve Turner and Mark Arm.

By 1987, it was all exploding as bands changed members more often than socks. There was little of the trademark flannel flying in those days either. Seattle, and in particular the hipster music scene, was still in the dying grasp of the Los Angeles glam revival, wrapped up in the tethers of Jane's Addiction's hair ribbons and the Cult's coifs and posturing. Many local musicians had already had a residency or two down south in California, and had greedily absorbed what they discovered there as an *alternative* to the casual clothes that the local lumberjacks, mechanics and Boeing plant production lines were wearing. However, as Nirvana sliced Interstate 5 between Aberdeen and Seattle, as Malfunkshun took the ferry from the islands to the mainland, as a hundred young upstarts got up on stage and manhandled their instruments, so the behemoth sound and the Rainier beer rendered all such niceties redundant.

The scene was exploding out in pinpricks, like a carbuncle shedding its necrosis, but this was a positive step. The American media might have turned a blind eye, but the little kids understood. Neither, though a handful of observers might have disagreed, was it strictly accurate to describe this as a local scene. The naysayers and the doom-mongers might like to pop everything into convenient little geographic boxes and isolate everything in the hope that the contagion would not spread, but the naysayers and doom-mongers were wrong.

There *were* other bands pursuing that vision. Even Sub Pop never confined itself to its immediate local environs. Oklahoma City's Flaming Lips, Denver's Fluid, San Francisco's Helios Creed, Cincinnati's Afghan Whigs, Ann Arbor's Big Chief all took early bows through Sub Pop's auspices; France's Les Thugs and England's Billy Childish moved in from even further out of bounds.

Beyond the label's grasp, too, the firmament was bubbling. What, after all, was Billy Corgan's avowed hybrid of Bad Brains, Jane's and a stack of Black Sabbath, if not a more esoteric take on Nirvana's purported impersonation of 'the Bay City Rollers being molested by Black Flag'? And as Sub Pop stretched its tentacles further, so it scooped up these other bands who at least understood…who at least acknowledged there might be some direction to take that didn't wash up where every other band had stumbled before.

In some cases, the linkage was intellectual – garage bands emerging from the east coast, the waves of grinding sweat that branded themselves forbears of a sort, and were accepted for their shared ideals of going against the grain as loudly as they could.

The Pacific Northwestern monopoly on Grunge was a part of it, of course. But so were scenes that had existed in isolation all across the country, elsewhere within the Smashing Pumpkins' own Midwestern constituency, where a new wave of garage bands – led by Soul Asylum and Husker Du – were taking local clubs to task and absorbing fresh waves of adolescent sweat; in the southwest, where the Red Hot Chili Peppers were putting the Funk back into Punk Rock, and Camper Van Beethoven were alchemising hardcore remnants with folksy accoutrements, to pioneer what would soon become the alt.country boom; back into the melodic sashay that would soon be making new stars of Green Day and Rancid; and, most precious of all, on the East Coast, where such veteran mavericks as Dinosaur Jr, Sonic Youth, and the Pixies had been banging their heads against the walls of mainstream ignorance for years.

It was no surprise at all that, as the 1980s drifted into a new decade, both Sonic Youth (the *Goo* album, the 'Cool Thing' single) and the Pixies (*Doolittle*, 'Here Comes Your Man') were making their first major inroads into the American psyche; that the Smithereens and Buffalo Tom were soaring to join them. And, as those bands' influence permeated deeper, so the East Coast hip that each so embodied leaked further westward.

For the most part, the acquaintance came slowly, via word-of-mouth. Bands would pass one another in clubs or cheap diners, or on the busted-down-van laden highways that circled every city, as they crisscrossed America paying penance for even daring to dream of pop stardom. Sub Pop first became aware of the Smashing Pumpkins through the enthusiasm of the Fluid, the Denver-based band who had been with the label since 1988 brought their *Clear Black Paper* debut. More recently, they'd been on the road promoting their seminal EP *Glue*, which is where they first caught sight of the Smashing Pumpkins, while passing through Madison, Wisconsin.

One state over from Chicago, Madison is another of those insulated Midwestern cities, a nearly straight shot west down Interstate 94 from lakeshore Milwaukee. Home to the University of Wisconsin, Madison is a smart, hip place, and a regular stop for hungry Alternative bands, each on their own musically tainted endurance marathon. The Fluid's own presence there was no coincidence, however; Madison was also home to Smart Studios, the increasingly (and deservingly) fashionable haunt of indie producer Butch Vig.

Vig himself is best known today as one fourth of Garbage, the band he formed with his Smart Studios cohorts Steve Marker and Duke Erickson in 1994 – the trio had already commenced cutting a swath across the contemporary remix market when they linked with Scots vocalist Shirley Manson and, making a quite unexpected leap out of the studio and into the live arena, set themselves up among the most vibrant bands of the 1990s and beyond. Studying their success, it is easy to forget that the members ever had any kind of life before they ran into one another; and easy, too, to forget that, without Vig, the 1990s themselves might have been a very different place indeed.

Born and schooled in Madison, Vig formed his first band, Spooner, in 1978, alongside school friends Erickson, Dave Benton, Jeff Walker and Joel Tappero. Although they diligently took their punked-out garage combo across the

Midwestern club circuit for nearly half a decade, they went nowhere and, in 1983, Vig and Erickson alone formed Fire Town with Marker. By 1984, however, that group, too, was moribund and Vig decided to shift his focus to the other side of the glass. In 1984, he and Marker opened Smart Studios, at 1254 E. Washington Ave.

Working closely with the Touch And Go label's roster of bands, Vig's first major project was the Madison Wisconsin based Killdozer's so influential 1985 *Intellectuals Are The Shoeshine Boys Of The Ruling Elite* EP, which married country twang and socio-political spit and spiked it with just a hint of complete and utter destruction. Word of Vig's accomplishments was not slow in leaking out – of all the producers working in the realms of the nihilistic guitar crunch that then permeated the underground, Vig alone seemed to understand precisely how to harness it, and turn its roughest edges to the music's best advantage.

The Rousers, the Laughing Hyenas and Die Kreuzen's dramatic *Century Days* all bore the hallmarks of Vig's eye for sonic detail and, by 1990, he was recording both the Fluid and Nirvana for their own latest Sub Pop efforts – indeed, the latter spent a week in Wisconsin in April 1990, recording the demos that they intended would shape the follow-up to their recently released *Bleach* debut album... 'Dive,' 'Breed,' 'Polly,' 'Stay Away,' 'In Bloom,' 'Lithium'... the album was to be titled *Sheep*.

The Smashing Pumpkins had already played Madison twice during 1990. On 9 February they landed at the O'Kays Corral, a venue which was notable for spotlighting bands hip to the underground but not to the mainstream. The 16 June, meanwhile, placed them at the two hundred seat Club de Wash, known to the locals simply as 'The Wash'. Vig was in the audience to see them, having been tipped off by the ever-supportive Mike Po. He had sent the producer a copy of 'I Am One,' so intriguing Vig that he made his own way to the show there to peruse a set that included early working versions of many of the songs that would end up on *Gish*, including 'Tristessa', and 'Window Paine', plus both 'Razor' and 'Try To Try', which would appear as 'Bury Me' b-sides.

Shortly after, he and the Pumpkins united again within the confines of Smart. The session flowed perfectly, as the band for the first time found themselves working alongside someone who didn't simply understand their sonic goals, but was capable of transforming them beyond even the Smashing Pumpkins' own ambitions – their own experiences of trying to recapture their sound, after all, had been confined to the demo studio or rehearsals. Beneath Vig's nimbly experienced fingers, however, the tentative victories that they had enacted alone were transformed to a triumphal arch, and Mike Po still remembers the excitement with which Corgan, Wretzky and Iha arrived at his apartment, having driven straight into Chicago from the final mixing session, to play him the still-warm finished tape.

The group cut two songs with Vig, the punningly titled 'La Dolly Vita,' and 'Tristessa,' a song whose title Corgan borrowed from a 1960 Jack Kerouac novella and which, though there is little common ground with the book's treatment of a junk-smattered relationship in Mexico, nevertheless revelled in several similar themes – love and loss are the biggest.

But there were other similarities: Kerouac used this book as a revelation of his growing disenchantment first with religion, then with life, situations that Corgan himself would soon be exploring within his own lyrics.

With Vig's enthusiasm for the Smashing Pumpkins echoing the Fluid's own entreaties, Sub Pop stepped in as a home for 'Tristessa.' Realistically aware that no larger stage would present itself for what was, after all, no more than their sophomore release the Smashing Pumpkins accepted the offer. However, hopes – subsequently repeated as fact by sundry other band biographies – that 'Tristessa' might be granted admission to the Single of the Month Club were to be dashed, as the label instead opted for the latest release by the Reverend Horton Heat, 'The Psychobilly Freakout.'

Released in December, 'Tristessa' remained a wonderful way for the Smashing Pumpkins to wrap up what had been an overall outstanding 1990 – a year which ended, on New Year's Eve, with a jam-packed return to the Cabaret Metro, sharing the bill with My Life With The Thrill Kill Kult, and premiering a set that was all but a dry run for what would become their debut album. With their eyes already focused on the future, the Smashing Pumpkins returned to Smart studios to commence piecing together what would become *Gish*.

CHAPTER SIX
THRILL KILL KULT WERE GOING TO BE MASSIVE

Sessions for *Gish*, the Smashing Pumpkins' first LP, ultimately ran until March 1991. Vig himself had already agreed to begin working on Nirvana's own next album immediately after, locking his Smart Studios door while he travelled instead to Los Angeles. History, of course, would ultimately be rewritten to so amplify Vig's work on that album, the soon-to-be seminal *Nevermind*, that anything else he ever recorded has been relegated to mere footnote status, his earliest work with the Smashing Pumpkins included.

It's an illusion that each of the Smashing Pumpkins has tried to shatter, as Wretzky reminds us; 'we worked with Butch before anybody knew who Butch was.' Even more importantly, any new tricks Vig perfected while recording *Gish* could not help but be refocused once he tried them amid the higher-tech surroundings of LA's Sound City Studios. But, if there was any sense of competition whatsoever between the Smashing Pumpkins and Nirvana in early 1991, it was neither musical nor commercial. Rather, it was simply the race to see who could get their album out first.

Nirvana, of course, already had a major advantage in those stakes – the massive Geffen label had staked its claim on their future and was confidently looking forward to a September release for the album. The Smashing Pumpkins, on the other hand, were still unsigned, and wondering what they needed to do to change that.

The *Gish* sessions themselves weren't always without trouble, as the band hammered through songs, new and old, in search of the perfect brew. Some performances came easily; others, however, went through twenty, thirty rewrites '…just over and over and over,' as Corgan put it. But both Vig and Corgan found that they worked well together. Vig remembers, 'Billy was really driven. He took a lot of pride in the arrangements and was extremely meticulous when it was called for in the studio.'

Chamberlin, too, was thrilled to be working with Vig, a fellow drummer who he admired tremendously, while Wretzky looked back affectionately upon the camaraderie that developed. 'We love [Butch's] ideas, the way that he worked.' Every musician has heard horror stories of how a producer will try to foist his own ideas upon their music, twisting and distorting their original vision in the hope of emerging with something that'll look good on his own resume. Vig, however, entered the sessions as a blank slate, committed only to working with the Smashing Pumpkins' own ideas and preconceptions for how the album should be, taking everything on board and becoming a part of the process. Not once the great maestro behind the curtain, he demanded only one thing – the highest possible quality that they could deliver.

That singular attention to detail, and the demand for quality work was a natural mirror, of course, to the perfection that Corgan, too, demanded from his band mates and – perhaps even more harshly – from himself. As the sessions got under way, Corgan's keenest ambition was to simply capture the spirit of the band's live performance. As time passed, however, he swiftly came to demand a second quality, a sense of the seamless rhythms which studio sessions allowed, to enable a finished product that would burn with righteous fire, but not fall flat with any of the sloppiness that live performance inevitably entailed. Indeed, it was in no uncertain terms whatsoever that Corgan defined his expectations for the finished product – 'If you want to see us fuck around, see us live.'

In the studio, there would be no fucking around, although that is not to say there would be no light-hearted moments. Taking a break from their own music, the Smashing Pumpkins laid down a cover of "Jackie Blue," a hit for those hoary 70's country-rockers The Ozark Mountain Daredevils, for inclusion on a forthcoming compilation schemed by another Chicago indie, Pravda Records. Modelled after the K-Tel-style hit compilations of an earlier era, *20 Explosive Dynamic Super Smash Hit Explosions* rounded up the likes of the Poster Children, Material Issue, the Young Fresh Fellows, Mojo Nixon and the Sneetches, to enact often gratuitously irreverent versions of the biggest hits of yesteryear – and did so with such success that there swiftly followed a second volume offering more of the same.

Compared with some of the concoctions that were delivered to the listening public (the Squirrels' medley of 'The Hustle' and 'Seasons In The Sun' come to mind), the Smashing Pumpkins' take on 'Jackie Blue' was remarkably respectful. But still it posed an oasis of light heartedness within Smart Studio sessions that were otherwise seldom less than deadly earnest.

Every band member excelled as *Gish* took shape, but it was Jimmy Chamberlin who, though frequently lost in the tumult, truly defined the album. Playing, he says, 'in terms of the song' he relished the opportunity to let his drums become 'really dry and natural...drums sound[ing] like drums,' laying down beats that provided a never-to-be-echoed backdrop for Iha and Corgan's guitar fury. It became fashionable, briefly, to compare the Smashing Pumpkins' wall of noise to the sound of early Black Sabbath. But, although that group did indeed inform the young Corgan's rock dreams, and Corgan would one day collaborate with guitarist Tony Iommi, the sound of his Stratocaster piling into Iha's Les Paul squashed any comparison, leaving 'Paranoid' sounding as tinny as a can of generic beer.

Corgan applauded Vig's intentions. 'I want our recordings to be perfect. An album is a permanent work of art, and to me, nothing should detract from that.' Even the band's newly-earned status as doughty road warriors was placed on hold as the sessions unfolded – they managed a mere handful of live shows during the three months they were recording, breaking for an East Coast sojourn that touched down in New Jersey, New York, Washington DC and Cambridge, Massachusetts. Less a break from the sessions than a chance to simply let rip on the material they'd just recorded, the Smashing Pumpkins' live set was a virtual mirror of all that wound up on *Gish*, topped off with a couple of let-your-hair-down covers, the Blue Oyster Cult's 'Godzilla' and Blue Cheer's 'Out Of Focus' among them. And then it was back to Madison to continue refining.

It takes only a cursory glance at the songs on *Gish* to reveal just how radically the mass market was going to shift, away from the glam rocking cocks and power balladeers. More concerned with feelings than feeling up some slick chick, Corgan's idealism ensured that the songs on *Gish* moved with the music, as he snarled and yelped his way through a sonic scape that was as textured as his own search for the truth in his soul might have been. What remained on tape as the sessions wound down was an album of absolutely breathtaking scope – beautiful and so strong through the music, yet somehow brittle and fragile at the same time.

Even among the confirmed live favourites, not every song recorded at the sessions would see an eventual place on *Gish* – 'Jesus Loves His Babies' almost made the cut to b-side, but was ultimately cast aside and placed into the vault. Both 'Slunk,' and 'Blue,' meanwhile, were shuffled out in favour of 'Suffer,' while the short 'I'm Going Crazy' survived only as an uncredited bonus track, to be discovered several silent minutes after the closing 'Daydream.' But, tracing back into the group's earliest repertoire, two 1989-era songs, 'Bury Me,' and Wretzky's vocal showpiece 'Daydream,' were revived, while the crowd-pleasing 'Rhinoceros' received its most dynamic restoration yet.

With so much attention paid to these seminal songs, it's odd that what Corgan hailed as 'the first true Smashing Pumpkins song' was allowed to stand as is. Plans to re-record 'I Am One' were, for whatever reason, shunted aside and Corgan still puzzled over that decision several years later – he was, he admitted, 'disappointed that I didn't take advantage of the chance to re-record the song for the album.'

Some of the perceived imperfections, however, were deliberate – even the accidental ones. Vig told *Vox* that several of the 'weird sonic things' were mistakes, left in the final mix because they brought new dimensions and colours to the sound. For example, Vig remembered recording 'Crush' and asking Corgan to take his jewellery off because it was rattling against his acoustic guitar. Corgan refused and, during playback, both men marvelled at the 'weird percussive thing' that was 'playing loosely in time with how [he] was strumming.'

Such minor happenstances notwithstanding, the sessions offered up little for even the meanest perfectionist to quibble over. Impressed by the rigidity with which Corgan adhered to his own vision of the group, Vig provided the backdrop for a wall of sound that eclipsed pretty much everything else on the market. Corgan, always astute, and acutely aware of the direction in which the musical climate was headed, had a very specific framework for how he wanted *Gish* to sound, to the point, he says, where 'I often get accused of being overly conscious. I knew where I wanted to be.'

With fluidity and grace combined with equal parts angst and spunk, *Gish* took shape over those few months and, from the Eastern flavoured breaks on 'Siva,' to the repetitive refrain of 'Rhinoceros', the Smashing Pumpkins ultimately crafted an album that would damn-near blueprint an entire genre. 'Rhinoceros,' in particular, would emerge one of, if not, *the* song that would place the band squarely in the emergent Grunge corner. But, in true Smashing Pumpkins style, it wasn't merely baited with the stripped down lo-fi guitar fuzz alone. That it was a mess of layered noise is without doubt; that it seethes and roils is without dispute. But what made 'Rhinoceros' such a multi-horned marvel was that Vig devoted a whopping seventeen tracks to feedback alone, to create what Corgan defined as the sound of 'World War I airplanes dive-bombing around your head.' And that was probably an understatement, although the song's impact was to the burgeoning of the Alternative scene what the Great War was to the reordering of Europe.

But 'Rhinoceros' was much more as well. With Vig and Corgan deliberately manhandling the steering wheel, it swerved again to became a bastard child of My Bloody Valentine; and again, delivered an absolutely uncanny premonition of the soon-to-be bigger-than-anything anthem of Nirvana's 'Smells Like Teen Spirit.'

Indeed, the echoes that lace the latter song are hard to miss, no matter which way you hear them, but even more devilish are the underpinnings that slot the Smashing Pumpkins themselves not alongside the garage bands and punk rocking flannel wavers of their peer group, but lay them instead among sundry post-Punk venerables who'd formed such a vibrant soundtrack to the Smashing Pumpkins' own adolescence. Echoes of the Psychedelic Furs, the Cure and Joy Division haunt 'Rhinoceros' in particular, and *Gish* in general without a trace of self-consciousness, a hint of revivalism.

Rather, as the album took its final shape, the songs converged to create a complex, complete sonic portrait that regurgitated all the Smashing Pumpkins had ever ingested, but laid it out as a new work, as new ground, as a new era. Indeed, no matter how far Nirvana pushed the commercial boat from traditional mainstream shores, it was only after the Smashing Pumpkins had handed them the ferry fare; as *Gish* changed not merely the face of Alternative music *circa* 1991, but the very fabric itself, cutting through the crap, cutting out the penchant for late 80's glitter, and cutting in a brutal basketful of blistering guitar and heavy, heavy beats.

Gish broke ground. Even though any number of the bands that were already tethered to the Seattle scene had hitherto laid down their rainy blueprints, the scene itself was as darkly insulated as the city. *Gish* was destined to bring the noise out of the rain, and into the glittering gem of mainstream eyes.

(As a vague aside to the album's immediate impact, the Smashing Pumpkins would completely re-master *Gish* in 1994, while they waited to join that year's Lollapalooza caravan, considering the album would be better served by beefed-up production and upgraded sound quality. The original pressing of the album was taken from the DAT tapes and didn't, in Corgan's estimation, sound as good as the original analogue recordings.

The new-look *Gish* would be released with no fanfare, would not be promoted as a re-master – it would just slot into the general stack, and Corgan explained, 'we're not going to make a big deal of it...we're not trying to rip people off...but I really take the opportunity to upgrade the sound quality.' Chamberlin continued, '[it's] not really that different. It's more like, if you recorded it and heard it as many times as I have, you'd be able to tell the difference.')

With the *Gish* recording sessions wrapped up in just forty-five days, the Smashing Pumpkins returned to the road in March 1991, the only blot on the landscape the nagging problem of just who would be releasing the album. Both Limited Potential and Sub Pop expressed an interest, with Sub Pop's already proven expertise in marketing LPs establishing them as a firm contender.

Nevertheless, the feeling that Sub Pop itself could best be regarded as little more than a stepping stone to eventually greater pastures was one that Nirvana had already proven. The label, although it was brilliantly promoting what was then regarded as the very best in Alternative music, was still seen as both a regional and a genre-specific label, with their roster of family bands, and the giants of Grunge at the top of the tree.

There was little room for any of the label's other signings to manoeuvre around what the media had already determined was Sub Pop's forte; in fact, signing to Sub Pop would have had the opposite effect, irrevocably marginalizing the Smashing Pumpkins within the grunge circle alone, and securing them within a straitjacket from which they might never be able to free themselves. Certainly Corgan's own, already firmly gestating plans for developing the Smashing Pumpkins' sound, of ringing the changes between style and substance, would fall on deaf ears, while there was something else that bothered Corgan. No matter how complimentary the Sub Pop team may have been, at the end of the day, 'they didn't love us like they loved Mudhoney.'

Besides, even in the independent market, Sub Pop was not the only game in town, while a handful of even better-connected labels had already shown some interest in the group.

Paramount among these was Caroline, the Virgin records offshoot with whom the group had already had some dealings, when the label's distribution department handled both 'I Am One' and 'Tristessa'; in fact, Limited Potential's Mike Po had himself recommended that his own contacts at the company move to alert their higher-ups to the Smashing Pumpkins' potential, demands that the success of both singles could not help but back up.

Of course, there were pitfalls to going above ground in search of a record deal, not least of all further fire for the critics who still condemned the Smashing Pumpkins for running out of Chicago before most bands could walk; for having friends in the kind of high places where most bands found blank doors; for having the temerity to admit that they were actually ambitious.

There was also the multi-volume handbook, compiled by countless bands over countless years, detailing all that could be sacrificed by signing up with a major – the loss of control over material, the derailing of creative energy, and the evil clutches of dollars over art. How many bands, even in the modern age, complained that they'd been signed because the label 'loved' them, then transformed into something that they themselves hated the moment they put pen to paper?

As the Smashing Pumpkins' newly-acquired management team of Raymond Coffer and Andy Gershon – overseers, too, of the now fast-moving careers of Cocteau Twins, Love And Rockets and the Sundays – began sifting through the offers that were coming in for the band, the Smashing Pumpkins themselves put in their own hard graft, trying to familiarise themselves with the ins and outs of the music business, and how record labels worked. They knew very strongly what they wanted, and what they didn't want to give up, and that made a difference when it came time to negotiate a deal.

With all this in mind, Caroline had attractions for the Smashing Pumpkins from the outset. Although ultimately bound to Virgin, the label nevertheless existed in a semi-no-man's-land, poised between major label subsidiary-hood, and the independent scene – in other words, enjoying all the benefits of one, without too many of the disadvantages of the other.

Caroline also had a proud history. It had been launched back in the mid 1970s as a semi-budget outlet for some of the parent Virgin label's more esoteric projects. The Virgin of the era was already highly regarded for the sheer eccentricity of its roster. Several years before they signed the Sex Pistols, such avant art concerns as Slapp Happy, Henry Cow, Gong and Kevin Coyne all parked their shoes under the alter. Caroline, delving even deeper into the British underground, and then reaching further afield towards roots-bound Jamaica, enjoyed a cachet of even more relentless experimentation. And though there was little room for such woolly-hatted mavericks on the Alternative scene of the 1990s, still the spirit flourished.

For unknown bands, labels such as Caroline (several other majors operated their own psuedo-indies) were an attractive proposition, the knowledge that success would inevitably see them transferred to the parent company, but failure would not necessarily see them peremptorily dropped, or else lost in the burgeoning indie-go-round. For the Smashing Pumpkins themselves, it seemed a natural transition in a career that, so far, had been built upon what Corgan reflected was a series of tiny steps upward, 'a stair step thing; one step after another, a little bigger, a little bigger.' By the time the Smashing Pumpkins hit the road again in June, for their first gigs since their week long East Coast stint in February, A&R man Mark Williams had signed them to Caroline, and *Gish* was on the schedules for August 1991. Around the same time a UK deal was hacked out with another Virgin subsidiary, Hut Records

This summery tour found the band in an understandably playful mood. Of course the imminent *Gish* dominated proceedings, but future John Peel session favourite 'Smiley' and an early variant on 'Rocket' were both in the set for their Chicago homecoming. The journey westwards towards California, meanwhile, saw the addition of 'Silverfuck' to the set, with audiences additionally treated to such unexpected joys as Corgan's take on Syd Barrett's 'Terrapin,' and teasing intros from Jimi Hendrix's 'Purple Haze' and the Dave Brubeck Quartet's 'Take Five,' prefacing the band's own searing songs.

By the time *Gish* gushed into stores in August 1991, much of its initial success was owed to the time the group was now spending on the road, scrunched up against equipment, eating what they could afford on their strict budget, and, more often than not, sleeping on whichever floors were made available to them.

With the band already fairly well-placed in the so-called key markets of New York, Los Angeles, Massachusetts and, revelling its brief day in that spotlight, Seattle, an already established fan-base greeted the arrival of *Gish* as a reward for having supported the Smashing Pumpkins for so long already – a little bundle with a bow delivered just in time for the kids to go back to college. Elsewhere, however, there were scores of people on the edge of such charmed circles, for whom the Smashing Pumpkins simply burst on to the music scene from absolutely nowhere at all – a nowhere that the band members themselves best remembered, as Jimmy Chamberlin put it, in terms of just one thing. 'We had this great broken down van for three fucking years.'

Now, however, the band was finally seeing some payback for that long stretch of busting their chops around the American club circuit, packing their gear in and out and in again at two to four hundred seat clubs around the country. Occasionally they could luxuriate in the presence of a favourite local band on the bill; and once or twice they might even run into a group that shared their own status in the growing revolution, such as the night they shared with Caroline label mates Hole at the Khyber Pass Pub in Philadelphia.

That band's label debut, the 'Teenage Whore' single, had just been released all-but side-by-side with *Gish*; their debut album, *Pretty On The Inside*, was looming, and rumours of a blossoming relationship between Corgan and Hole's colourful leader, Courtney Love, were already nudging the grapevine. After seven years, Corgan and girlfriend Chris Fabian had separated. It would turn out to be a temporary break, but the already rapacious gossips flagged Alternative's new supercouple nonetheless.

Neither were the benefits musical (and personal) alone. Non-stop touring not only helped the band hone their craft, it also helped them stockpile money. The goal for the Smashing Pumpkins, Wretzky has said, was not to sell out (although you wouldn't guess that from the snippy comments that still circled the band like so many mealy vultures). But 'we were wanting to make a decent living...we love what we're doing and we [didn't] want to have a workaday job.'

Still, the speed with which *Gish* moved out of the 'unknown indie band' bag and onto a palate of wider appreciation astonished many industry observers. The Seattle based journalist, Dave Thompson, recalled, 'if you asked anybody what the big hits of the forthcoming [autumn] were going to be, it was things like the Blue Aeroplanes, MC 900 Foot Jesus, Swervedriver....The big names were Robyn Hitchcock, Love and Rockets, Camper Van Beethoven, Richard Thompson...there was an entire layer of bands who were gnawing at the mainstream, "Alternative superstars" who were just beginning to show up on MTV, and places like that.

'Everyone thought Thrill Kill Kult were going to be massive. Then you'd look at bands like Hole, Soundgarden, Nirvana and the Smashing Pumpkins, all of whom were on major-ish labels at that time, and they simply weren't in the picture. Sonic Youth's last album [1990's *Goo*] made number ninety-six in the chart, and that was considered a major success.'

It was easy to see why few people rated such records. Jane's Addiction notwithstanding, the pop charts of the day had little time for leviathan slabs of heavy guitar, raunchy intensity and driving energies. But just a casual sniff proved that there was a sea-change in the air that caught even Alternative industry insiders off-guard. When *Gish* rose to the top of the CMJ music chart, it was the first even halfway-independent album to achieve that honour in over three years and, by the time the first week of September rolled around, *Gish* had cracked the Billboard Top Two Hundred.

It dropped out again the following week, but still *Gish* was pushing at frontiers that had hitherto seemed impermeable and, as the Smashing Pumpkins bathed in the unaccustomed limelight of a suddenly intrigued national media, it would have been easy for them to adopt the mantel of standard-bearers, bold pioneers, settlers on musical plains as windswept as any that surrounded the infant Chicago. And then Nirvana released *Nevermind*, and the entire picture changed overnight.

CHAPTER SEVEN
FRIED UP EXTRA GREASY

The Smashing Pumpkins sauntered into Seattle at the end of the summer. It was not their first encounter – they passed through in January, in the wake of the Sub Pop single – but still there was a certain synchronicity to their latest visit, two shows three days apart in late August, 1991.

Unable to even imagine how much its life would change in the coming months; unaware, as the month burned on (for the city can be as hot in summer as it's wet in winter), that Seattle was luxuriating through what would become the final summer of its cultural innocence, the heaviest-hitting of the local rock hierarchy, Alice In Chains, Soundgarden, Tad, Nirvana and the pre-Pearl Jam Mookie Blaylock, were hitting the bar rails for the very last time. Looking at the gig guide in the week before the Smashing Pumpkins' shows, theirs was just another name on the calendar and, the first night they played, 20 August at the Ballard neighbourhood's Backstage club, that's all it was.

It was the second show that really mattered, to onlookers and participants alike; the night when the Smashing Pumpkins decamped to the darkness on the edge of downtown, and walked into a grimy, greasy, heavenly dive just under the highway that cleaved the city.

The Off-Ramp, never as well known to outsiders as some of the city's other sights, was in its own way just as important a testing ground for bands that came through town, and also for those whom Seattle herself was ready to disgorge. Dark and twisty, a maze of nooks and crannies and painfully overloaded when two hundred and fifty people crammed inside, the Off-Ramp was a bar's bar, full of the scene's up-and-comers, but without the posturing that would soon dominate many venues in the city. It was open, casual, and full of dreams, sticky to the touch across tables and floors soaked with sweat, beer and tears.

And it was even more so that August. Hot outside and hotter than hell in, it felt like the very city was pulsating, shimmering in waves that were quelled by an occasional cool puff from the water of the sound. As more mainstream folk were preparing for the end-of-summer music festival, Bumbershoot, those who preferred to move in the shadows were streaming into the Off-Ramp on 23 August. Some were aware of the Smashing Pumpkins' innovative sound, but many were not. They squeezed in on cheap tickets, cheaper beer and the club's famous after-hours hash browns, fried up extra-greasy to sop up the alcohol before its patrons stumbled home.

Barely knee-high off the dance floor, the stage was small and narrow, rear-ended with a curtain that, if pulled back, revealed the glamour of the 'dressing rooms.' It left little room between patron and star, and the Smashing Pumpkins' gig felt communal, the energy was even more palpable because of it. Brion, a club regular who stood at the foot of anyone on stage, described that night as 'incredible! It was incredible, man. I'm not into guitar heroes, but I'd never seen anyone play like that before. Corgan just ripped it up.'

He truly did. Confidently – even arrogantly – aware of his youthful good looks and his towering height that was only exaggerated in the close confines of the club, his voice raced to soaring heights before steadying to grind his trademark screech down to a barely audible hush. The audience was floored. Just stunned. Sure, they'd all seen Alice In Chains at the Vogue, the nascent Nirvana here and there, Soundgarden at the Central Tavern, these folk were no strangers to crash-and-burn. But this, these Smashing Pumpkins, were like nothing they'd ever seen before.

Across 'Siva,' 'Tristessa' and 'Window Paine,' great swatches of the new album, the Smashing Pumpkins did more than deliver. The air inside the club was heavy, with the music and with sweat and smoke, but the claustrophobic crush was so infused with the Smashing Pumpkins' energy, that any discomfort was transcended to ecstasy. Lauren, a Jane's Addiction kind-of-girl at the best of times, and a Dee-Lite day-tripper in more private moments, remembers, 'it was one of the best shows I'd ever seen. I had no idea who these guys were, my boyfriend at the time dragged me out to see them, he'd been at the Vogue show and had seen them down in L.A., so I went along to the Off-Ramp. It was amazing.'

Who would have thought that a handful of relatively unknown musicians from Chicago – of all places, the onlookers grimaced in their ignorance – could sweep into the centre of the belly that birthed Grunge, and out-grunge the masters? That's an easy question to answer. Anyone who'd been following the Smashing Pumpkins since their earliest gigs could have predicted the outcome of that hot night in Seattle without the slightest hesitation and, in less time than it takes an eye to blink shut, to close the aperture. And, anyone who started following them after the Off-Ramp show knew precisely where the future began, for the Smashing Pumpkins and for Grunge alike.

You thought the 70s were sticky and the 80s inedible? The 1990s were barely eighteen months old and already the vultures were circling. The economy was in chaos. Housing prices plummeted and, with them, the property values that had hitherto stood as the final bulwark of insurance against anything disastrous. As a fresh generation came squeaking out of the halls of academia, they hung their finally-out-of-school diplomas in the cupboard, then joined a real world they'd never been educated for.

But did they complain? Did they object? Did they even dream of rebellion? No, they'd just stumble back to their apartment at the end of the shift, put on the Fine Young Cannibals, and wish the world would go away. They needed a break, they needed a change, they needed something to hope for. But most of all, they needed a kick up the pants to remind them that sometimes, you had to suck it up and just grab all that for yourself.

Grunge – lightly in the maw of *Gish*, screaming through the paws of Nirvana, and unavoidable via the host of screaming wannabes who descended from every compass point thereafter – would deliver that blow.

Why? There had been regional scenes before and there would certainly be regional scenes thereafter. Even the mid-80s advent of college radio and the college tour circuit had not really changed things – a handful of bands...REM, Pylon, the B52s...broke out of Athens, Georgia, to convince the world that the South had risen again; indeed, Billy Corgan, always ready with a warm remembrance for REM's jangled pop, was himself a part of that revolution, ranking them as one of his high school favourites.

New York and Los Angeles, too, had always bubbled in a ferment that only occasionally escaped the city limits, and then only because the ferment itself took place in the industry's own back garden – it's hard to miss a band if they're always standing outside your office door. The difference was, in a country the size of the United States, national stardom can arise only when an act espouses a mood that the nation itself can identify with. Existential angst may sound great on a coastal college campus, but it doesn't translate to the mid-western farmsteads. Ironic androgyny hangs heavy in Hollywood, but it doesn't make sense in a Colorado K-Mart. And so on.

Grunge, however, touched a chord that everybody could identify with, from the Valedictorian who left college with a PhD, and still ended up wearing a paper-hat and a shit-eating grin; to the kid who thought he'd inherit the family farm, and instead was bequeathed a few acres of debt. Hopelessness and homelessness stalked the land of the free and, for the first time in history, the feel-good optimism that is America's natural state of mind was beginning to question its very own soul. Grunge, the music of the underdog, the dance of the dispossessed, did not have the answers to that question. But it did let the questioner know that he was not alone in his isolation.

And the Smashing Pumpkins were in the heart of it.

Looking back, it is difficult to recall with any kind of precision, just how it felt during the six weeks or so that divided the release of *Gish*, the Smashing Pumpkins' answer to a virgin's prayer, from *Nevermind*, Nirvana's revelation that that sweet young thing wasn't as naïve as we thought. Reviews of *Gish*, after all, were largely handled by writers who were themselves already well-versed in the primal stew of fuzz guitar and hard hitting rock that the Smashing Pumpkins espoused and had long since accustomed themselves to talking knowledgeably about the grunge school of music that was spreading like a damp stain away from the rain-soaked northwest. To their ears, the Smashing Pumpkins' musical achievement was remarkable, but really no more than anyone had expected.

It was the album's absorption beyond those quarters that raised eyebrows – the sudden shock of switching on the radio, tuning it to any one of the countless college-rock style radio stations that littered the dial, and suddenly being assaulted by 'Rhinoceros' or 'I Am One,' when the most you'd been expecting was REM or the B52s. It was settling down on a Sunday night to watch MTV's Alternative flagship *120 Minutes*, expecting the umpteenth rerun of the Sundays' first single, and instead being assaulted by the sensorial firestorm of 'Siva' with its combination of startlingly low lighted candles and ship's figureheads, while Wretzky emerges from water like an Ophelia in reverse and the band themselves resembling some sort of psychedelic train wreck.

It was all these things and more, the knowledge that, for the first time in a long time, the patronising pat on the head that was the industry's acknowledgement that there was a sub-basement beneath the underground's lowest tier, had actually been upgraded to something a little more, but not too, familiar. The Smashing Pumpkins neither invented Grunge, nor especially adhered to its tenets. But *Gish* ushered in its advent regardless, and ensured that once Nirvana emerged out of nowhere, a lot of people already knew where nowhere was.

Indeed, for all the Smashing Pumpkin's steadfast avoidance of the grunge tag, they nevertheless found themselves shovelled right in there, despite the direction of 'Siva,' and despite such delicate gems as 'Daydream' and the wonderfully, acoustic 'Bye June' – a demo that would cap November's *Lull* EP, a fan's-favourite round-up of the album cut 'Rhinoceros,' plus the *Gish* outtakes, 'Blue' and 'Slunk.'

None of that mattered once Nirvana's *Nevermind* hit the streets – never mind, it was all over, as the media sustained whiplash *en masse* and shuffled a batch of bands together like a bushel of apples. The Smashing Pumpkins were sucked right into the vortex and Corgan, for one, was a little grumpy about it.

The band weren't ungrateful for all the hype, of course. It was just that Corgan wasn't 'altogether happy about the direction it was coming from.' Neither was he surprised by the haste with which the Smashing Pumpkins were scooped up in the new craze. As he himself admitted, 'we're a pain in the ass to describe, we're so specific and distinctive that it causes a lot of problems.'

Given the critical loathing for any loose ends when it comes to pretending that every band has its place, it was better to just lump them in with the rest of the pack. Easier, and as events played out – safer too.

However, there was another dimension to the entire issue. Even within his discontent, Corgan could not help but absorb, and inwardly celebrate, a sense of community quite unlike any he had hitherto felt, or even envisioned, in the past. From all corners, it seemed, a new wave was gathering, one that drew its energies and impetus from all over the United States.

That was the wave that the Smashing Pumpkins now found themselves riding, surfing on a generational mudslide that nothing could resist. 'The Beatles and the Rolling Stones redefined [the music industry],' Corgan explained. 'Before the Beatles, bands didn't [even] write their own songs.' Looking around at the groundswell that surrounded him, Corgan believed a similar revolution was imminent today. And, though he didn't know how the pieces would fall together, still the conviction was inescapable, not only that a great new musical movement was inevitable, but that its progress was also inexorable. And it didn't matter whether or not the Smashing Pumpkins wanted to be a part of it or not. They were along for the ride regardless.

It wasn't only on a musical level that the Smashing Pumpkins found themselves being hauled into a bout from which, for the time being, there could emerge just one winner. That same autumn, Kurt Cobain and Hole's Courtney Love emerged as lovers, the King and Queen…or the John and Yoko? Opinions really were that divided….of the Grunge scene. But who had Love been visiting the evening she met her future husband? None other than Billy Corgan.

'She's told everyone that she flew out to Chicago to see Nirvana,' Corgan revealed years later. 'And that's where she hooked up with Kurt. The truth of the matter is, that she came out to see me; I flipped out, ended up making her leave my apartment. She goes to the show, gets completely fucked up, goes home with Kurt, fucks Kurt, calls me the next morning and begs me to let her come back over to my house. That's the way it happened.'

Naturally, the speculation surrounding both Corgan's protestations and Love's denials have – and will – never be suppressed by anything so mundane as a reasonable explanation; neither would that speculation ever heal the bitterness that allegedly sparked one-sidedly between Cobain and Corgan – the Nirvana frontman apparently went to his grave referring to Corgan as the 'Pear-shaped box,' while scandal-lovers the world over still believe Hole's 'Violet,' with its snarling chorus of 'go on, take everything,' was targeted personally at Corgan.

None of which matters a jot. Love and Cobain wound their way together, and Corgan eventually reconciled his troubles with Fabian. And that was that.

For his own part, Corgan – no matter how goaded he has been over the years – has said very little regarding his time with Love, and neither should he.

Private lives are private. He's always maintained that the real Love, like the real Corgan, is very different to the public perception, and lets it go at that. It's the rest of the world that refused to leave the story alone, resurrecting it constantly throughout the remainder of Cobain's lifetime; again when Love and Corgan were reunited in the studio in 1998; and on sundry occasions in between times.

Although Hut Records had not scheduled *Gish* for a European release until early in the New Year, a 12-inch of 'Siva' had impacted hard in the UK, while the excitement swirling around the band back home only exacerbated the sense of expectation. Long before Grunge became a household name in America... long before most people thought of The Pacific Northwest as anything but the last outpost of apple-pie, a cup of coffee and TV's *Twin Peaks* before you hit the Canadian border...Sub Pop had become a near-household name in Britain, championed by a music press that itself had long despaired of Britain ever counter-acting the country's own shambolic terrors.

The last years of Margaret Thatcher's government, as even her own ministers seemed convinced that she had finally let go of reality, saw the nation slip beneath a gloomy shroud that made one positively nostalgic for the discontent that had once sparked Punk Rock. But only the maniacal escapism of the Madchester clan seemed even halfway prepared to battle those chimeras, and not every social problem can be remedied with drugs.

Crossing the ocean on imported wax, Grunge, on the other hand, packed a morose universality that everyone could share in, a sense of brutality that – again – may not have had the answers to all of life's most awful problems, but promised relief from them regardless, in the communal merging of the mosh pit, in the brain-charring bludgeon of guitars-on-fire and drums-on-stun.

It was just a fleeting moment – six months on from *Nevermind*, and Suede were already taking their first glamour-pussed footsteps into the gaping holes of rock'n'roll's heart. But nobody knew that was going to happen and, though the Smashing Pumpkins' visit that September 1991 was little more than a smash and grab, the advance word on their one London show regarded the band like incoming deities.

Flying in from Ghent, Belgium, following a handful of shows in the Low Countries, the Smashing Pumpkins had two dates to take care of – their UK live debut at the Camden Underworld on 6 September...where *Melody Maker*'s Cathi Unsworth praised their 'freshness, an acerbic enthusiasm...[a] vicious/delicious flurry of love beads, hair, leather and stardust'; and a John Peel session on 8 September. It was, from Billy Corgan's own account, to prove a hair-raising occasion.

Better remembered, perhaps, as drummer with 70's rock legends Mott The Hoople, Dale Griffin had been producing sessions for the BBC since the early 1980s, turning in some of the best-loved outings in the entire session library.

He was already aware of the Smashing Pumpkins; thought 'the band was astounding,' and singled out Chamberlin as – and he should know – a truly 'great drummer.'

His encounter with the band got off to a bad start, however, first when what Corgan dismissed as 'a technical misunderstanding' saw the band arrive late for the date; then when they realised that the great John Peel himself would not be waiting to welcome them into his world. Miscommunication then piled onto misunderstanding. Griffin remembers the first battleground came as the band inspected the equipment. 'Billy Corgan seemed to think I was trying to short change him in some way, like I was only using "the cheap mics" on their session.' In fact, Griffin continues, 'we were using beautiful old, but perfectly restored ribbon mics of the highest quality' – mics that he himself had hand-selected for their ability to 'give guitar bands a powerful, rich sound.'

Corgan, however, could not be convinced. 'Billy wanted any mic, but the ones we chose carefully for the session. He seemed to want to try out all of the mics in the studio, just in case. Or he thought I was some dumb fuck.'

Further confusion flowed around the strictly regimented, and tightly-scheduled nature of Peel sessions themselves. 'The Beeb sessions are strictly timed and we had no time for that kind of "making an album" state of mind,' recalled Griffin, pointing out that even the most organised band in the land had trouble cramming more than four completed songs into their allotted time. With the dispute over the microphones having already eaten up precious minutes, the Smashing Pumpkins were always going to be racing against the clock. But when Griffin pulled the plug with just three songs taped, they simply couldn't understand why they couldn't work on and, when Corgan came to reflect on the night a couple of years later, his disappointment was still raw to the touch. He described the Peel session as 'probably number one on our all time worst experiences list.'

'Wild,' responds Griffin. 'Anyone would think we'd had a big argument – we didn't. Great band. Fucked-up fellow.'

Not that the session itself suffered from the catalogue of errors that surrounded it. Broadcast less than a week later, on 13 September (and released as a stand-alone EP the following summer), the recording found the group in fiery form, kicking out a dramatic revision of 'Siva,' plus two previously unheard tracks, 'Smiley' and – surprising many people, but scarcely a shock selection, a cover of Eric Burdon and the Animals' 'A Girl Named Sandoz.'

Originally released in April, 1967 as the b-side to the Top 20 hit 'When I Was Young,' 'A Girl Named Sandoz' was Burdon's paean to the psychedelic era's then-drug of choice. Sandoz was the Basle, Switzerland-based pharmaceutical company where Albert Hofman, so fondly remembered as the man who discovered LSD, was working when he made his so influential breakthrough. Recast as a tender love song, but drenched in giveaway acid-flecked fuzz, the song emerged as a multi-layered journey through one hell of a trip; a voyage that the Smashing Pumpkins themselves recreated with beguiling fortitude. Retaining the sleazy guitars and Hendrix-y bass lines that nailed the original to its own purposefully hazed, dazed lethargy, Corgan even modelled his vocal delivery on Eric Burdon's prime performance. The result was the session showpiece, and the drawing of a taut thread between 1960's Acid Rock and the rise of Alternative groove.

It was, of course, a thread that the Smashing Pumpkins would continue merrily twanging deep into their future.

CHAPTER EIGHT

YOU GET A LOT FOR YOUR QUARTER

The Smashing Pumpkins were back out on the road again almost the moment they returned home, wrapping up the final dates of their own summer tour, and then reversing the van back out of the garage to join the Red Hot Chili Peppers' latest outing. The Los Angelino funksters' *BloodSugarSexMagik* album had itself just transformed the Peppers from an under-achieving practical joke, into elder statesmen of the Alternative scene – the band had been around since the early 1980s, they'd just scored their very first Top 50 album. And the excitement that swirled around the band was evident in the size of the venues where they were now touching down – arenas and auditoriums all around the United States.

The Smashing Pumpkins were not the first choice openers – both Soundgarden and the all-girl L7 were also considered for what was shaping up to be among the most prestigious tours of the year. The Smashing Pumpkins were finally invited on board after top Pepper Anthony Kiedis caught them performing on MTV's *120 Minutes* and was blown away by 'this very different, beautiful, musical aesthetic.'

Once aboard, they wasted no time in making their mark. Pledging a live repertoire that would shuffle around from night to night as the material settled into these unaccustomed new surroundings, the Smashing Pumpkins joined the tour on all-but home turf, leaping into the fray on 16 October for their first stadium gig at Madison, Wisconsin's Oscar Meyer Theater – named for the manufacturer of a range of popular luncheon meats.

A week later, with every intervening night an absolute triumph, the two bands were joined by Pearl Jam, eagerly anticipating the January 1992 release of their own debut, *Ten*, and themselves acknowledging the impact of the Smashing Pumpkins' arrival with an album whose debt to *Gish*'s refusal to camouflage its heritage was unmistakeable. The Seattle band had already tentatively scheduled a club tour for the New Year, to coincide with *Ten*, but the opportunity to tour with not one, but two of the hottest bands of the age saw them abandon those plans without a second thought.

The three bands rocked the country through November with nearly a show a night, city to city across the United States, and everyone upped the temperature a little – on 1 November, the Smashing Pumpkins and Pearl Jam even joined the headliners onstage for the encore, to help celebrate Anthony Kiedis' twenty-ninth birthday – mercifully, Corgan and co. chose not to follow Eddie Vedder's lead, and appear onstage naked bar a strategically-dangling sock.

Other nights, the Smashing Pumpkins remained true to their word and jiggled each show a little, to deviate from a straight *Gish* set – although those songs still represented the lion's share of material. However, the band did preview 'Drown' a song they would gift to the 1992 *Singles* soundtrack, and reprise 'Smiley', as well as the marvellous 'Obscured', which was recorded during the *Gish* sessions and would ultimately wind it's way onto the 'Today' single later on.

By the time the Smashing Pumpkins peeled off the tour in early December (to be replaced, with vibrant serendipity, by Nirvana), it was as much an acknowledgement of their own soaring status, as it was the need to return to plans that had already been laid – more than one reviewer, and many thousands of gig-goers, confessed that even before the Red Hot Chili Peppers came on stage, the audience had already received its money's worth from the bill. Almost a decade later the magic of those evenings was recaptured when *Rolling Stone* magazine included this leg of the tour amongst 'the greatest concerts of the 1990s.' Kiedis told the magazine '[the Smashing Pumpkins] had sort of a feminine dynamic. Even when I wasn't watching, when I was listening when we were getting ready backstage, I could tell that [Corgan] meant it.'

Riding the adulation that spilled out from those shows, the Smashing Pumpkins launched into their own west coast outing during December, breaking in a handful of new songs, but also winding down from a tumultuous year. By Christmas, the two week break that loomed ahead of them was a Christmas gift in itself, and the now traditional New Year's Eve show at the Cabaret Metro was less a gig than a near-all-night party. It was only when you stepped back and actually looked at the four musicians, bathed in sweat and drenched in triumph, that there was even a suggestion of unease playing around their eyes, and only when you caught them off-guard that it was possible to vaguely sense the tensions that would soon be edging their way up to the surface.

That *Gish* managed to crack the Billboard Top Two Hundred – admittedly peaking at a creaky number a hundred and ninety-five – was a remarkable feat for a band that was all but unknown in the mainstream market that dominated the American Pop chart; and even more remarkable that the Smashing Pumpkins themselves were an oddly-named band from the Middle West.

But, with this feat tucked into the scrapbook, *Gish* was not simply an indication of all that Grunge already was. It was a beacon for all that it was capable of becoming, just as the Smashing Pumpkins were never comfortable being described as a grunge band, when everything they aspired towards looked beyond the simple bandwagon that was picking up pace all around them.

Blending Corgan's 70's rock love affair with the gritty fragments of Punk and a host of private demons, the Smashing Pumpkins ultimately emerged through dirt clouds and barbed wire with a whole new battery of energies. Yet, they were shackled to the movement regardless, with the likelihood of escape only diminished by their own on-going fascination with the commercial mechanics of all that it entailed – a fatal attraction that was proven when the band agreed to supply that one song to the soundtrack of the forthcoming movie, *Singles*, and confirm their figurative marriage to the Seattle scene.

And the only excuse that they could possibly deliver in their own defence is the fact that they had no idea just how huge the movie was set to become; just how readily director Cameron Crowe's love-story-with-flannel would become the aperture that split Seattle wide-open in the eyes of the outside world, confirming the city's ascendancy to those who were already aware of it, and introducing it to an entire new audience that wasn't on track with Alternative music. Rightly or wrongly, *Singles* took a single interpretation, ran it through the rosy glasses of Hollywood, and transformed it into gospel. Crowe then further backed its vision with ferocious sounds, and sold it to the world.

The movie not only used Seattle as its backdrop, tracking its action from the O.K. Hotel to the low-rent apartments on Capitol Hill, it also rounded up a crop of local bands, and audiences as well. With actor Matt Dillon wrapping his own short hair in stubbornly-greasy grunge-laden locks, and fronting the fictional band Citizen Dick, (Pearl Jam's Eddie Vedder was recruited as his drummer; Jeff Ament's wardrobe was hijacked for the star's), the timing of the film could not have been better.

Though it was conceived and, indeed, shot months before any of the future had hit the fan – the wrap party was held on 25 May 1991 – it would be another nine months before the entire project was complete, by which time everybody involved knew precisely what they were letting themselves in for, and by which time the entire scene with all its attendant players was beginning to move on as the inevitable strains of sell-out danced merrily around the periphery.

For the local bands that starred on the soundtrack, a role call that included Soundgarden, Pearl Jam, the Screaming Trees, Mudhoney and Alice In Chains, the world that *Singles* illustrated was one to which they were already irrevocably bound. For Paul Westerberg, former frontman for Minneapolis' Replacements, inclusion confirmed his already burgeoning role as a godfather-of-sorts to the Alternative scene in general. And for Jimi Hendrix and Mother Love Bone, it really didn't make much difference how people perceived them.

For the Smashing Pumpkins, however, perception remained their most solid link to the success that had so far attended them, and, when the group entered Waterfront Studios, in Hoboken, New Jersey, to begin recording their own contribution to the soundtrack, 'Drown,' it was surely in the knowledge that participation in the movie could easily drown them.

As it turned out, and for whatever reason, the Waterfront sessions did not go well; weeks later, the group were back on the more familiar soil of Butch Vig's Smart set-up, and trying again to nail the eight-minute masterpiece with which they would be gracing the film. And this time, they cracked it. 'Drown' slipped effortlessly in alongside Pearl Jam's 'Breathe' and Mudhoney's 'Overblown'; slid in, too, amongst the half-dozen or so soundtrack morsels that were pulled away for radio play by 'Alternative' stations around the US. But, while the Smashing Pumpkins – and radio itself – pushed hard for the song to be culled as one of the singles that would help push the soundtrack...having already agreed to a radical edit, Corgan even professed himself 'willing to make a video'...they were denied at every turn as Epic, the soundtrack's label, shoved their own conglomerate's bands into the spotlight.

It didn't really matter. The group were left with the knowledge that, in 'Drown,' they had cut one of the greatest hit singles that was neither a hit or a single and, though they never put the song on album (it was eventually rounded up for inclusion on *Greatest Hits With Judas O*), it became a regular visitor to their live set during the latter half of 1992 and into 1993. The song would also make a dramatic reappearance during the band's 2000 Machina, Resume The Pose, and Sacred and Profane tours, and always merited a war whoop cry from the audience. And Corgan laughed as he observed, 'when we play the song now, the reaction is like it was a hit song. Eight minutes – you get a lot for your quarter.'

Singles seems almost painfully old-fashioned today, quaint in the same way that those late 50's American teen rock'n'roll films are – 'hey gang, let's put the show on here! And who cares if our moms and dads don't like it, they're all square and they don't understand.' And, in many ways, the Smashing Pumpkins' participation was not misguided, as the film turned out to be a perfect mirror of their own relationship with the grunge scene – completely absorbed by the aura of the era, completely representative of the genre it showcased, yet somehow utterly out of step with the pack, and watching everything with the quizzical eye of the outsider.

But whereas a movie is allowed to step outside of its imagery, a band rarely is. And henceforth, when the Smashing Pumpkins protested at the lazy critics who simply lumped them in with the grunge brigade, it was difficult to respond with any realistic sympathy. They hadn't exactly fought against it, after all.

Away from what would, as the year progressed, prove itself one of the toughest battlegrounds upon which the group would ever find itself – or, one of the greatest challenges, depending upon how deeply one wants to try and analyze the quartet's motives – the Smashing Pumpkins returned to Europe in January 1992, kicking off a month long tour in Hilversum, Netherlands, with an in-studio gig for VPRO Radio – broadcast on 15 January, it caught the group performing 'Snail,' 'Siva,' 'Crush' and 'Silverfuck' before Corgan wrapped up the airtime with a short interview.

From there it was on to Belgium, for a return engagement in Ghent, where they were joined by the support band with whom they would spend the next four weeks, the fast-rising English combo Catherine Wheel.

It was an inspired pairing. Itself newly released to raw applause, the Great Yarmouth quartet's *Ferment* LP debut was a worthy partner of *Gish*. Part distorted shoegazing miasma, part Black Sabbath inspired rock and roll, and seldom less than a full-on frontal assault, Catherine Wheel were catapulted to attention via the unstoppable *Black Metallic* EP in the fall of 1991. And, although the two bands' music was intrinsically different, still they shared a passion that was scarily similar as Corgan and singer Rob Dickinson captured, from opposite sides of the ocean, the raging vitality of all that rock'n'roll pledged the new decade.

Informed by 70's icons and completely corrupting their message – how ironic that Dickinson's own cousin should be Iron Maiden's Bruce Dickinson – and blasting their emotions through a wall of fuzz pedals and wah-wah guitar solos, both Catherine Wheel and Smashing Pumpkins had the ability to assault their audience with a continuous barrage of riffs and licks, while never losing sight of the fragility and beauty that lingered just below the surface. Same ideal, completely different intent. It couldn't have been better than that.

Catherine Wheel bassist Dave Hawes remembers, 'I, personally, had only seen [the Smashing Pumpkins'] name in the music press and hadn't heard any songs, so I was [most] excited because we hadn't played in Europe before...and we got a real tour bus to boot! This was a bit embarrassing because when we arrived outside the Belgian venue for our first date, the Pumpkins and their road-crew were all travelling in what really was an over-sized Transit van!'

He continues, 'it was the usual headline/support band practise of not really speaking to each other until the third show. By the end of the tour, I was closest to Jimmy...there's a great photo of the two of us passed out on each others' shoulders in the bar at the Columbia Hotel in London at the end-of-tour party. He was easily the most accessible.

'D'Arcy, I found quite introverted at first, but as we got further into the tour we always would end up having a chat. She was a big Iggy fan, so Punk would often come up.' Among Hawes' enduring memories of the outing is the sight of her in the dressing room before a show, head down and her long blonde hair covering a copy of Marion Zimmer-Bradley's *The Mists Of Avalon* – one of his own favourite books.

'James I have no real recollection of conversing with in any length. It was always a nod, smile and "How you doing?" when we passed. And Billy was...Billy. Probably just the same now as he was then. Leader of the pack! I'm not saying that in a derogatory way by any means. He was always very focused on the "task in hand." Most of the time convivial; sometimes laconic' – and, one night mid-tour, in such desperate need of downtime that Chamberlin, Wretzky and Iha all boarded Catherine Wheel's bus instead of their own, just to give him some space.

There were dramas nevertheless. In Lund, Sweden, the Smashing Pumpkins' show was so beset by technical problems that, according to Hawes, 'I think they managed two songs, one of which was pure feedback, and then stormed off stage...' but only after Corgan informed the solidly sold-out venue precisely what he thought of them and their country, before vowing never to play Sweden again. And, sure enough, the following night's show in Stockholm was cancelled.

In stark contrast to that, Hawes concludes, 'Billy had a stinker of a cold in Birmingham and everyone was sure he was going to cancel, but he showed up and performed like a real trouper.'

The Smashing Pumpkins' presence across Europe throughout January and February – they also visited Germany, Switzerland and France, before returning to the UK – was timed, of course, to coincide with the long-awaited European release of *Gish*. Those in the know had already been savouring the album via import for half a year, but the remainder had only been teased, by memories of the 'Siva' single and the September Underworld show, or the critical word-of-mouth that flowed across the ocean from America. February, however, brought a staggering one-two punch as, first, the *Lull* EP hit the stores, three months after its American appearance; and then *Gish* swung into shimmering view.

With the band seemingly constantly on the road, *Gish* would ultimately go on to sell a whopping seven hundred thousand copies worldwide. But, outside the hallowed corridors of the sales and marketing team, Corgan and his band mates had other things to think about – like the genesis of their next album. Breaking away from their European dates, the Smashing Pumpkins returned home via their first ever trip to Hawaii (for a show in Honolulu) in early March.

They'd sewn up the present, now it was time to begin embroidering the future.

CHAPTER NINE
BALEFUL PANDEMONIUM

Immediately after returning to Chicago, the Smashing Pumpkins booked themselves into the local Soundworks studios, to begin working up material that would predict, if not wholly embrace, the directions towards which they were aiming their next album. Their first task was to record b-sides for what Hut had already decided would be their next UK single, 'I Am One.' With Corgan co-producing alongside Kerry Brown, drummer with the local Chicago band Catherine, the Smashing Pumpkins cut four songs: 'Plume,' 'Starla' and the instrumentals 'Hope' and 'Bullet Train To Osaka.' Corgan has since disparaged the inclusion of both 'Plume' and 'Starla,' indicating that they were only ever really intended as demos, and that they were brought to play when the band needed to fill out the UK single b-sides.

The following month, April 1992, saw the Smashing Pumpkins back on the road as they were ushered into the oddest in-concert pairing they had yet been subjected to, opening for Guns 'N' Roses for two shows on their *Use Your Illusion* tour – a widescreen warm-up in Oklahoma City on 6 April, followed by what could well have been an utterly tremulous triumphal homecoming, three days later, at the Rosemont Horizon in Rosemont, Illinois.

Here they were, after all, psychedelia-tinged grunge gurus, opening for the most mainstream, white-bread, watered down version of the Los Angeles glam scene to have survived its implosion. The very prospect should have made smaller bands quake – Axl Rose and Slash were living up to their larger than life reputations, and, across much of the country, Guns 'N' Roses were still quite the stuff in the early 1990s.

For Corgan and the Smashing Pumpkins, though, it was a chance to rock – on the largest stage they had ever walked, with a completely different audience. There would be no approving yowls from the Alternative crowd here. It was balls-out metal time and the Smashing Pumpkins weren't going to let the moment pass them by. Withdrawing from the set anything that even looked like a gentle ballad, a tender moment, a precious oasis of restraint and taste, they redesigned their offering as an armour-clad leviathan – and, if the end result didn't blow the headliners off the stage, it at least ensured that the audience wouldn't be howling the Smashing Pumpkins off it either. If there were any dissenting voices in the crowd, they were drowned beneath the volume that the band kicked up from the outset.

The Smashing Pumpkins returned to more familiar realities as they launched their own headlining series of shows through the mid-west that summer, plucking support bands from within their own circle of friends. Kerry Brown's Catherine, Oklahoma City's Chainsaw Kittens and fellow Chicagoans Red Red Meat were all invited to fill the opening slots. All, of course, would go on to play their own significant role within the Smashing Pumpkins' future career.

The Chainsaw Kittens' Tyson Meade recalls 'we were about to start making our second record, *Flipped Out In Singapore*, and the label [Atlantic subsidiary Mammoth] wanted us to have Butch Vig produce it. We didn't really know who he was, because he hadn't done the Nirvana record yet. But we said we'd check him out. He was doing *Gish* at that point, and he got our first record, *Violent Religion*, in the mail and I guessed he played it for Billy, and Billy totally loved it – "Oh Butch, you've got to do this band." And, from then on, the Pumpkins more or less took us under their wing. They were rising really fast, and we were still travelling pretty much at a snail's pace.'

Red Red Meat, meanwhile, were riding the self release of their debut LP, an impressive manipulation of Chicago's famous Blues, recorded with Jimmy Chamberlin on drums. Formed the previous year by vocalist Tim Rutili and bassist Glynnis Johnson out of the wreckage of their post-punk outfit Friends of Betty, the band's rising profile was certainly assisted by the summer gigs with the Smashing Pumpkins. So, however, were the destructive forces that had been plaguing Red Red Meat since its inception, as Rutili and Johnson's own personal relationship shattered. Out of the band, Johnson, who was in the final stages of AIDS related illness, passed away not long after. The Smashing Pumpkins would record their own tribute to her, 'Glynis,' for the *No Alternative* AIDS benefit album the following year.

The Smashing Pumpkins' live sets were still filled with favourites from *Gish*, but there were other songs filtering in as well now, as they began to try out some of the new material that was gestating. In Milwaukee, Wisconsin on 9 June, the band played a meandering, but magical set seemingly designed to the same specifications as the venue itself. The Unicorn, on 300 W. Juneau Ave. was located underground, a dark ramble down a close staircase and through multiple rooms. The Smashing Pumpkins' set, too, took its witnesses through some unfamiliar twisting corridors. 'Disarm' made an early appearance, alongside 'Frail And Bedazzled' and the still unreleased 'Bullet Train To Osaka' while the band also turned in a cover of Steve Miller's party anthem 'The Joker.' (The band also serenaded Jimmy Chamberlin, who would turn twenty-eight on the 10th, with a rousing rendition of 'Happy Birthday.')

The Midwestern excursion over, it was then back to the United Kingdom for a handful of shows in the days leading up to their appearance at the annual Reading Festival at the end of August. With the re-released 'I Am One' hot on the shelves (it would crack the UK charts in early September) the band should have been flying high. Their day-out at the festival, however, would come close to completely undoing them.

That year's three day gala was packed to brimful with an even more eclectic mix of bands than was the festival's usual want. Inspired by the example of Perry Farrell's all-American Lollapalooza – which in turn, so famously, was inspired by Reading itself – the weekend's billing swirled from the still new but swiftly ascending Suede, to hardcore rap progenitors Public Enemy, from the Wonder Stuff to the Fatima Mansions and on, inevitably, to a healthy contingent of American Grunge, played out via the so-called riot-grrls of L7, primal sludge merchants the Melvins, Sub Pop demi-gods Mudhoney and, topping the whole pile off, Nirvana.

For each of the bands filing in to fly the flannel flag, Reading would prove a triumph. What happened to the Smashing Pumpkins, however, would go down in their – and everyone else's – diaries as one of those inevitable days of infamy when anything that could go wrong turned out even worse than that. By the end of the day, Billy Corgan was reportedly on the verge of packing it all in.

As the Smashing Pumpkins took the stage late in the afternoon, they already knew that they had some big shoes to follow. Whereas the rest of their be-flannelled compatriots, the headlining Nirvana included, were billed to appear on the third day, a western bloc that amounted to a mini-fest in its own right, deranged scheduling placed the Smashing Pumpkins at the climax of a clutch of sets by some of England's own then-most popular acts – Suede and the Manic Street Preachers, Sunscreem, the Farm and EMF... it was Party Central party-time, flamboyant, flaming and flirtatious. And then out came the Smashing Pumpkins, still in tempestuous post-Guns 'N' Roses noise-mangle mode, and any groovy vibes aroused by the last two hours of non-stop celebration were ground into the thick Reading mud.

From the very outset of their performance, the band were plagued with the technical troubles that Corgan so desperately hated and, no sooner was one feedback-screeching gremlin erased, than another would clamber into another piece of equipment. Chamberlin recalled 'in the middle of the second song – boom! – the wheel falls off the cart. Billy broke his guitar, threw it into the audience and it hit our record company president in the head.' Desperately trying to hold themselves together, but knowing from the look of the audience that the whole thing was falling apart, the Smashing Pumpkins stumbled through a lacklustre set that included 'Bury Me' and 'Siva' from Gish, tried to raise the temperature with a clutch of new songs...'Geek U.S.A' and 'Hummer' among them...and dropped in a playful 'Hello Kitty Kat.'

But they were already dog-tired from way-too-much touring, and all the peripheral fuss that follows a band as it tries to rise. And Corgan, for his part, was just plain old at the end of his ropes, assailed by the first of the personal demons that would ultimately see him diagnosed with a bout of massive depression. But even his temper tantrum went awry. Whipping his guitar into mic stands and amps, during and between songs, it took the better part of the set before he was able to actually destroy the instrument, by which time the audience had had more than enough of the pouting prima donna who'd turned up to trash their good mood.

'Fuck the Smashing Pumpkins!' festival-goer Dolores Scott wrote to an American friend after the show. 'I was so desperate to see them cos you love them so much. Next time they play, I'll make sure I'm babysitting.'

The audience was bitter, reviews were rough. But Corgan was furious, stalking off stage and, according to several supposedly knowledgeable sources, he came close to shattering the band on the spot. Three years later, however, in 1995, he told Q magazine, 'That's all bullshit. One gig is not going to make us break up. That's English journalists over-hyping the importance of an English Festival.' Nevertheless, he conceded, 'we were upset with each other because it was one of a handful of times where we've let each other down,' and as their bus drove away from the festival grounds Wretzky and Chamberlin were loudly vowing they would never be in each other's bands ever, ever again. Corgan concluded 'in seven years we've probably had about three or four bad gigs and that was number one.'

Yet there was to be no respite for the road-weary warriors. Limping off for a handful of dates in Belgium and the Netherlands, the Smashing Pumpkins were back in England in the middle of September, to tape a seething 'Rhinoceros' for the BBC's *Late Show*, and play a thunderous set at the Manchester International. The band that Billy Corgan was only dreaming of putting together when he met New Order in Chicago, were now selling out that same band's hometown, and Peter Hook reflected paternally, 'lo and behold, years later, I was watching the band he was thinking of forming, the Smashing Pumpkins, sell out arenas in Manchester.'

The band also played shows in Nottingham and London and Corgan, reflecting upon his own personal credo that 'great ideas often have a nasty habit of going horribly wrong,' later recalled one of his own favourite nightmare experiences. 'When we played London I thought it would be really funny to come out for the encore dressed in a clown suit. I dunno, it was one of those things which seemed like a great idea when I first thought about it – "Okay, I'll wear the clown suit." But then I was backstage putting it on, knowing that within minutes I'd be walking out in front of four thousand five hundred people with a red nose and a funny hat and big floppy shoes, and suddenly it didn't seem such a great idea. Only by then it was too late.'

The way he told writer Dave Thompson the story, you would have expected a grisly ending, beer and spit hurled at the stage by sweaty limbs, with Corgan creeping off stage to be known evermore as "Bozo." However, the backfire backfired and, Corgan continued, 'a friend who saw the show told me afterwards that once the initial shock had worn off, he forgot I was even wearing it, and just got into the music again.'

Back from Europe, at long last, the end of the road was in sight. Gratefully returning to Chicago, the Smashing Pumpkins would play a meagre handful of shows between the end of September and the close of the year, as they battled instead to put themselves back together. Everyone was exhausted, shattered beyond the realms of simple tiredness, and entering that arena where even keeping your thoughts straight was an impossible task. Corgan himself was convinced that he was losing his mind. So the last thing he wanted, as he tried to get some sleep, was a reminder that *Gish* was now more than twelve months old, and it was time to start thinking seriously about following it up.

The Soundworks sessions had been successful, the new songs that were squeezing into the live set were great. It should be no problem at all to begin pulling a new album together – or would it? Only Corgan truly knew that the handful of new songs was just that – a handful; and that he'd not done a thing to increase that quantity in half a year. Nearly two years of solid touring had left the band precious little time to look forward to their next adventure, let alone write songs. Neither had they had a chance to rework the bare bones of the new songs into something that the studio could shape into anything workable. He had no intention whatsoever of simply wandering in and banging 'em down – that wasn't how the Smashing Pumpkins worked, it wasn't how he himself thought.

Yet the alternative was equally gruelling, the idea that he could delve into a brain that felt drained of all but life's most instinctive emotions, and pull out anything that would not shatter in the daylight. Exhaustion turned to panic, and his already incipient depression was poised to absorb another fear into its blackness.

It wasn't simply exhaustion that was weighing the Smashing Pumpkins down. Their own personal relationships, too, had taken a heavy beating over the past year.

Ricocheting from town to town, from country to country, from van to plane and then back round again, the Smashing Pumpkins found themselves undertaking a tour that would have lasted – off, but more often on – for the better part of a year and a half. It was the closest they'd ever been to one another, and the longest they'd spent in one another's company. And, if the public face of their career was racing towards the sky, behind the scenes, matters were somewhat more frail.

The pressures came in from two directions, crushing the band in a pincerlike grip from which it was difficult ever to find some respite. Externally, the musical movement that had embraced the Smashing Pumpkins, and which they themselves had embraced in return, was a straitjacket within which they were never too comfortable. The ruthless totalitarianism that strikes at every genre was no surprise, of course – as far back as rock'n'roll's first emergence, audiences had baulked viciously at any artist's attempts to swerve away from their public's preconceptions, and the annals of pop history are littered with the corpses of bands that pressed on regardless.

For, just as their own audience might react with betrayal, so others might respond with distrust. The Smashing Pumpkins' own intentions to distance themselves from the Grungewagon upon which they'd blithely ridden so far were no secret, of course. But, neither was the alacrity with which they'd taken the ride. At least half of the problem facing the band as they attempted to piece together their next generation of songs, was the knowledge that they needed to walk a very fine line. And one misplaced footfall could doom them forever.

How easy, however, would it be to take that misstep, as Iha and Wretzky, emotionally involved for much of the Smashing Pumpkins' lifespan so far, began to disengage, breaking up as the touring ground on, in an environment that seemed purposefully designed to prevent them from ever gaining the personal distance they required. Simply trying to play together on stage while their own private conflicts were coming to a head, while they were trying to untangle and separate the emotions of their relationship, was almost too painful to bear. A break-up in the real world is bad enough, but wrapped up in the stringent rigors of a never-ending tour, it was magnified tenfold.

Iha summed it up most cogently: 'All the normal stuff that would happen between a boyfriend and girlfriend who had broken up after a long time relationship was happening, only we were stuck together.' And, indeed, they were absolutely stuck together. With the buzz and hum thrumming around *Gish* and the tour, gruelling as it had become, looking to finish with more than a modicum of success, it seemed improbable that either Iha or Wretsky would actually be able to take any time out, or time apart. The Smashing Pumpkins had become a living, breathing being on the road, and all the band members had spent far too long on that process to shrug off something as tetchy as a break up.

But it couldn't have been that offhand, really. Although both Iha and Wretzky have remained largely mum on that period of their lives together, one can only imagine how messy it must have been for the pair, slogging through those last days on the road, cramped in the tour van, camped out in hotels, on floors, and on stages probably a little too small for their immediate liking. But, in spite of a look here or turned back on stage there, the shows continued apace.

Life behind scenes remains cloaked in silence, and it's only for the band to know what the energy was like as Iha and Wretsky struggled to come to terms with the blow up of their relationship and to sift through the remains in order to put together the friendship that would emerge from the wreckage. The break-up didn't appear to affect their musicianship, from the outside at least. If anything, both parties could direct frustration straight through fingers to strings and finally out of the stacks of amps that broadcast their pain and anger, angst and grief to the assembled multitude.

If tensions between Iha and Wretsky had reached any kind of head, one only had to look in front and behind them, for both Corgan and Chamberlin were ticking faster as well. These tensions were high throughout the last months of the tour, and the Smashing Pumpkins shrugged them off as best they could, to brandish sword-and-scythe across sets that did more than prove their rising eminence. But worse was to come as Corgan continued mourning his separation from Chris Fabian. According to *Creem* magazine, Corgan took refuge in food, 'eating himself into a state of bloated oblivion, a little human butterball who used to write great songs.' And, just when it seemed that things couldn't get worse, they did, as Jimmy Chamberlin announced that he wanted to quit the band, to take care of drug and alcohol problems that themselves had been exacerbated by so long a time on the road.

Finding himself increasingly unable to control his own mind and body, and with the rest of the band increasingly concerned not only for his health and well being, but also for the upcoming sessions and the very existence of the band itself, Chamberlin entered a Los Angeles area rehab clinic for twenty-eight days of treatment.

He told *Q* magazine in 1995 that 'it's weird because you're young and someone hands you a bunch of money.' Alongside those bags of cash comes the unwritten and unfortunate subtext of rock'n'roll that has derailed many a musician – that being a total fuck up and drug addled wastrel keeps the popularity meter ticking. Chamberlin felt, too, that it was easy to 'buy into' the whole myth. Still fresh-faced, now hooked, the means to indulge whatever whim he fancied quickly led into a downward spiral that crippled, and continued crippling. Chamberlin admitted, all those years later, that beating demons was 'still not easy, it's an everyday thing.' With what would quickly reveal itself as an awful prophecy, he confessed, 'sometimes I need to go out and fucking tie one on.'

In later years, as commentators looked back upon the life of the Smashing Pumpkins, the sheer tumult that hit the band...and kept on hitting it, for this was only the beginning of their travails...was frequently reduced to little more than a soap opera, a succession of events through which the four band members could only grit their teeth and plough on, secure only in the knowledge that no matter how bad things seem today, they were bound to become even more complicated tomorrow.

How infrequently, on the other hand, did those same commentators pull back to consider the fact that, behind the press releases and grapevine gloss, these were real people dealing with real lives; that their personal problems were not simply a sideshow staged for the delectation of the watching hordes; and that a lot more hung in the balance than simply giving Corgan something new to hinge his lyrics around.

For, as grotesque as it was to watch the group jerking haplessly to the strings of a malevolent puppeteer, it was far more vicious to read the critics lining up not, simply to imply, but to actually insist that the crisis points plaguing the group were part of the Smashing Pumpkins' own *modus operandi*; that they were physically decaying to a preconceived strategy, that they literally thrived on strife.

It is true that the day-to-day living of life as a band did have a hand in shaping their destiny; true that, had they been simply four friends who met up for a drink every Friday, things might have been very different for them all. And it is true that, without the friction and fire-burn of that life, Billy Corgan's lyrics and James Iha's guitar licks might never have attained the emotional frenzy that, in turn, communicated a reality to everybody who heard the music and felt, they thought, exactly the same way. Indeed, it was that perceived angst in Corgan's lyrics, and the tortured guitar sounds that bled out around them, that would become synonymous with the Smashing Pumpkins – an existentialist agony that transcended mere grungy rock and roll, to become as endless a cycle of swelling and falling as the group's own career was destined to appear. And that, in turn, inspired Corgan to speak of a 'guitar power that puts you in a different universe.'

The universe that the band were living in, however, was the same one that everyday folks lived in; and the bubbles they inhabited were those that we're all familiar with, comprised of precisely the same emotional components – life, love, happiness, hopelessness. The nature of their calling, of course, amplified those emotions somewhat. But it also deadened them. When a plumber breaks up with his girlfriend, nobody knows and less people care, and they can both deal with the parting in their own private ways. When a rising pop star breaks with his or hers, everyone knows, everyone cares, and privacy went out of the window months before. Their bubble becomes a goldfish bowl. And the Smashing Pumpkins' was shattering.

It is impossible, either from without or within the Smashing Pumpkins' own immediate circle, to quantify the magnetic attraction that the group seemed to hold for disaster; for whatever crazy reason that calamity not only followed them, but actually hid behind their greatest triumphs, to howl down their pleasures with its baleful pandemonium. Yet they did, it did, and, even as the Smashing Pumpkins should have been celebrating a mercurial rise in which everything had gone right for them, they were instead left to count the personal cost of all the things that had gone wrong.

CHAPTER TEN
NOSE PICKING AND SCREAMING

Bruised and battered by the events of the past months, the Smashing Pumpkins were in desperate need of rest. But copping out and dropping out wasn't an option. There had to be a way to make it all work. It looked more and more like it would be a matter of writing and recording as they went along – and hoping that the techniques of one might somehow compensate for the deficiencies of the other.

Jimmy Chamberlin shuddered at the memory, recalling how the group 'ended up locking [them]selves in a rehearsal space for…months and working on nothing but new music eight hours a day.' As autumn turned into early winter 1992, the band slaved across sessions that slowly, but ultimately, sorted themselves into demos that they could submit to the record label.

Nearly half of the songs that would eventually appear on *Siamese Dream* were included there, from the broken-in concert newcomers 'Silverfuck,' 'Hummer' and 'Geek USA,' to new gems 'Cherub Rock,' 'Today' and 'Spaceboy.' (An early version of 'Meladori Magpie' was demoed as 'Doorstep'; so was a version of 'Set The Ray To Jerry,' another song written in the immediate wake of *Gish*, and a favourite blast in rehearsals. Destined never to end up on a Smashing Pumpkins album, it would grace the '1979' single. But though Corgan would attempt to resurrect the song later on, it ultimately never made the grade.)

Against all the odds, the sessions really did go some way towards healing the battered breeches which had assailed the band on the road; reminded them that, whatever other secrets their relationships with one another held, at the end of the day, they possessed a chemistry that had a life force all of its own. As the demo process came to an end, they were 'eighty percent satisfied with the songs,' and that seemed enough.

But even when they met up with producer Butch Vig in Toronto, the Canadian city they had selected as a suitable base of operations, uncertainty continued to assail them, and Vig himself acknowledged that it was going to be a hard grind. 'Billy felt a lot of pressure before that record came out. We postponed the start [of recording] a couple of times, primarily because he didn't feel he had all the material done. We went to Toronto with the idea of working up there. We would be riding around in the car, and he'd play me a little bit of a song and then take it off. I just got this feeling that he was not real confident with the material yet.'

Vig's recruitment to the project was a carefully studied decision. Although Corgan had already tried his hand at self-production, with Kerry Brown alongside him, Vig had proven from the very first day the Smashing Pumpkins set foot at Smart Studios, that he completely understood the group's creative make-up. He knew when to push, and when to hold back. And, with Corgan and Vig's instincts firing every synapse, the band had taken their debut farther than they'd expected. It stood to reason, then, that for their sophomore release, Vig would take them even further still. However, it also stood that the symbiosis between band and producer would allow the Smashing Pumpkins to collapse a little – provide them a smattering of home comfort and a place where they wouldn't have to break in someone new, crush preconceptions of who they were, or explain themselves to.

Toronto, however, wasn't working out, and the band began casting around for a fresh location. They found it at Atlanta's Triclops Studio – a decision that would quickly reveal itself as little short of genius.

Located in the northern part of the state, far from the mossy ocean inlets of Savannah, Atlanta is steeped with a musical tradition that encompasses the rich R&B sounds of home-grown talents James Brown and Little Richard, as well as the more contemporary rock'n'roll of the Black Crowes and the Indigo Girls. Certainly it was a far cry from the pressure-cooker of fans, friends and gratuitous hangers-on that would have surrounded the band had they remained in Chicago or Madison ('way too many distractions,' as Chamberlin put it); a far cry, too, from the bitter winter weather that bound that city to its furnaces all season long. As Chamberlin continued, with more than a small pinch of good humour, 'being cold and having to run from a van to the studio in the morning all the time is not very conducive to creativity.'

The temporary relocation also brought the Smashing Pumpkins somewhat closer to the groovy southern vibe that infused the near-by-ish Athens community of REM, Pylon and so forth, with their inestimable spirit – a spirit that Corgan remained in awe of. Michael Stipe, in particular, had always impressed Corgan; had always impressed upon him a sense of kinship even before he started to appreciate the similarities between Stipe's damnably, but so deliberately, murky vocal deliveries and his own often misinterpreted lyrics. He also openly admired the way in which REM nearly single-handedly shaped the modern college rock arena – indeed, Corgan even credited Stipe and co., with being more influential to American modern music than the ubiquitous channels of Punk. That, while perhaps not the ideal historical painting, certainly cannot be disputed.

It is an inalienable truth that Punk fuelled the seeds of revolution in the UK. However, this dangerous fire that fed on the corruption of successive local governments, and ignited the righteous to stand up for their beliefs, for their idols and their youth in a raucous battle cry that went so beautifully in tandem with the three chords that drove the music, didn't fully translate Stateside.

Punk did percolate through the musical underground, and eventually managed to go overground as the sonics were co-opted by American bands thirsty for a new direction. Some of that angst, that modern folk revival, was washed into the South, landed in Athens and was reborn in the jangled tangle of that city's distinctive sound. The slash of guitar, the pound of drums were washed clean and revitalized, creating a new sound – a Punk of sorts for the newest breed. It was a movement spearheaded by REM, and a banner now being flown by the Smashing Pumpkins. The mere proximity of Atlanta's own febrile ferocity could not help but inform their own immediate aspirations.

Triclops Sound Studio was co-founded by childhood friends Rick Meyer and Mark 'Rooster' Richardson, the latter a man whose own musical heritage read like the history of Alternative Rock in its own right. Based in New York during the mid-1970s, he was among the stunned witnesses to the rise of the CBGBs generation of Patti Smith, Richard Hell and the Ramones. A year later, he was in London in time to catch the first bursts of Punk from the Sex Pistols, the Clash and the Damned. And, by the early 1980s, he was in Los Angeles, championing the then-unknown Red Hot Chili Peppers.

A sonic engineer who'd since worked with a prestigious roster of musicians that included the Brains, Kool & The Gang, Joan Jett and Drivin' 'n' Crying, Richardson demanded microscopic detail from his studio and was esteemed as an engineer. The instruments he kept scattered around for resident musicians to play with had been tweaked across a variety of genres, and his work ethic was a good match for the Smashing Pumpkins.

'Mark was very meticulous,' remembered his friend and assistant Guy Goodman, following Richardson's sad death in 2002, after a two year battle with cancer. 'He was precise about the placement of the microphones, getting the recording levels straight before rolling tape.' That, too, was something that Corgan certainly would have appreciated.

Nevertheless the sessions were not to pass off completely without some discomfort. Wretzky later compared the experience to 'being in a prison camp or something.' Removed from friends and family, ensconced within the studio for up to fourteen hours a day, she felt 'completely cut off.' The problems that would arise as the sessions proceeded, she mused, grew directly from this isolation. It was, she said 'a really unhealthy thing to do.'

Again recording over a December – March span, the band rolled a year's worth of experience into the New Year, with what they hoped would prove a minimum of fanfare. Having finally pulled together sufficient material to lay down the album in quickish time, the Smashing Pumpkins were understandably feeling confident in all that they intended to do. It was only when they looked outside, as sometimes even the most focused minds must, that they again came face to face with the realities of what their audience expected from them.

Corgan, in particular, found that his absence from the front pages could not remove him from excruciating examination, and an apparently permanent place alongside Nirvana's Kurt Cobain, as the voice of the angsty-pants Gen-X-ers everywhere. With the success of *Gish* having outpaced even the most generous of expectations, and with a buzz following the Smashing Pumpkins like a swarm of bees, the band was under greater pressure to perform the second time around, more so than if their debut had been released and tanked.

'We were working on the album, and there were all these people from [the label] coming round, to find out how things were going. So, to get them off our backs, I decided to give them one song, "Today". And they loved it. The next thing we knew, all these people were shooting their mouths off about how great the album was going to be, what it was going to sound like, and all on the strength of this one song. We're sitting in this studio in Atlanta, and all we're hearing is that the album's a killer.'

Elsewhere, Corgan mourned, 'People expected me to make The Important Second Smashing Pumpkins Record. The record we'd become "the second Nirvana" with.' All he wanted to do, hackneyed though it sounds to say it, was make sure that they remained the first Smashing Pumpkins and not the next anything. But, although the band had been jostling in and out of the music rags for three years now; being showered with praise or scrutiny wasn't going to be easy. Through no fault of their own, the Smashing Pumpkins were moving into mythic territory, that grey area that lurks between mere fame and superstardom, in which an artist is not feted for anything he or she achieves, but rather, is measured up against what they represent. Nirvana, of course, had it worse – and would ultimately react accordingly.

But they, at least, had a major label and heavy-hitting management behind them, to sop up some of the excess. In those terms, the Smashing Pumpkins weren't even in the same ballpark – and Corgan was reeling under the pressure. Always upfront about his penchant for wobbling into depression in the face of what he perceived to be high stress situations, Corgan balked even harder as the *Siamese Dream* sessions progressed. And, though the media focus was always on him, his band mates were not having an easy time, either. 'Everyone in this band is a perfectionist,' Chamberlin admitted and, in that assertion, so there was layered another coat of expectation. 'We knew we had to make a great record – not for anybody else, but for ourselves.'

He, too, pointed out that, whereas with *Gish*, no-one really cared whether the band performed sales miracles or not, when it came to the recording of *Siamese Dream*, expectations were high. Although Chamberlin admitted that the band's A&R rep. 'was in the studio [for just] one day out of the four months,' there was still pressure. 'It's hard to be in a studio and know you're spending all this money and go "o.k., turn on the creative machine, now".'

The pressure started to build and, for a moment, Corgan panicked. 'Then I realized that I just had to get on with what I was doing, and not care about what everyone else was going to say. Of course, I remained aware that the album was going to be scrutinized, that people weren't just going to put it on and say, "yes very nice," so I really went out of my way to trim the fat, listening to a playback and saying to myself, "It's a good song, but is it a hit...does it have that necessary...."'

Yet even that requirement was to hang tantalizingly out of reach. Coming off tour, the Smashing Pumpkins found themselves drifting apart and, despite a prior pledge from all four of them to work together as a band on their second album, Corgan found himself ever more frustrated by his band mates' own...what? Refusal to see things as clearly as he believed he did? Ability to live lives that did not revolve a hundred percent around his personal vision? There was a distance, Corgan perceived, not only between their individual goals – that had always been a part of the Smashing Pumpkins' chemistry – but between the lengths to which they were willing to travel to attain them. Soon, Corgan was working all-but solo in the studio, first writing, then playing, and ultimately recording all the parts for the album, while his band mates did, in his eyes, nearly nothing. So he decided 'to throw away all the pressure and to just never take offence anymore. Fuck the media, fuck the band. And I just started writing what I wanted to hear and what I wanted to play.'

But nobody could deny that there was dissention in the ranks. The band as a whole were tired – touring had taken a lot out of them, Iha and Wretzky were still healing, and Chamberlin was sifting through his own stack of problems. And, with the sessions well under way, the three were often incognito and hard for anybody to pin down. Corgan, too, was picking up the pieces of his own personal life. But, rather than simply surrender to the temptation to curl into himself, Corgan chose, as he most often did, to face his perceived problems head on – to throw himself into recording *Siamese Dream* full throttle.

He told writer, Dave Thompson, 'Everything that mattered to me seemed to have gone out of the window, I was changing details that I wouldn't normally have changed. But at the same time, I had to hang on to what made recording so special to me in the first place.'

That sense of what was special dated back to Corgan's youth, when the fourteen year old clapped on his headphones, not for 'a straight-ahead punk roar,' but 'little bits that went off in one ear and made you think, "Wow".

'The thing about recording is, the essentials are really basic. Drums sound like drums, guitars like guitars. So they have to be embellished, and that's what I enjoy the most, the things you can do so that a drum sounds like something *more* than a drum, or a guitar sounds like something more than a guitar. Or more than just one guitar.

'I knew all along that some people would criticize, because there's so much going on in each track. I can understand people criticizing a song because they don't like the music, or the lyrics. But to hammer it because I made a deliberate attempt to beautify it, because I didn't just release a backroom demo with the guitars mixed too high, that's like criticizing me for the way I walk. Besides, I always got off on Prog. Rock!

Corgan, kept himself segregated from other music while he was writing; he didn't often listen to anyone else's stuff while he worked on his own songs 'because,' he said, 'I find myself subconsciously stealing things from whatever I'm listening to at the time – riffs, tiny inflections, things like that.'

However, there was one exception to that monastic isolation, Corgan's recent purchase of an Electric Light Orchestra compilation, a characteristically lavish cherry picking of the symphonic majesty that was once draped over Jeff Lynn's Beatle-oid daydreams. Butch Vig explained, 'I remember Billy got the ELO [collection] and we listened to a lot of that stuff. And we were just amazed how cool some of the production was on those tracks.'

Any recording process has its moments of frustration, as well as moments of blissed out 'wow' – and the sessions in Atlanta were no exception. Corgan had already made the decision to abandon some of the brash clatter band of *Gish* to explore moods and genres a little more fully. 'We were doing "Spaceboy," he recalled, 'and it really wasn't going anywhere.' Suddenly, he discovered a dusty, long unused mellotron in the studio, and Vig suggested he give it a go. 'I did, and, after that, I wanted to put it all over everything.'

Restraint ultimately prevailed, but still the creaky, tinky instrument was layered into 'Spaceboy' – a song written in tribute to Corgan's younger brother Jesse, who was born with an odd chromosome disorder. It was another step out of the grunge frame the band had been painted into, and a step closer to the sounds that rocked a younger Corgan's world.

Sometimes the process became so personal that he could not allow others to intrude – though Corgan is traditionally coy regarding the genesis of his lyrics, preferring to defer to the everyman amalgamation of experiences for his creative pool, he acknowledged that 'Soma' was rooted in his break-up with Chris Fabian. And, even if his head had resisted, his heart insisted that the song be done 'correctly,' and that translated, in his mind, to doing it himself.

This was, in fact, nothing new. According to Butch Vig, Corgan had played 'probably eighty to ninety percent' of the instrumentation on *Gish*. This time, however, it was not Corgan's attention to detail and focus that dictated his enthusiasm. It was fear.

'I was so scared to let someone else do something, that I didn't give them a chance,' he reflected, but when he turned to his band mates later on, to ask their opinion of things that he'd done, it seemed as though nobody had that much to say. Which led Corgan, in turn, to shunt them further out of the picture, convincing himself that, if the album was ever to be completed to his satisfaction, he'd have to complete the thing himself. And then, he snarled in interviews afterwards, 'when they were interviewed, it was "yeah, it really sucks," all this. Complain, complain, complain. And then I thought, "what are you fucking complaining about?" A situation like that creates a lot of misunderstandings and hate' – both external and, as he now discovered, internal.

Finally the album took shape as a whopping forty songs were completed, enough not only for the group's next album but also a stockpile that would come into play even further into the future.

Looking ahead to the Smashing Pumpkins' third album, *Mellon Collie And The Infinite Sadness,* the instrumental 'Mellon Collie' was an early version of 'Infinite Sadness,' while a rough cut of 'Bullet With Butterfly Wings' also survived to fly another day. 'Pissant,' meanwhile, was, Corgan said, 'one of the few things we have ever recorded live.' Cut during the Triclops sessions, it was seriously considered for *Siamese Dream* – Wretzky was especially keen to include it – but it was destined to become nothing more than a b-side. So was 'Siamese Dream,' the album's *de facto* title track, included finally on the 'Disarm' single.

The band also brought several guest musicians on board during their stint at Triclops, broadening their sound even as they broadened their horizons. Among the most notable things that set *Siamese Dream* apart from the more ragged moments of the Smashing Pumpkins' debut was the inclusion of lush orchestral strings to 'Disarm' and 'Luna,' with long-time Kansas violinist David Ragsdale and cellist Eric Remschneider (who would go on to play with, among others, the Scratchie label's Fulflej and guest on James Iha's *Let It Come Down* solo album) supplying the symphonies. REM bassist Mike Mills, meanwhile, added piano to Corgan's 'Soma' lament.

Still, those 'misunderstandings and hate' that Corgan alluded to remained, and misunderstandings, of course, only offer further food for the rumour mill to grind into 'fact.' The media picked up on the band's internal stress very early on and, even before the new album was on the streets, was littering its pages with a grim portrait of the grunge-gods imploding, of Corgan as uber-dicatator, striding around the studio with crop and cap, literally browbeating his comrades into following his instructions.

For someone who, in so many interviews, was rarely less than affable, seeing himself then reconstructed as 'this weird, crippled character' was so absurd that, finally, he began to live that role for every journalist, knowing that if he gave them what they wanted to begin with, he might actually have a chance of getting his points across. "Hi, it's your favourite jaded rock star!" became a classic Corgan ice-breaker as he sat down, or, as so many pointed out ad nauseum in print, 'folded himself' into whatever piece of furniture was at hand, and it was up to the writer where they took things from there. Shame to say, a lot of them seemed to believe him.

A lot more felt they knew his band mates as well, and their interviews, too, took on a surrealness that left friends staring in bemusement at the printed page, wondering precisely who the journalist had been talking to. Those writers who were out to crucify Corgan whispered conspiratorially of palace coups and behind the scenes intrigues, with Corgan a mad Rasputin character, moments before the assassins plugged him full of poison and bullets; those who leaned in the other direction, and regarded the Smashing Pumpkins as one talent and a bunch of friends, then hawkishly watched Iha, Chamberlin and Wretzky, awaiting that one moment of absent distraction.

It was a projection that filled the slathering newshounds with ecstasy, and one that would ultimately hurt the band's own image – with the foundations laid for subsequent interviews to take band members' words and warp them for armchair titillation, Corgan responded to these jibes with ever more acidic comments. Those then, would be wrapped back around his neck, constricting him to the point where he felt that whatever he said would be re-touched.

Such a shame that it was usually the journalists' observations alone that made it into print, however. The incident may be apocryphal (but one sincerely hopes it isn't), but those industry circles that smirk at the discomfort of journalists still speak of the day that one hatchet-bearing scribe suggested that Wretzky apply as much dedication to her bass playing as she did to putting on her make-up. A few weeks after his story hit the news-stands, the same wretched soul unwisely, but utterly unsuspectingly, appeared backstage at a Smashing Pumpkins concert – there to be confronted by a still-seething Wretzky, armed with a brand-new lipstick, which she proceeded to apply – all over his face.

But, if Corgan was beginning to shy away from the media spotlight, he continued flaying himself open for the public regardless, immersing his own soul in the spotlight through his lyrics, as the convoluted messages and often impenetrable meanings of the songs on *Gish* yielded to compositions that rank among the most honest Corgan had ever written. And there was a wry irony there, in the knowledge that, as he erected the walls between himself and the press, he then tore them back down in the context of his songs.

Infamous for bottling it all up – despite the cries of confessionalism that trailed behind him like so many battered puppies – *Siamese Dream* saw Corgan vow to just let it all go, explaining that 'now my emotions are very open in my songs.' Indeed, scanning the mass of words that made up the scattered lyric sheet in the album, it was clear that Corgan was beginning to cast off the protective walls of his childhood, when he kept his emotions well in check, maintaining the distance that followed him through adolescence and on to his crafting of himself as rock star and a poet. He argued, of course, that he was 'just an ordinary guy like everyone else,' but outward appearances rendered him much, much larger than life. Pearl Jam's Eddie Vedder in his flannel and jeans was just an ordinary guy. Mudhoney's Mark Arm was an ordinary guy. Billy Corgan was not. One look at the style of the Smashing Pumpkins revealed a world where glam was in and glamour filled the open spaces.

Even when garbed later for an entire tour in his infamous Zero T-shirt, Corgan still wore silver PVC pants. Just an ordinary guy indeed! Of course, in his own world, well away from the glare of the public eye, it was another matter entirely. But when the spotlight flickered on, so did Corgan's innate understanding, and love, of showmanship, the knowledge that while a singer can sing and a guitarist plays guitar, a performer *must* perform. For what other point is there to even getting up on stage?

And performance, by its very nature, demands stepping away from the mundane humdrum of everyday life; stepping out of the shadows of Everyman anonymity, and giving the people something to think about, talk about, to dream about. Damn that discipline of pop stars who insisted 'I'm just like you,' damn the ugly ordinariness of icons with all the personal appeal of the boy-or girl-next-door. If you're not going to put on a show when you play, you might as well invite the audience back to your house to watch you watch television.

Corgan understood this instinctively. What he did not understand was the difficulty that so many people experience when it comes to separating an artist's public persona from his private life. Tearing it down and building it up was all for art. And, it was funny, but even that Zero T-shirt caused so much talk, speculation and deep interpretation that, when Corgan obtusely insisted it was representative of no statement more portentous than his 'lack of any direct sense of style,' the questioning didn't stop. Finally, pushed a little too hard by *Big O* magazine, he delivered a quip that spoke volumes about image and art. 'If I shit on this table, now that's a statement too. It's all art. Every single bit of it. Down to the nose picking and the screaming. We live and learn. And forget, and live and learn and forget again.'

CHAPTER ELEVEN
CUTTING UP THE LITTLE CHILD

The Smashing Pumpkins finally emerged from Triclops in mid-March 1993, to play Atlanta's Center Stage, blazing through a set that cherry-picked the very best of both *Gish* and the forthcoming *Siamese Dream*. Their first live show of the year would also be their only appearance until they hit the tour circuit again in June, as they then leaped into the laborious process of actually sorting out the material they'd recorded.

With so many songs in the can and with the entire process seriously, if not dangerously, behind schedule, the band switched their venue, taking the tapes to Rumbo Recorders in Canoga Park, California. Located in the West San Fernando Valley outside of Los Angeles, Rumbo Recorders had been opened in 1979 by Daryl Dragon, better known as the 'Captain' in Captain & Tennille. The studio's mission was to provide a place where artists could relax and work in an atmosphere that fostered creativity. And it certainly provided Corgan with just that. There, Corgan would tweak the final mix over the course of a month, while welcoming a new face into the Smashing Pumpkins family as English producer Alan Moulder signed on to work the mix down.

One of the things that Corgan wanted very much for the final sonic assault of *Siamese Dream* was 'a real sense of depth, without necessarily using delays or reverbs – to use tonalities instead.' Moulder, then, was the perfect choice. A pioneering producer at London's Trident studios, working as an assistant alongside Brian Eno and Chris Thomas, Moulder was fascinated by sounds that used highly stylized technology, that spliced electronic wizardry with classic rock riffing. Alongside engineer John Loder, he had shaped Jesus & Mary Chain's seminal *Psychocandy* LP during the mid-1980s, pushing the band through paces that emerged with the snarling fuzz fuel that almost single-handedly hauled the decade out of its post-Punk malaise.

Indeed, Moulder himself would quickly become regarded among the whiz kids of the age, sprinkling his glitter dust over late 80s classics as far apart as the Sundays' *Reading Writing Arithmetic* debut, and My Bloody Valentine's ambitious and highly anticipated sophomore album, *Loveless*, before swallowing the beginning of the circle with a fresh re-mix of Gang Of Four's 1995 'I Parade Myself'.

By the time the Smashing Pumpkins caught up with him, he had so well defined his working fingerprint, and honed his skill to such an art form, that his style bled beautifully into *Siamese Dream*, augmenting the band's already substantial timbre with a fleeting, and beautifully morose undercurrent.

Together, the band and Moulder created a sound that, having mined all that it required from *Gish*'s monstrous riches, concentrated now on an audacious overhaul of everything that had made the band precious in the first place – and would ensure that they became even more so in the future. The very nature of *Siamese Dream* was an heroic reversal of expectations that could easily have become a reversal of fortunes. That the group had the ability not only to pull the switch off, but to become all the bigger for doing so, surely ranks among the Smashing Pumpkins' all-time greatest achievements.

Long before the record was finished and certainly before its contents were finalised, there was a furore among industry insiders surrounding the upcoming release. Given the strong start to the Smashing Pumpkins' career-so-far, anticipation for the band's sophomore effort was at an almost feverish pitch, all the more so because of the outspoken deliberation with which Corgan moved not only to set himself apart from the pack, even as he was keeping step with it, but also because of the band's penchant for ignoring everything except what their own inner voices told them to do.

Indeed, for all the struggle and strife that had gone into its creation, *Siamese Dream* would emerge an immediate, sizzling triumph, a sonic culmination of all the tension, personal demons, and non-stop touring that the band members had worked through for the last two years. The album was a product of everything that had gone before and, even before it capped its two million copy US sales mark, its brutal refusal to bow down to anybody's expectations had placed the band on top of the world, under a spotlight of champagne and glitter and more scrutiny than they'd probably ever anticipated.

Even as the group worked on the final tweaking, Corgan, in particular, was under no illusions about the weight of expectation bearing down upon the group. Just as things stood two years before, the Smashing Pumpkins' new album would be squeaking into the stores just one month before the latest Nirvana record. But whereas, back then, neither band had meant much more than a hill of beans to the average Joe, this time around, the situation was very different.

All year-so-far long, even as the media buzzed curiously around the weird scenes inside the Smashing Pumpkins' goldmine, so it went into overdrive in anticipation of Nirvana's latest offering, as rumours flew out of the sessions to suggest that, even more than Billy Corgan, Kurt Cobain intended ripping his past alliances to shreds. *In Utero* was, in the words of more than one supposedly informed industry insider, 'commercial fucking suicide,' with even the band's choice of producer, Midwest noise merchant Steve Albini, indicative of the trio's distrust and disgust with their media profile.

Of course, the finished album – September's *In Utero* – would not emerge anywhere near the snarling mass of disgruntled discordance that was being so widely predicted. But the Smashing Pumpkins were not alone in ensuring that their own latest album was released safely out of reach of the Nirvana disc, and the fall-out that would inevitably attend it.

The week that puppy hit the stores, after all, there'd barely be a spare dollar in the record-buying public's pocket to spend on any other record, and not a spare eardrum left to listen if there were. With a full four weeks gap between the two, however, *Siamese Dream* would at least make itself heard for a month.

Neither was it the media, and the public alone who would be scrutinising *Siamese Dream*. Virgin Records, the band's ultimate paymasters, too, were preparing to place the Smashing Pumpkins under the most powerful microscope – any future that the group hoped for on the label was, in every way, dependent upon *Siamese Dream* for its successful execution and, as Corgan and Moulder worked, the singer found himself 'changing details that I wouldn't normally have changed.' However, he was equally adamant that he would 'hang on to what made recording special to me in the first place.' Whether it was layered guitar, a drum beat amplified, a fuzz of bass awash through a riff, whatever, it was those moments, those 'little bits that went off in one ear' that gave those who spun the Smashing Pumpkins and attended their shows, shivered moments of pure sonic bliss.

Finally the job was complete and, with everyone breaking for a little much-needed rest and recreation, Corgan felt settled, happy even. He and Chris Fabian had reunited during the sessions for the album and, as the Smashing Pumpkins emerged from the studio, the couple wed that spring. Yet the respite from the business of the Smashing Pumpkins would not be a long one. Preparation for the album's launch continued apace, and the band knew that if they did not involve themselves in every decision that needed to be taken, somebody else would be making those decisions for them.

Even the matter of selecting the first single from the album became impossibly complicated, as the group locked horns with Hut over whether 'Cherub Rock' or 'Today' should have the honour of launching *Siamese Dream*. In Corgan's eyes, 'Cherub Rock' was the obvious choice, even though it was one of the easiest songs he had ever written. 'I wrote "Cherub Rock" in half an hour. I heard it one day while I was driving up the road, and it was one of the last songs I wrote before we did the album.' However, Hut were pushing hard for 'Today's brand of hooky-happiness' and, in Corgan's eyes at least, that seemed a weak move, that a song he'd dashed off in just ten minutes as a snarky response to strained band relations in late 1992, should take such a prestigious slot.

Indeed, he later admitted that 'Today' had been penned 'during a very difficult time in my life.' The band had toured for fourteen months straight to support *Gish* and once off the road, Corgan had to snap into writing, and, rather than diving in with a flurry of paper and pen, he was holed up in a crappy apartment and was in 'probably the worst writing slump that I've ever had.'

He also wondered whether such precipitously penned songs could even be considered complete; 'there's parts of me that wonder what would have happened if I'd spent four hours writing [them], and not done something else. How much better a song would [they] have been?' Of course, there was no answering that question.

Corgan would win the battle over singles, and 'Today' was shelved for dessert, but Virgin would end up with the last laugh anyway. Although 'Cherub Rock' easily marched up the UK chart that summer, coming to rest at number thirty-one – thirteen places higher than 'Today' would muster later in the year, it was another story entirely in the US. There, 'Cherub Rock' sank without a trace following its (delayed) Stateside release in October 1993. 'Today', on the other hand, with its so-dopey ice cream truck video, became one of the strongest 'Alternative' hits of the year.

Corgan thought it was funny that 'Today' became such a massive, feel-good smash. Written in response to the desperation that he felt, he explained later that 'although the main lyric is "today is the greatest day," it's not the song you think it is. It's pretty much like a joke song about how I want to kill myself, but of course nobody ever gets that 'cos they get very fixated on the positive lines.' Recounting the song's genesis on VH1's *Storytellers* years later, though, he copped to the fact that the song was positive as well. 'But of course, at this point in my life, it is a positive song because you know, it's about survival.'

Moving now towards the album's release date, the Smashing Pumpkins finally opened the promotional portion of their world tour in London in June, with a live appearance on MTV's *Most Wanted* show, steamrollering through 'Cherub Rock' and 'Disarm' – and, of all the songs on the forthcoming album, they could not have made a more appropriate choice. 'Cherub Rock,' in particular, was very much the keynote of the entire *Siamese Dream* album, 'a monstrous emotional piece of art,' as Corgan put it, and a song that posited directions far from the grunge mindset with which most reviewers approached *Siamese Dream*.

Long since positioned in the very heart of those fires by the American (and, to a lesser extent, British) media, advance speculation placed *Siamese Dream* firmly within the realms of the now near-traditional Sound-vana In Chains wall of disaffected noise. And, seduced by the no-nonsense barrage of 'Silverfuck,' it was so easy to shut one's ears to the group's advances elsewhere, and accept *Siamese Dream* as simply one more subtle twist on an already-familiar musical theme. But the wisdom of bringing Alan Moulder on board was displayed, as the Smashing Pumpkins swung 'Cherub Rock' into a fuzz busting bitterness. 'Disarm,' meanwhile, pinned down Corgan's lyric not with scything guitar, but by simple acoustic strumming and orchestral swells – liberally scattered touches that, again, would edge the Smashing Pumpkins ever further away from the fray.

From the hallowed halls of MTV's London studios, the Smashing Pumpkins travelled next to Paris, France, where they treated fans to a live acoustic set at Studio 10S, and offered up another taste of the quartet's eclectic musical forbears, when they swung into a cover of Thin Lizzy's funk-laden 'Dancing In The Moonlight' – the late Phil Lynott and co were undergoing the first glimmerings of a major musical rehabilitation in the US, with Henry Rollins, among others, readily championing their street-smart hard rock. The Smashing Pumpkins' acknowledgement of Thin Lizzy as an early influence could only strengthen the Irish band's status. Then it was back to the US towards the end of the month, prefacing the 27 July release of the album with another live acoustic performance at Tower Records' Chicago branch on the twenty-sixth. The show, which featured new songs 'Rocket', 'Cherub Rock' and 'Today,' was simulcast on Chicago's 93 WXRT Radio station.

Siamese Dream debuted at number ten on the US chart, and Corgan admitted, when he heard the news, 'I started leaping up and down in an airport somewhere.' It was not, he added, 'something I like talking about, because I don't want people to think that success is all I care about.' But it was a moment of sublime personal triumph regardless.

Certainly the release of *Siamese Dream* catapulted the Smashing Pumpkins into another period of absolute frenzy, beginning with a whirlwind tour that would keep them on the road until the following September, and barely permitted them more than a handful of reinvigorating pauses along the way. And, again, heavy touring would bare its snarl and exact another toll on the band's energies, as the initial novelty of being back on the bus first lost its excitement, then its edge and, finally, its very soul.

It was exhausting, it was claustrophobic. Bravely, Corgan acknowledged that such grinding repetition was 'all part of the game,' and he admitted that, compared to some of the things they could have wound up doing, it was a game that they were all mightily pleased to find themselves playing.

But writing and recording, and being in a band for a living was not only the realization of all the goals the group had set. At the end of the day, it was still a job. Plumbers plumb, burger boys flip meat and musicians make music. And the night-after-night routine of gigs, travelling, hotels, diner food and rawk'n'rawl can be just as tedious as asking someone day in and day out if they'd like that wrapped and thank you very much. Glamour was easily supplanted by tedium, although Corgan did agree that being on the road often sparked 'ideas and inspiration.' And out of that ferment there arose other determinations, the single-minded belief that the Smashing Pumpkins were on the verge of blowing the closeted world of 'Alternative Rock,' 'Indie Rock,' 'College Rock,' Call-it-what-you-will Rock, out of the water forever.

Casting his mind back to the days when the very release of *Gish* was the most exciting thing in the Smashing Pumpkins' universe, Corgan reflected on the many rigors that they would no longer need to, or be required, to subject themselves to. 'We will no longer be an opening band,' he celebrated, 'going out there with [our] tail between [our] legs, [to] accept whatever fate is cast upon [us].' Neither were they to be bound up within the circle of catty holier-than-thou one-upmanship that characterized Alternative circles, and which was just as brutal as the mainstream industry from which the Indie standard bearers so conceitedly held themselves aloft.

The same petty name-dropping, the same 'who's cooler than who' debates, the same authentic lumberjack flannel vs. store-bought name-band pandering. It was all about who you knew and, if you knew them, did you play with them? '[It's] no different from the Paula Abduls of the world,' Corgan growled. 'They sit in their little castles and say, 'well, you're not *cool* enough and you're not *this* enough.' And the more the Smashing Pumpkins saw of those castles, the more they were adamant that they would never enter their keeps.

The Smashing Pumpkins were more concerned with *how* their music sounded, if it was good, if it was great, if it was God-like. They didn't give a fuck who they knew and who hung out with whom. Going out on stage was the important time. Even, perhaps *especially,* in their days as the perennial opening act. Strong seeds sown early were probably not the best ways to win friends and acquaintances, but even if only in the most selfish of ways, the Smashing Pumpkins' conviction was absolutely on the mark. Because, hopefully, ideally, the essence of a band is the desire to play music, a desire that, in turn is born out of a need to please themselves. If other, outside, contingents want to listen, all the better – and if they didn't, tough shit.

'This is my forty-five minutes, and you're gonna listen,' Corgan affirmed. If the vibe was good, the audience was given a jacked up show. If the vibe was sour, well, then – watch out. 'When the audience is out of it and the band is out of it, I just start pushing those buttons to get a reaction.' Back in 1992, pushing *Gish* to a crowd of eight hundred Parisians, the vibe coming out of the audience wasn't healthy, wasn't hostile, wasn't anything at all. Sixteen hundred eyes, all staring, not applauding. The group could have been playing in a mortuary for all the feedback they were getting from the dance floor. So the Smashing Pumpkins decided to send some feedback back to them – four songs painfully protracted into forty minutes of noise and chaos.

On the road that fall, on both sides of the Atlantic, the band blasted through some of their most invigorating performances yet, and some of their most distinctive – shows that seemed designed to draw the audience as far out of its own expectations as they could, yet without ever losing sight of what those people had paid their money to see. The group were active, too, on TV and radio, including a disarming rendition of 'Disarm,' recorded for UK television's *The Word* in September. (The performance was broadcast the following February as the song was released as a single).

The band also cut their second John Peel Session at the BBC on 12 September, with in-house producer Ted de Bono – Dale Griffin's sound engineer on the first Nirvana session back in 1989. An infinitely smoother ride than their 1991 debacle – and that despite Corgan's on-going frustration and hesitance to relax in the studio – the Smashing Pumpkins cut another three songs, ripping through 'Disarm,' and then marching into unknown territory with a couple of cover versions, a straightforward acoustic reading of Fleetwood Mac's 'Landslide,' a Stevie Nicks song that Corgan had always adored; and Depeche Mode's 'Never Let Me Down Again,' nodding to another of the group's more unlikely influences.

'We did it in one take,' said Wretzky, 'it was surprising how well it turned out. Dave Gahan said some really nice things about it. I was very intensely into Depeche Mode when I was around seventeen.'

Despite Wretzky's enthusiasm the song was a surprising choice, but not an altogether inappropriate one. Originally released in 1987 on Depeche Mode's groundbreaking *Music For The Masses* LP, the vaguely homoerotic 'Never Let Me Down Again' was one of the songs that pushed the band into the completely new direction that would come to epitomise the next stage of their development, as they shrugged off the teeny bop cliché they'd worn for nearly a decade, and transformed themselves into hollow-eyed and empowering spokesmen for the out and proud gay club generation and the disillusioned post-Punk Goths who followed them.

With the Smashing Pumpkins themselves taking a similar giant step, Depeche Mode were a role model that only fools would have overlooked, and the version lavished down for the Peel session captured all the significance of the gesture, Corgan breathy and languorous, beaten back by both Wretzky's throbbing bass and Chamberlin's drums. Even with the guitar cut at the end, the song shoves the original's dishevelled energy aside to pick instead at the sexy, sleepy undercurrent that haunted, but never quite stood out of Depeche Mode's original version. (This performance would subsequently be reprised on the 1998 *For The Masses* Depeche Mode tribute album.)

Back in the States for the American leg of the tour at the beginning of October, the Smashing Pumpkins opened their account with an appearance at MTV's *No Alternative* benefit concert, taking their place alongside the cream of the current Alternative crop, to raise funds for the Red Hot Organization's fight for a cure for AIDS. From the Goo Goo Dolls to Australia's Straightjacket Fits; from Uncle Tupelo to Patti Smith and the Verlaines; from Nirvana to

Soundgarden and Matthew Sweet, there were few key names left behind.

Setting an early precedent for what would become an ongoing penchant for philanthropy, the Smashing Pumpkins recorded a set at Soundworks in Chicago that included the three *Siamese Dream* singles as well as 'I Am One' and 'Geek U.S.A.' A live version of 'Glynis', the band's tribute to their friend, Red Red Meat's bassist Glynnis Johnson, was ultimately gifted to the accompanying album.

Another notable television appearance followed at the end of the month, as the group made their debut both on the long-running comedy show *Saturday Night Live*, and on American national television itself, on 30 October. Purposefully contrasting their performance with the more relaxed, and certainly more esoteric offerings they made in Europe and elsewhere, the group performed nothing more adventurous than straightforward versions of 'Cherub Rock' and 'Today,' the first two singles from *Siamese Dream*. And they were rewarded for their forbearance with a sharp sales spike the following week.

The band wrapped up the American leg of the tour on 12 December at the Universal Amphitheatre in Los Angeles, California. The set, which featured a jolly version of the holiday classic 'Rudolph The Red Nosed Reindeer', was taped by the local KROQ radio station to be broadcast as their Christmas concert. That outing sewn up, the band were able to gratefully snatch a couple of weeks off, for Christmas and some much-needed recharging. Looking back over the events of the past few months, it was readily apparent that, had anybody sat down to actually plan out their course of attack, the Smashing Pumpkins and *Siamese Dream* were following it to the letter, brick-beating any last doubts that remained regarding the quartet's staying power into the dust.

Siamese Dream had unfurled in the summer sun, shooting into the Billboard charts, before finally coming to rest at the tip of the Top Ten. It fared even better in England, securing a plum number four slot and landing all three of its singles in the charts. And, while the Smashing Pumpkins may not have captured the mass hysteria that was suddenly the lot of certain other bands on the same circuit – Nirvana, now riding the shocked acclaim that greeted their latest album, *In Utero*, and Pearl Jam, as they shunted aside the distrust of so many critics, and grasped the great unwashed underbelly of rock instead – what the Smashing Pumpkins achieved, they did off their own backs, and on their own terms. They would not compromise and they were playing the shows of their lives.

Indeed, as 1993 finally faded into the hour glass, Corgan himself was buzzing so hard that he admitted, 'if I didn't have to be on tour, I'd start on a new album tomorrow.' In the event, it would be a long, long time before a new Smashing Pumpkins album hit stores – and, by the time it did, in 1995, things would be very, very different. The face of Alternative music would have changed forever.

CHAPTER TWELVE
LO! YOU STINKING MASSES,
THE NEW MESSIAH

The Smashing Pumpkins launched their 1994 touring itinerary on 21 January in Parklands, Gold Coast, New Zealand, with an appearance at the third Big Day Out festival.

An idea originally hatched by indie concert promoters Ken West and Vivian Lees, the Big Day Out was launched in January 1992 to spotlight some of Australia and New Zealand's biggest, loudest and most energized rock and rollers – a direct kick in the face for a local mainstream music market that remained content to spew out tired rock 'n' insipid pop, in a country that had mined some of the modern era's most influential acts.

Playing just one city, Sydney, that opening year, the first Big Day Out recruited a glamorous coterie of both international and local acts, including Nirvana, Celibate Rifles, Died Pretty, Violent Femmes, Beasts Of Burboun, You Am I, and Henry Rollins, who joined the Hard Ons for the occasion. Some 10,000 fans streamed through the gates and, with the Big Day Out living up to both its name and the underground anticipation that accompanied it, the 1993 event was expanded to include additional shows in Perth and Adelaide.

Ten bands, including Nick Cave & The Bad Seeds, Carter USM, Mudhoney and Sonic Youth toured the three dates, augmented by scores of local bands picking up the slack stages in each city. But the 1994 event was to be even bigger than that, expanding to two further venues in New Zealand, Auckland and Gold Coast, and a combined audience of over 100,000.

It was a grandiose affair – aside from the Pumpkins, performances from Soundgarden, Bjork, the Ramones, the Breeders, Teenage Fanclub and local heroes You Am I and Straightjacket Fits, rounded out the headline fare; Cruel Sea, Urge Overkill, Def FX and DJ Pee Wee Ferris & The Meanies made up the numbers. Taking a multimedia leaf out of Lollapalooza's book there was a 'techno rave room' and art exhibition space.

From one of the biggest festivals in the world, the Smashing Pumpkins returned to the UK to play one of their longest engagements, five solidly sold-out nights at the London Astoria in February, where the band tickled the audience with a version of Depeche Mode's 'Never Let Me Down Again'.

Their current single 'Disarm' was now storming up the chart. It would peak at number eleven, although plans for the band to consolidate the triumph with an appearance on *Top Of The Pops* were scuppered when the song's lyrics were deemed too strong for the show's intended audience. According to *Record Collector* magazine, it was the line 'cut that little child up inside of me' that aroused the BBC's ire. Perhaps if the Smashing Pumpkins had just worn the thongs a little tighter, they might have got away with it.

From there, it was back to the United States for a further series of heartland gigs, plunging their message even further into the depths of middle America.

Busy promoting the album, whipping every successive audience into a wild frenzy with a show that dripped blood, the Smashing Pumpkins then confirmed their now blistering ascendancy by cementing their presence on the European festival circuit as they signed up for Nuremberg's near-decade old Rock Am Ring event in May. Staged at the infamous stadium where Hitler once addressed the Nazi rallies; but where, too, international auto racing had done much to drive away such bitter memories, Rock Am Ring was an event whose sheer musical diversity spoke volumes for each of its attractions' ability to transcend whichever musical box that the critics may have slid them into. Playing alongside the Smashing Pumpkins, who were slotted fourth on the bill, were such oddly assorted old-school rockers as Aerosmith, now firmly into the swing of their latest renaissance, Australian art poppers Crowded House, the venerable Peter Gabriel, and frat-boy rockers The Hooters.

If the Smashing Pumpkins felt at all out-of-place amid such bizarre companions, however, they never showed it. A bang-on set rounded up the very best of *Gish* and *Siamese Dream*, then closed with a brutally riffing recounting of the epic 'Silverfuck,' burning white hot to a conclusion that saw everything wrap up in gripping chaos, with both Corgan and Iha rampaging, wrapped in feedback, across the stage. It was a scintillating performance, one of the most intense that the Smashing Pumpkins had ever inflicted upon a European audience. And there were reasons for that intensity which, though nobody in the Smashing Pumpkins' camp dared mention their name, hung on everybody's lips regardless.

Just weeks before the Nuremberg show, early in the morning of 8 April, a workman called in to upgrade the electrics at Kurt Cobain's home in Seattle, discovered the singer's body in a room above the family garage. A shotgun lay beside the corpse; a suicide note sat in a heap of soil tipped out of a nearby flowerpot. It was a grotesque tragedy that would, of course, become even more grotesque by the time the media and the rumour-mongers had finished picking through the shattered, bloody remains of Kurt Cobain's state of mind. And the Smashing Pumpkins would find themselves wrapped up in the midst of it all.

As the earliest days of 1994 rolled through the haze and hangover of the New Year, it was already apparent that the year was not going to be a comfortable, or particularly good, one for Kurt Cobain. Nirvana were still very much at their peak, with *In Utero* still rolling through what would ultimately become an 87 week residency on the American charts.

A European tour was looming, a string of long sold-out shows that ensured the group's already established pre-eminence was only going to grow stronger. No less than the Smashing Pumpkins, Nirvana had more than they ever dreamed possible nestled in their sticky palms. But, unlike the Smashing Pumpkins, Kurt Cobain, the undisputed King of rawkus DIY Grunge, was hating every minute of it.

It was, in many ways, guilt that pushed Cobain during these increasingly fraught times, and into an overwhelming downward spiral. Guilt that he'd lost the uncompromising vision that had once seemed so holy; guilt that, in his eyes, he was unable to be a good father to his infant daughter, Francis Bean, or a good husband to his wife Courtney Love; and guilt that, in the throes of the Nirvana-mania that had impaled the band on the peak of the musical Everest, Nirvana themselves had already fulfilled the prophecy of sell-out forecast by the cynical masses.

Pressures came to the trio from all sides – from the media, from the labels, from the band's own agenda. It was hard being under such a microscope. Musing later on Cobain's downward turn, James Iha remarked bitterly, 'what did people talk about Nirvana? They talked about Kurt, they talked about Courtney Love, heroin abuse and smashing guitars. They never talked about how good the songs were, how good the lyrics were.'

Corgan, too, mourned Cobain's plight, privately if not publicly. "I found him at times to be a total brat, and other times I found him to be really engaging. But, like me, he was a Pisces and with Pisces, you never know what you're gonna get." He regretted, however, that the two were never able to get past the blocks that their respective positions had placed in their way. "He was a very difficult person to get to know, he was just a very intense person. And in my particular case, we were basically rivals, so when you're in your mid-20s and rivals, you don't just sit down and have a chat over a Coke."

Ensconced in the beginning of the year in Europe for a handful of dates, it was clear that Cobain was not in good shape. Wracked with stomach pain, under enormous stress to perform, and just plain tired from having cameras relentlessly jabbing in his face for the past nearly-three years, Cobain was increasingly self-medicating himself in a staggeringly horrific variety of ways.

With wife Love and band mates Kris Novoselic and Dave Grohl able only to look on as Cobain struggled against the demons with which stardom had stuffed his soul, each of them wracked by a sense of absolute helplessness, the first months of 1994 were rocky – and were only going to get worse, as Cobain's increasing agony shoved each of them, in turn, to the edge of the abyss, where they teetered, only able to look at the void that waited below. Not one of them, however, could imagine what was about to play out as, early in the year Perry Farrell invited the band to headline that summer's Lollapalooza festival.

To most observers, it was no more than Nirvana deserved; indeed, just as their admirers could point to the group as the single-handed saviours who hauled 'Alternative music' out of the shadows forever, so Lollapalooza demanded equal credit for an equal accomplishment, not only pushing the music into a corn-fed American mainstream that had hitherto known nothing more challenging than another spoon-fed dose of roots, rock and easy-listening pap, but also cutting across the petty marketing boundaries that themselves divided the Alternative minority into so many even tinier boxes.

In the massive shake-up of musical mores that rocked America as the 1980s were shattered by the sonic explosions of the 1990s, the advent of Lollapalooza filled a void, brought music to the masses and used the medium to fulfil founder Perry Farrell's overly ambitious dreams. He conceived Lollapalooza not simply as the greatest American festival, but as the ultimate. In so doing, too, he would become an unwitting participant in the great passing of the mantle, as the exploding tatters of his own Jane's Addiction bowed down to the rising insurgency of the flannel and denim denizens of Grunge.

Lollapalooza's origins dated back to Spring 1991. Jane's Addiction were still in the throes of a massive tour. It was a gig with no signs of ending in the foreseeable future, and, truth be told, Perry Farrell was getting cranky. He'd been touring non-stop with his band for years now, and he was tired. But the bookers never stopped booking, the promoters never stopped promoting... only when it became painfully apparent to all that Farrell had reached the end of his tether did anybody sit back to sweeten the pill. Farrell recalled being told he could do 'whatever I wanted. [They said] "We're giving you the license to do with your tour whatever you want".'

What he wanted was a tour that brought together every arena of art that he considered worthwhile. He wanted stages full of multimedia extravagance, music that spanned generations and genres, rest areas, food stalls, body piercing, and information booths. He wanted every opinion in the world to converge into one massive travelling circus, to take its message to the mobs. He wanted a Lollapalooza.

Festivals were nothing new, of course. From Monterey to Reading, from Glastonbury to Big Day Out, and onto Cult frontman Ian Astbury's Gathering Of The Tribes (which unknowingly test-drove almost every idea that Farrell himself had lined up for his own show), multi-band...even multi-venue...festivals were already part of the landscape. But Lollapalooza was different from the outset, an absolutely monumental combination of music and idea that united rocker and rapper, singer and sledgehammering headbanger, rising superstar and struggling nonentity, warmonger and peacenik, hippy and heavy, a rainbow coalition with Greenpeace at one end, the NRA at the other, and all convinced that their messages would be heard.

Lollapalooza 1991 would become a summer of glory days stacked up against one another, as the Rollins Band, the Butthole Surfers, industrialists Nine Inch Nails and Ice-T took their place alongside Jane's Addiction; and, emboldened by the phenomenal success that greeted the entire outing, Farrell looked to repeat the excursion the following year. By 1994, Lollapalooza was the healthiest four year old in the land, the excitement building from the moment Farrell announced the new year's line-up, then sat back to laugh while the world debated his choices.

This year was no different. By January he had already sewn up a line-up that stretched from the twin pole of George Clinton and P-Funk to Nick Cave and the Bad Seeds, with punk japesters Green Day thrown in the middle. Inevitably, such extremes raised many a hackle-laden eyebrow, but the addition of the Smashing Pumpkins certainly calmed a few nerves, and the invitation to Nirvana settled everyone.

Everyone apart from Nirvana's themselves. As Perry Farrell later admitted, Cobain never actually said he *wanted* to headline Lollapalooza; he had, in fact, already complained that he was already under too much pressure to do too much, and a 40+ date tour during the summer, on the heels of Nirvana's own schedule, tipped the balance too far.

Such objections, of course, did nothing to calm the rumour mill, which placed Nirvana at the top of the bill before Farrell himself even issued the invitation, as though the weight of expectation alone would push the band to come through for the kids. Good old Kurt, he'd never let them down.

But, as Lollapalooza trundled along toward the final planning stages, Cobain's last weeks on earth were already playing out in Europe. In Italy, early in the month, Cobain overdosed in his hotel room, with the country's camera crews seemingly already on standby to beam images of a shattered Courtney and a comatose Kurt onto televisions around the globe. Back in the US at the end of March, Cobain entered the Exodus Recovery Center in Marina del Rey, just outside of Los Angeles – then discharged himself just two days later, and vanished off the face of the earth.

Frantic with worry, Courtney Love, herself in the midst of her own promotional stint for Hole's forthcoming *Live Through This* LP, spoke with Farrell. He told *Spin* '[she] asked me if he was at my house. He ran away from rehab, and she thought he might be heading my way.' He wasn't and, given what people were now construing as his own feelings towards Nirvana's involvement in Lollapalooza, he wasn't likely to. Just days later, Nirvana's management company, Gold Mountain, issued a pointed, and very public statement, announcing that Nirvana had pulled out of the Lollapalooza line-up.

None of the people who hoped that such a pronouncement might draw Cobain back into the world could have known that it was already too late. According to the coroner's report into Cobain's suicide, his body was already lying in that quiet garret, patiently awaiting its eventual discovery.

Gone was the frontman for the only band in America with sufficient charisma to launch earthquakes. Lost was the leader of a revolution that redefined all that modern music was – and could become. Overnight, a generation had lost their king, had lost their spokesman, had lost, it seemed, their very own hearts. And, overnight, Lollapalooza had lost its headliner.

At first, there didn't really seem to be any problem replacing Nirvana at the top of the line-up – just add another band to the bottom, and then bump everyone else up a place. But, when the fruit was offered to George Clinton, he turned it down. 'You know, they were going to give Nirvana $100,000 a night and give us $15,000 a night. Then when they wanted *us* to headline, they were going to give us $25,000 a night! I mean, we can take a joke, but we said "Fuck No!".'

Farrell turned next to the Smashing Pumpkins – and surely wondered why he had not approached them first of all. It was already apparent from reading the music press that the death of Cobain had created a vacuum that was simply begging to be filled; and that whatever, or whoever, filled that vacuum was not going to be drawn from the same pack of Seattle-shaped superstars that already prowled in Nirvana's wake... Soundgarden, Pearl Jam, Alice in Chains, they all had their virtues, but not one of them possessed that ineffable spark, that chameleon charisma, that could truly absorb the pressure and the scrutiny of the throngs of downtrodden wannabes who were wailing for a new figurehead.

Billy Corgan, however, possessed all of those qualities; was already equipped with the ability to incite exactly the emotional response that his audience demanded; had indeed already done so. Likewise, when you actually studied their story, the rest of his band. Already, the Smashing Pumpkins' legend read like a rock'n'roll fairytale – from nowhere to nuclear in under three years; triumph over tribulation every step of the way; a bleeding heart and a sensitive soul, *the original tortured genius effect*. As a person, Corgan was nothing like Cobain. But as spirits, in terms of the strength of their convictions and the power of their emotions, the pair were as close as blood brothers. The kids, looking for a fresh leader, had already absorbed that similarity, were already preparing to pass Corgan Cobain's crown. Lollapalooza, by elevating the Smashing Pumpkins to the peak that Nirvana vacated, would become the new king's coronation.

There have always been leaders for the disenfranchised, spokesmen in song for the delirious lay-armies, saviours who are expected to voice, through music and lyric, the thoughts and essence of the populace. In the 1950s, Elvis Presley led the rebel armies to storm the gates of civilisation. In the 1960s, it was John Lennon, in the 1970s, Johnny Rotten. And, as the 1980s stepped for the first time out of the hour glass, it was Joy Division's Ian Curtis who wrapped himself in the crown of thorns and wire that was Rock's greatest gift to its most preciously anointed.

Like Cobain, Curtis held millions in thrall, hanging onto his every hair-shirted word, his voice, his actions. And, like Cobain too, Curtis was tired, depressed and bewildered by the shattering bouts of his recently diagnosed epilepsy, yet was still grinding beneath the leviathan pressures of his band's career. Like Cobain, he was walking a line that strayed dangerously close to madness. And, like Cobain, he just couldn't hold on until it got a little easier.

It was devastating to his fans, and shocking to the public when Curtis' lifeless body was found hanged in his home on 18 May, 1980, a copy of Iggy Pop's so-purgative *The Idiot* ceaselessly spinning on the turntable next to him. Immediately the rally cry went up, as grief stricken youth called for a new Ian, a new era, a new presence to give their dreams voice and vocation – and answered its own prayers when someone stepped behind the Cure's Robert Smith and shoved him, pitchfork to the back, into a spotlight too black to behold. Lo!, you stinking masses, the new messiah has come! Of course it was a cape that Smith didn't want, not at all. But it was the way it had to be, the prophecy had to be fulfilled.

Smith railed against the honour, but found himself powerless to resist. 'I hate the idea that you'd die for your audience, [but] I was rapidly becoming enmeshed in that... the idea that Ian Curtis had gone first, and I was soon to follow.' Now Billy Corgan found himself in a similar position and, like Smith – another of his own musical idols – there was little he could do about any of it, including the demand that he drive himself into the ground creating music that would match the moods that his new status demanded.

In the two years that followed Curtis' passing, until he finally found the emotional reserves to shatter the Cure, in order to rebuild afresh, Smith wrote and recorded what remain two of the most gruelling albums ever released in the name of mere rock'n'roll, the self-immolating torment of *Faith* and *Pornography*. Across the same span in the wake of Cobain's suicide, Corgan began sewing the seeds of the almost-indefinable *Mellon Collie And The Infinite Sadness*, a megalith that would itself come close not simply to destroying the Smashing Pumpkins, but almost wiped out the musicians themselves. But first, they had a festival to prepare for.

Lollapalooza wasn't unique only in its approach to presentation and diversion. There were also genuine attempts made to ensure the physical wellbeing of the concert-goers themselves; an desire to treat them not like so many pigs on their way to the slaughterhouse, to be prodded and poked into barbed wire enclosures, and charged the earth for the most basic human requirements...five dollars for a bottle of warm water, five hours queuing for a stinking portable toilet, five miles of mud between campsite and stage. Traditional festival arrangements weren't simply inhumane, they were self-defeating. As Corgan pointed out as Lollapalooza drew closer, 'if you're playing at the end of the show, do you want to be playing for a bunch of sunburned, crabby people who are tired, or people who feel it's a positive environment and they are having a good time?'

'Our basic principle is to give good, solid concerts,' he affirmed. But they demanded a good, solid audience and, as far as it was possible, it was the Lollapalooza organisers' duty to make sure that they got one. Then the Smashing Pumpkins would take over, and they knew precisely how to behave. 'If someone's gonna serve me twenty thousand kids who go to high school and think they're Alternative, I'm going to give them a dose of Pumpkinland. I wish there had been Nirvanas and Pearl Jams and Smashing Pumpkins when I was fifteen.'

CHAPTER THIRTEEN
PSYCHODRAMA SKITS AND THE AMIABLE POOCH

Wrapping up the last leg of their spring 1994 tour with the reconstituted Red Red Meat, the Smashing Pumpkins finally detached themselves from *Siamese Dream* and checked into Chicago's Gravity Studios, to begin working on the two dozen instrumental demos that would shape their next album. Some of the songs laid down during this period – 'Tonight, Tonight' and 'Jellybelly' among them – would survive all but intact into the actual recording sessions; others would require time in which to metamorphose; and plenty more wouldn't ever be taken any further, haunting completist compulsives with tantalising titles that describe little more than their chord progressions. Such wastage, however, did not matter. What was most important was that the band had an opportunity to spread out its wings without feeling sandwiched by a sound check or an encore.

Some of those newly discovered wings would accompany them onto the road, as the Smashing Pumpkins stepped into Perry Farrell's alterna-universe in July. Since the first announcements back in early spring, the Lollapalooza bill had expanded into one of the most captivating (but still, of course, controversial) in the festival's entire history. Joining the Smashing Pumpkins, Nick Cave, Green Day and George Clinton for the opening show on 7 July, in Las Vegas, Nevada, were the Beastie Boys, A Tribe Called Quest, the Boredoms and L7. Offstage, a host of new interactive excitements awaited – a rain room, in which concert-goers could be cooled off by moisture and a constant temperature of fifty degrees Fahrenheit. There was the Revival Tent, dedicated to scheduled forums on a variety of subjects, as well as a venue for more spur of the moment discussions and performances from members of the crowd. And there was the traditional Lollapacircus of travelling lobbyists, information stands and membership drives.

Neither was there any shortage of takers for the tickets. In the years since the first Lollapalooza proved that a then-widely proscribed downturn in the market for live shows was, in fact, nothing more than people staying away from a lot of lousy concerts, industry insiders had continued to prophecy the festival's decline and seized upon each year's bill as advance warning that this was the year in which the bubble would finally burst. And every year, Lollapalooza proved them wrong.

The New York shows, at the end of July, were already sold out by the middle of June; and city after city followed suit. Soon, rather than count the empty seats, the organisers were having to find ways of filling more than they'd ever bargained for, adding a clutch of further shows to the bill and, for the first time, extending the tour far beyond its customary summer season lifespan, and into early September. And, when legendary street poet funkers, The Last Poets, joined the Beastie Boys on stage in Las Vegas, for an unscheduled performance of Gil Scott Heron's inflammatory commentary 'The Revolution Will Not Be Televised,' they set the stage for the entire venture. A lot of it probably *would* be televised – every local news channel in America seemed to have cameras at one show or another. But the revolution was blazing regardless.

There were surprises elsewhere. In Philadelphia, Courtney Love shrugged off the widow's weeds within which the media seemed intent upon binding her, to take over the main stage for solo acoustic versions of 'Doll Parts' and 'Miss World.' A few nights later in New York, she repeated the performance and James Iha, keeping a voluminous tour diary to relay the entire experience to fans, noted 'Courtney Love performed twice...with just her and a guitar. Really minimal, but powerful and cathartic.'

Iha commented kindly, too, on the always dashing Nick Cave, as he brought style and jangled class to the shows, opening the afternoon in his trademarked suits and Cuban heels and howling out his black heart at the shimmering heat and sun of an American summer. As a teenager, Iha believed Cave could do no wrong. Catching him now, his adult self realised that the teen had known what he was talking about.

There came another, more personal, highlight in Los Angeles, when Iha joined the Breeders on stage to perform that band's classic 'Divine Hammer.' It was a blistering occasion, as guitarists Iha and Kelley Deal wailed away, handling twin leads like some cock-rocked seventies studs. It was another one of those outstanding, hyper-energized moments with which every stop on the tour seemed to overflow, and which every act in turn seemed determined to provide, as this Lollapalooza – perhaps more than any – set out to steamroller the barriers that infest modern music, and keep ears from hearing all that they should.

Most white, middle class kids had barely even heard of George Clinton, for example, let alone comprehended how he revolutionized the way soul bred into funk during the 1970s. Perhaps they would have recognized snips of Clinton's songs imbedded in samples from the current crop of rap super sellers, but even that was to assume they had ever heard the songs to begin with. At Lollapalooza, they finally had their chance – and audiences responded. Clinton was hot, carousing on stage, venerating a genre of music that middle class values and white bread record moguls had spent the better part of two decades trying to suppress. It was an absolute triumph but, again, it was not the only one. If the main stage was rocking, after all, so was the second stage with its rotating roster of mixed and matched performers.

The Flaming Lips, Verve, and Luscious Jackson were among those who kicked off the first two weeks of the tour, with the Lips in particular tearing it up every night, throwing such an eccentric mix of covers into the blend that even Billy Corgan, no stranger to the art of the unexpected, could not help but stand amazed. Queen's 'Under Pressure,' A Flock Of Seagulls' warped 'Space Age Love Song' – those were songs that the Smashing Pumpkins themselves could have appropriated to equal effect.

Guided By Voices and The Palace jumped on stage for the Chicago and Detroit shows. Hot hopefuls Girls Against Boys took the tour through to New York City; Lamb, the Boo Radleys, Stereolab, Shonen Knife and the rappers Fu-Schnickens came on board later.

'I had fun this summer,' Iha later reflected. Writing again in his tour diary, he summed up the experience through his own eyes, and exercised his iconic reference points in a startlingly astute way. 'I always imagine the 70s to be kinda like Lollapalooza, when you had amazing bills like Foghat, the Steve Miller Band...and people played Frisbee, danced in the mud and wore sandals. Years from now, people will kinda remember how the Smashing Pumpkins played with Beasties. Or was it Foghat with the Doobie Brothers?'

The Smashing Pumpkins themselves entered into the spirit of fiery free enterprise that characterised the Second Stage, by making their own surprise appearances on that platform, before taking to the Main Stage for their own scheduled set. Dallas, Texas, on 21 August, San Diego (25 August) and Mountain View (27 August) were all treated to these virtual guerrilla raids, a thrill for everybody who'd just been hanging around to see if anything might transpire, but an absolute nightmare for all the devotees who'd already staked their places by the Main Stage, in readiness for the band's advertised set.

Yet not every observer shared Iha's enthusiasm for Lollapalooza; and not every one seemed to accept the Smashing Pumpkins as any kind of replacement for Nirvana whatsoever. A couple of kids from Seattle followed Lollapalooza all the way down the west coast, and reported back with almost bitter betrayal. 'The Smashing Pumpkins sucked rather badly', singling out then 'Disarm' and 'Rocket' as special disappointments, while 'Cherub Rock,' according to one attendee, 'was played so fast that my roommate insisted that they hadn't played it at all.'

Others, meanwhile, complained that Corgan was too whiny, pulling a 'Jim Morrison/Perry Farrell invective monologue about how his life sucked, how we sucked...blah blah blah.'

Of course such discourses were familiar to the Smashing Pumpkins' regular audience. Lollapalooza, however, brought them out in front of crowds who might never have attended an individual group's gig, but viewed a big muddy field full of music as the summation of teenaged experience. For them, anything that did not conform to the masturbatory ideals they hatched in the privacy of their own warped enclaves had no purpose but to be howled down.

For Corgan and the Smashing Pumpkins, however, the prickly endurance course of uneducated audiences was part of the appeal of Lollapalooza itself. Once again, they were shuffling off the anticipated course, doing their own thing, making their own glorious noise and taking shit because of it. Almost gleefully, Corgan acknowledged, 'We took the high road and it caused a lot of problems, because the youth of Lollapalooza didn't want real rock & roll.'

Neither would he apologise for this. The foundations of the Smashing Pumpkins' very meaning is built on the band's penchant for agonizing the pettiness of society, for disdaining the Gen-X pity parties, and for stomping hard on an entire generation's feeling that somehow, somewhere, they have been massively, and royally screwed over. Life sucks...so suck it back. There's just no pleasing some people.

In fact, an almost shockingly optimistic Corgan later reported, the Smashing Pumpkins swallowed all of their exhaustion and blasted through the tour, playing 'damn honest.' At the end of the day, of course, 'Lollapalooza certainly soured me on the shows' – no matter how many great experiences came out of it, forty plus nights in such a high-pressure goldfish bowl could not help but drain all but a saint. But it wasn't disdain for the road that fired the Smashing Pumpkins' new found frustrations. It was a yearning to get back to the business of being a band, rather than being part of an 'experience'; an almost physical itch to return to the studio, to continue preparing the songs that were bound for *Mellon Collie And The Infinite Sadness,* and with the songs, to rekindle the mood or mood*iness*...that would characterise its greatest moments.

The tangle of emotions, and the raw and rampant media speculation that followed Cobain's suicide, dogged the Alternative music community throughout those summer months, even dampening a little of the spirit that Lollapalooza intended. No matter how well the Smashing Pumpkins performed, few people could forget that they could have been watching Nirvana instead – and, there is no question at all in history's mind that many more people saw the Smashing Pumpkins as they rode the Lollapalooza shebang than ever caught Nirvana in the flesh.

But Corgan himself refused to rise to any of the suggestions that, in realising this, he was himself accepting the dubious crown he had been offered. Rather, he retreated further from the arenas in which he traditionally battled the media, insisting that, 'after what happened to Kurt, opening yourself to the press seems even more ridiculous than ever.' Cobain's suicide would, in part anyway, start closing the door between Corgan and the media, between his personal torments and the fans' hands that reached to bridge the gap between their reality and his own.

In any case, the opportunities for such questioning to be pursued were fast drying up. Following their final gig in Carson, California on 5 September, the Smashing Pumpkins headed east, back to New York City, for an appearance at the MTV Music Awards on 8 September. And then they all but vanished from view...a few weeks personal downtime, a few months sequestered in the studio, the occasional concert to sweep away the cobwebs...between the end of Lollapalooza in 1994, and the beginning of 1996, the Smashing Pumpkins would play no more than two dozen gigs anywhere in the world. The rest of the time was devoted to the studio.

The initial groundwork was already done. In addition to the rough demos that the band recorded during the early summer, Corgan had been turning lyrics around during the tour – including the future classic 'Bullet With Butterfly Wings.' He admitted that he 'started working almost immediately after Lollapalooza. When you haven't written in a while, it's really hard to write more than a couple of hours a day.' But he quickly expanded those two hour bursts into four hours, then coupled that advance with another long stretch of rehearsal. It was draining, but it was also energising, building up such a groove that, by the end of the sessions, Corgan found himself up most of the day and night. It was crazy, he said, but 'it kind of builds to that.'

He also revealed that 'Bullet With Butterfly Wings' itself grew directly out of the Lollapalooza experience, specifically the line 'despite all my rage, I am still just a rat in a cage'. 'I'm not blaming Lollapalooza but the thing is this: your own ambition puts you in a situation where you think "I'm finally getting what I want." And when you get what you want, and you realize that you're not really equipped to completely deal with it. Then you have to fight all those feelings. And then it just became a larger parable for life, like you have some shit job and you hate it and you want to kill everyone but you never say it.'

That autumn brought further songs to bear, as Corgan tuned in and turned up at his own recently completed home studio, Sadlands. He had matured blissfully into his own voice during the gestation of the first two albums – now, rather than having to force himself to sit down and write, with often painful blocks and bouts of self-doubt, by 1994 he found himself looking forward to it, relaxing into the process.

He'd been relying on himself more and more often over the years, leaving behind the lessons of the other great writers and instead tapping into his own resources to pull out the lyric, to pull out the pure pleasure. 'I've been down the road,' he said, 'where you're learning on what somebody else has carved out for you,' the process, of course, that everybody follows, as they obey that most natural of creative inclinations and study all that has been done before, in order to reinterpret it in their own right. Corgan, however, now realized that 'you cannot create your own language until you escape that' – until you understand the creative essence which is itself the magic that makes those other 'great' artists worth learning from in the first place.

It was during these first sessions that the Smashing Pumpkins laid down many of the ideas that would eventually transform themselves into the lengthy 'Pastichio Medley,' itself finally completed during autumn 1995. A vision of absolute psychosis, the twenty-three plus minute 'Medley,' comprised entirely of snips, bits and riffs of almost every unused song recorded for *Mellon Collie And The Infinite Sadness*, but which didn't, ultimately, make the grade. Rather than waste them on the cutting room floor, however, Corgan 'randomly ran small bits all together to create a pastiche of madness....'

Fellow Lollapalooza performer Nick Cave, interestingly, had recently enacted a similar construction around a series of extraordinarily productive ad-libbing sessions recorded over the previous couple of years. Titled simply 'B Side,' it offered up close to twenty minutes of discordant and disorientating snips and clips, collage art rock in its purest form. 'Pastichio Medley' regardless of whether it was inspired by Cave's example, nevertheless followed in its footsteps, even echoing 'B Side's' mode of delivery by appearing as part of the chunky seven song *Zero* EP. There, it nestled alongside the *Mellon Collie And The Infinite Sadness* out-takes 'God' and 'Zero,' an early-in-the-sessions attempt to wrap the band's sound around a burst of Cybermetal.

Zero was also notable for fulfilling a threat that the band had long promised, as it served up the ferocious 'Tribute To Johnny,' the Smashing Pumpkins' honorarium to the modern blues guitarist Johnny Winter. Notable for his work with Muddy Waters and brother Edgar, as well as for his own solo work, the albino Winter carved an unmistakable swath for himself across the mainstream American rock scene of the very late 1960s and 1970s. He might never have come close to eclipsing brother Edgar's 'Frankenstein' success, but still Johnny landed fifteen albums on the American charts, and racked up a pair of singles as well, covers of 'Johhny B. Goode' and 'Jumpin' Jack Flash' in 1970 and 1973. Billy Corgan never ceased to be amazed by Johnny Winter's abilities – rhapsodizing on Winter's performance on the 1992 Bob Dylan Tribute Concert, Corgan reported, 'even James Iha, who could give two shits about Johnny Winter, had his mouth hanging open.'

Several small interludes punctuated the major sessions for the album, as autumn 1994 turned to winter, and the writing continued – indeed, as first the weeks and then the months passed, it became evident that this new undertaking was going to be a lengthy one. Corgan had long ago hinted to the press that, among his most fervent ambitions, the desire to create a double album was one of the most pressing – a comment that was usually greeted with a laugh and a snort by whoever was listening in. This was Alternative Rock, after all, and Alternative Rockers *just didn't* release double albums. Leave such bloated conceits to the likes of Yes, ELP and the Electric Light Orchestra.

The earliest buzz, though, continued to sniff out hints that the next Smashing Pumpkins project was going to be a behemoth. Cooked up in Corgan's head partly as a ploy to fly in the face of the party line, and, partly, simply because he wanted to, the very suggestion of releasing a double LP stirred vicious debate long before the final tracks had even started to shuffle themselves into such contentious form; and long, too, before the waiting ears realised that it wasn't simply the form book that the Smashing Pumpkins intended tearing up.

The band's very direction was undergoing a remarkable shift, with new songs that were shaping up to be so vibrant, so vital, and so pregnant with ambition that it was clear that there could be no hurrying this process – no matter who was doing the hurrying. Virgin, of course, were desperate to capitalize on the success of the band's Lollapalooza showing, salivating behind the door for the next release, but Corgan was not to be drawn from his intended course. There would be no new Smashing Pumpkins product until he, and the band, were good and ready.

To that end, to appease everyone, two notable releases appeared in October 1994, as Virgin pulled out the only stopgap measure at their disposal, to keep heat on the band. It was a two tiered punch, the *Vieuphoria* video collection, and a Corgan-compiled collection of b-sides and rarities, *Pisces Iscariot*.

The album itself was not an altogether original concept – Nirvana had pulled a similar rabbit from their hat two years earlier, when their own next album seemed unlikely to appear any time soon. But *Incesticide*'s gathering of demos, out-takes, BBC sessions and the like, barely bit into the American Top Forty. *Pisces Iscariot*'s round-up of almost identical provenance wound up galloping to number four, the Smashing Pumpkins' most dramatic chart placing yet. Even more rewardingly, radio grasped onto the BBC session take of Stevie Nicks' 'Landslide,' and drew that into the Top Twenty airplay charts, without it ever being released as a conventional single.

Vieuphoria, meanwhile, showcased ten live tracks that had been recorded between 1993 and 1994. These were supplanted with in-betweens that ranged from tantalising glimpses of Corgan's days with the Marked, odd psychodrama skits, and even little clips recorded in Iha's home 'Bugg Studios.' It was the latter that produced his electronically twisted, New Orderish snip 'Bugg Superstar' – named for, and after, his amiable pooch. As amusing as these interludes were, however, the most attention was focused on the full-length live performances that drew from shows recorded as far afield as London, Europe and the Far East, as well as Chicago and Atlanta.

The Smashing Pumpkins crossed cultures and datelines too often to keep track of whether they were coming or going, and in the process, audiences were regaled with songs that only emphasized what a sizable presence they were live and raw and in the flesh. With an ever-changing array of psychedelically tripped out shirts, Corgan cavorted across the stage, or droned into his mic, providing an intense foreground that bled away to Wretzky's long blonde hair swinging over her bass and picked out in the lights, to Iha's studied face, set over his guitar and, back even further still, to Chamberlin, decked to the nines behind his kit. The city, country, venue, weather changed, but the image of the band on stage did not – becoming on video a moving collage of snapshots as the band played for their lives.

The video, then, was a successful attempt to whittle the Smashing Pumpkins' experience down to a 'set' that would give the armchair viewer as much of a thrill as the concert-goers themselves. On disc, across their two studio albums, the band was often close to revolutionary, carving a myriad of styles into shreds and then reassembling them via their own manifesto to something completely vital, urgent and utterly contemporary.

Live, however, the Smashing Pumpkins were nearly unstoppable, delivering a raucous cacophony that transcended everything for which they were already renowned, to become a force that would endure long after the rest of the scene that produced them had imploded. Indeed, so successful was the package that, nine years later, and nearly two years after the Smashing Pumpkins themselves ceased to exist, *Vieuphoria* was released in dramatically expanded form for DVD, an intimate and – given all that had transpired during the intervening decade – often pertinent examination of the Smashing Pumpkins as they hovered on the very brink of the superstardom that would, ultimately, dog them into disintegration.

CHAPTER FOURTEEN
BEHEMOTHS, LEVIATHANS, AND A
LITTLE SPAZZMATAZZ

As 1994 wound down, everybody was in agreement that the rough sketches for the Smashing Pumpkins' third album, *Mellon Collie And The Infinite Sadness,* were already in place. Confidence was high as they prepared for their longest haul yet in the studio, and their most ambitious; even from within the insulation of the innermost sanctum, the weight of expectation hung heavy – the Smashing Pumpkins were gearing up for their glory moment and they knew it.

They also knew precisely what was expected from them; knew that their image – or, at least, an approximation of their image – was now so firmly imprinted in the Alternative psyche that the only common debate in the outside world revolved around whether Billy Corgan was the sweetest guy you could ever hope to meet... or the lousiest shit you could ever hope not to. The band's own reputation followed suit.

Iha, reflecting upon the year-or-so that the group had just lived through, sighed resignedly, 'Billy caused a lot of those problems with the first slew of interviews he did...the media just played to it, and that was the angle on the whole last album.' But he was also aware that image always walks hand in hand with public persona, and the Smashing Pumpkins' public persona was one of edgy confrontation, four souls united in a fractious marriage, while their frontman spilled his guts out in the most brightly lit forum he could find.

Much of what was freshest about Rock in the 1990s revolved now around the confessional self-flagellation that had seemed so out of step when the Smashing Pumpkins first burst onto the scene – a revolution that Corgan had certainly played a major role in fermenting. Far beyond the acknowledged standard-bearers of the bruising, a pantheon that itself now stretched beyond the acknowledged grunge-aholics of Kurt Cobain and Eddie Vedder, to embrace everyone from America's Liz Phair to Ireland's Whipping Boy, an evening with the hottest bands in America was akin to a night spent in an especially prickly psychiatrist's office, fly-on-the-walling while the pain and torment of a twisted soul wafted into the stagnant air.

Neither was it always easy to differentiate precisely where the music ended and the reality began – the bitter tragedy of Kurt Cobain's suicide saw to that, as his own much-publicised litany of personal traumas and private grief, hitherto bookmarked by so many critics as just another platinum pose, was suddenly revealed not to have been a pose at all. Nobody was willing to take that chance again; suddenly, the most insincere sounding bleat had to be accepted as a genuine cry of pain, for fear that another lifeless body would be staked out in the morgue, while another generation bled tears of futile rage. No wonder Corgan himself, surveying the human wasteland over which he presided, complained that 'nowadays rock stars are too human.' Short of selling your soul to the unbridled hedonism of Britpop, soaring so high in the United Kingdom, but still little more than a sideshow in America, the fantasy world of rock'n'roll had never strayed so close to the pain of actually living.

Yet Corgan was not necessarily about to resign his position. Acutely aware that he was perceived by many fans to be a (if not THE) voice of the generation, he admitted that 'I don't feel a responsibility for the youth of America. But I [do] feel a responsibility to best articulate what I feel.' And, if others took his own words as a form of gospel, then that only increased the responsibility, no matter what his intentions may have been at the outset. 'The rock mythology that I have is the reality of the me – the temper tantrums and the failed love affairs I've had. But that's nothing I've created on purpose.' It was nothing to hide or to be ashamed of. It was simply, just his own self, his own life, distilled.

Whether deliberately or otherwise, there was little about this latest rock god that did not find its way into print, into the rumour mill or into the common mythology archives that collected and dissected thoughts and deeds twenty-four hours a day, and that played into the Smashing Pumpkins' renown as well. As 1994 finally shuddered its last, raspy breath, the Smashing Pumpkins galloped away with any number of honours, including a few they might never have expected. Dominating the indie rags' year end lists was not an unfamiliar sensation. But taking Band Of The Year from the traditionally conservative *Spin* certainly was.

Holed up inside their Pumpkinland rehearsal space, the new year began as the old one ended, with the band running through versions of songs before the actual business of the recording sessions commenced in March, then giving the repertoire a public run through when they took over Chicago's Double Door for a four night residency in February.

Located in the Wicker Park neighbourhood, the Double Door had hosted some of rock'n'rolling Chicago's greatest nights. With admission prices that remained stubbornly easy on the wallet – five bucks at the low end, and rarely more than twenty dollars at the top – the venue had thrown open its doors to everyone from the Rolling Stones to the latest local hotties. Given the somewhat experimental nature of the proceedings, the Smashing Pumpkins set ticket prices at the low end, then donated their own share of the proceeds to charity.

Few of the songs on display over the course of the four nights would be familiar to anybody standing on the dance floor, as the group powered through a selection of *Mellon Collie* works-in-progress ('Speed,' 'Towers Of Rabble' and 'God' were among the best-received previews), a clutch of old b-sides, a fabulous cover of David Bowie's 'Never Let Me Down' and, to the delight of future archivists, a handful of songs that never would make the cut from studio to album, among them the magnificent 'Mouths of Babes.' Written and toyed with during the *Siamese Dream* tours, the song was, according to Corgan, 'a favourite at sound check' even if it would never see an official release. And why was that? Because there simply wasn't room for it.

In stark contrast to the ghastly gestation of *Siamese Dream*, Corgan now found that, once he started to write, he couldn't stop. With songs biting through his brain at a horrific pace, he had already confirmed to the label that the new album would indeed be a double; had confirmed, too, that the nature of the new material was such that any preconceptions laid down about the Smashing Pumpkins-so-far would need to be swept away.

Corgan was undergoing yet another sonic shift, consciously fulfilling another promise he'd made to himself. Further amplifying his admiration of REM, Corgan openly admired what he perceived the band to have done for modern music, and more importantly, for their audience. He, too, would walk that same path.

Commenting that, over time, he'd seen bands like U2 moving away from their own personal roots and toward what, and who, they perceived their audience to be, he praised REM for their own contrary push 'to lead...and see who followed.' It is one of the stark truisms of rock'n'roll that few of even the greatest bands are ever able to escape the trap of their audience's expectations; that, two...three...at very best four...albums into their career, they abandon the unbridled creative crunch that gave them their voice, sound and motivation, and turn instead to recreating those sensations, knowing that that is what their audience demands. And so U2 make U2 noises, Pearl Jam make Pearl Jam noises, Sonic Youth make Sonic Youth noises.

REM, on the other hand, have never fallen into the sonic maw that other bands build with every successive album; have never simply sat back on their laurels and agreed, 'they seemed to like it last time, let's just do it again.' Not only did they fly by the seat of their pants, time and again they first selected the most unfashionable pants they could find, just to see what would happen. The slew of gold records on the wall of the band members' home answer that question, as the group's audience not only applauds REM's continued inventive courage, but acknowledges that, contrary to the opinions of so many other industry analysts, they are eminently capable of accepting change, so long as that change is enacted with respect.

It was a lesson that Corgan had long ago taken to heart; that was now being implemented as the new album took shape. *Siamese Dream* had already moved in large increments away from *Gish*, and the mysterious gauze and crash of the developing *Mellon Collie* would prove to be a massive push away from *Siamese Dream*.

Yet Corgan was not altogether confident that, where REM walked, the Smashing Pumpkins could follow. Opening a window that he would certainly come to regret in later years, once his fears had been proven groundless, Corgan openly hinted, from time to time, that *Mellon Collie And The Infinite Sadness* would spell the band's death knell – although Wretzky was later quick to affirm that the knell was, perhaps, a little more metaphorical than Corgan suggested, and others assumed. The purpose of recording and releasing a behemoth like *Mellon Collie And The Infinite Sadness* was, she said 'to bring everything we've tried to do in the past seven years to fruition.'

Part of that shift, that reach toward fruition and whatever kind of closure it heralded, would be instigated with the band's choice of producer. After the intense focus upon 70s era rock'n'roll smashed into the contemporary Alternative riffing that had been pulled along by Butch Vig's own sense of the band's sound, Corgan dramatically pulled back from the rawk and turned his attention instead toward a dreamier sound, one that would resonate not only across two groundbreaking discs, but which would reach back, too, to the lush early cine-style techniques of the album's keynote videos.

Recalling Alan Moulder from the final mix of *Siamese Dream*, the band also recruited Flood, the English producer best known for his partnership with dark rocker Nick Cave, and the teasingly tempestuous camp of Marc Almond and Depeche Mode. Separately, the two producers' credentials were impressive. In tandem, and married to the Smashing Pumpkins, they would prove unstoppable. Although few of the eyebrows that raised so questioningly when the partnership was first announced could ever have predicted that success – and with good stylistic reason. Yet hindsight dictates that there could not have been another choice; as Iha put it so succinctly, 'the last thing we wanted to make was an Alternative rock guitar album again!'

What they did want to do was explore new territory and, while the band's long-time partnership with Butch Vig had not been sullied in the slightest, the Smashing Pumpkins needed to stretch their frontiers, a challenge that the combined forces of Flood and Moulder would certainly force them to face, both in stylistic terms and in terms of execution. It is unwise for any band to work with the same producer over an extended period of time – again, patterns emerge, ruts develop and sometimes it's easier to do the same thing year in and year out than step out of the box, shake the tree and take a flying leap into a different direction. Iha laughingly recalled the days when Vig and Corgan would spend hours together, tweaking a take, a riff, a note, and then contrasted that with Flood's preferred method of eschewing the quest for 'the perfect take,' in favour of 'the take that feels the best.'

With Corgan relaxing into the creative process, and Virgin now resigned to allowing the band as much time as they required in which to complete the project, the group found themselves relishing not only the freedom with which they now controlled their own destiny, but also the now-bandwagoning whispers from without, that the only point of such an ambitious undertaking was to finally accomplish everything that Corgan had been promising from day one – to break down the band for good.

For their own part, making this album in this way was the fulfilment of another of Corgan's mantras altogether, his constant assurances that they should 'just do what you want to do. Just do what you want to do.' The making of Mellon Collie And The Infinite Sadness was simply the next step on the rung. They'd paid out enough dues to have the opportunity to finally explore the tweaks and twists at which they'd only hinted in the past. And they responded with glee – whatever outsiders might have imagined was taking place in the studios as they worked, there was certainly no subversion or internal dissolution on the Smashing Pumpkins' own part. Indeed, by all accounts, it was just the opposite.

With the producers in tow, the Smashing Pumpkins spent several weeks in Pumpkinland before their arrival at the Chicago Recording Company at the beginning of March. This not only allowed the band to take a dry run through what they intended bringing into the studio, it also allowed Flood to hear what the band had written, and to think about it before the session got underway for real.

The recording sessions stretched from March 1995 through August and would continue into the fall as the album was mixed. It was the longest break from touring – or any other duties – that the band had enjoyed since their inception and, with that heavy schedule completely cleared, so the group's own internal chemistry flourished, as working relationships began to shift in a surprising number of ways.

Ideas and music flowed in directions that the band had never hitherto dreamed possible. Attitudes towards one another's suggestions, towards the very tone and timbre of the songs themselves, were more open than they had ever been in the past. The personal demons that had previously so plagued the quartet were beaten back into the shadows for the time being; and, while Corgan was still writing the lion's share of words and music, for the first time the Smashing Pumpkins emerged as a real collective, a group mending their rifts, sealing the cracks with spit and fire, and layering the patches with dreamtime imagery and haunting guitar. Mellon Collie And The Infinite

Sadness would reflect that, and would emerge as vibrantly vivid as the flames that fed it.

The album itself was recorded in intense bursts. Spread out over the Chicago Recording Company, the nuts and bolts of *Mellon Collie And The Infinite Sadness* marked a different tack for the band. Iha recalled that 'we had two rooms going at the same time...Billy had his room, me and D'Arcy had our room, and it was three months of two rooms going at once.' And where was Jimmy Chamberlin in all this to-ing and fro-ing? He was everywhere, popping in and out of each room in turn, keeping everyone in stitches and up to the task.

Flood himself ensured that the musicians had no time in which to succumb to any of the traditional malaise of protracted studio time. Even the customary regimentation of a booked studio was not sacred as the producer staggered the individual players' start times, so that he could get a drum sound down or a guitar piece locked into place before everyone else arrived. It was this attention to detail, coupled with Corgan's unerring vision for how *Mellon Collie And The Infinite Sadness* should sound, that brought the album to life.

Two rooms, two discs, two moods, and two months into the heavy recording sessions, the band were already shuffling songs into test albums – and still it would be close to a year before *Mellon Collie And The Infinite Sadness* finally shuffled itself into its two distinct parts. The first, Iha explained, was 'more like a standard Smashing Pumpkins record, more what people would expect.' The second, however, 'just goes off the deep end, becomes even more bloated, and becomes unrecognizable, so that when you actually pull it out of the drink, it just looks like some sort of cattle mutilation.' It was a description that, once thrown to the wolves on the pre-release interview circuit, led to any amount of unease and dire predictions, but Iha certainly tossed the image out there with the very best of intentions. How else *could* you describe an album of so many shifts, so many moods and so many moments of absolute defiance?

Although the bulk of *Mellon Collie And The Infinite Sadness* was recorded at Chicago Recording Company, the final album would also pull from sessions at Pumpkinland, Corgan's Sadlands and Iha's home Bugg Studios. Then, once the songs were finished, Corgan, Flood and Moulder decamped to the Village Recorder in Los Angeles to mix it.

Carved out of a roaring twenties era-Masonic temple in the heart of Los Angeles in 1968, the Village Recorder has been host to musicians from all walks of life. From Steely Dan to Supertramp, and onto Bob Dylan and Tom Petty, the studio has an almost kinetic energy, and these latest denizens were swift to add their own spectre to the soup; the feedback of guitars that bled into strings too beautiful to imagine as Corgan's voice railed and cracked with a tempestuous and beautiful fragility.

Simply figuring out what should go onto the album was itself a mammoth task. There was so much to choose from, and so much to include. 'It's a lot,'

Corgan said of the lengthy sets. But, neither he, the band, nor the producers expected people to sit down and listen to the entire album in one uninterrupted swath. That would be too much to hope for. But they did hope that fans would put the album on and play bits and pieces, a few songs here and there. They hoped that people would absorb the songs and the album's intention, that they'd discover new bits to digest each time the discs were spun.

The album itself became the ultimate journey through the psyche's dark underbelly in ways that the Smashing Pumpkins' peers couldn't even begin to touch with their heart on sleeve hit 'em hard style. Layers upon layers could be peeled off *Mellon Collie And The Infinite Sadness* to reveal yet more underneath. Depressive, excessive, obsessive, the songs on the album reeled off like so many neuroses – but self indulgent as it was, it was also entrancing and absolutely exquisite in its rendering.

With strings and some of the band's quietest interludes yet subverted by the heavy wailing of songs like 'X.Y.U.' and 'Jellybelly,' the album was punctuated by twisted gnarls that took every genre-specific tag the band had ever boasted and threw it back up in a fresh re-invention.

While Corgan worked on putting the final touches to the album, Iha stayed back in Chicago, linking up with Kerry Brown to begin the enormous task of sifting through all that was left over, close to two dozen further songs, to choose the b-sides that would accompany the stream of singles that would inevitably be culled from *Mellon Collie And The Infinite Sadness* itself. Not all were strictly out-takes and off-cuts – several numbers were recorded after the album's final running order was deemed complete; others, including 'Ugly,' which Corgan told *Guitar World* was 'an interesting interpretation of what had essentially been an acoustic song,' were originally included within that running order, only to be excised when *Mellon Collie And The Infinite Sadness* was shortened from thirty-one to twenty-eight songs.

There were other notable cast-offs. 'Spazzmatazz' and 'Methusela' were dumped from early incarnations of the album, in favour of the gospel-tinged 'Jupiter's Lament' and 'Believe' – recorded, Iha explained, 'the day after the music for the album was done'. Another of Iha's favourite exiles was '...Said Sadly,' a further late-in-the-day recording that pre-supposed the guitarist's own personal leanings. Indeed, like the *Let It Come Down* solo album that was gestating in his mind even then, '...Said Sadly' featured Veruca Salt's Nina Gordon on vocals, representing a band that Iha had long publicly applauded. 'Nina and Louise [band mate Shapiro] are energy fireballs. Nina has like twenty times more energy than I have,' he enthused. 'They can sing, play, they do it all.'

Jimmy Chamberlin also took advantage of this period, as he linked up with Skid Row vocalist Sebastian Bach, The Frogs' Jimmy Flemion and Breeders' bassist Kelly Deal to form The Last Hard Men. Like Corgan's Starchildren, it was a very ad hoc arrangement, but the group made its mark on the soundtrack to the movie *Scream* with a searing cover of Alice Cooper's 'School's Out.' The aggregation would remain a going concern long enough to record a full album for Atlantic Records, although ultimately the major chose not to release it. The self titled LP would finally see release as a limited edition on Kelly Deal's own Nice Records imprint in 1998.

Although the Smashing Pumpkins themselves remained out of sight, and out of the loop, as they worked towards completing *Mellon Collie and the Infinite Sadness*, news and, less creditably, rumour continued percolating through the press, keeping the group's name firmly in the spotlight.

Few of these tales had too much grounding in fact; others simply grabbed the wrong end of whichever stick was being proffered, and ran with it – such as the British *New Musical Express'* announcement, on 22 April 1995, that the Smashing Pumpkins were to join the likes of Low, Moby and Mazzy Star on a forthcoming American tribute to Joy Division. In fact, Billy Corgan alone would be taking part in the project, as he chose the Manchester band's 'Isolation' to ring down the curtain on a project that he, Iha, tour manager Bob English and Kerry Brown had been flirting with for several years now, the aptly-named Starchildren.

A strictly casual operation that Corgan built solely around the availability of time, inclination and other musicians (Brown's Catherine band mates, guitarists Neil Jendon and Mark Rew were also occasional players), Starchildren had played live no more than a handful of times, frequently running through original songs that Corgan determined would never fit into the Smashing Pumpkins' repertoire, but better known on the Chicago club circuit for the slew of memorable cover versions with which they peppered their performances. Gary Numan's 'Cars,' John Lennon's 'Give Peace A Chance' and the Cure's 'A Night Like This' were all proven Starchildren favourites, while their one stab at a serious recording, Corgan's 'Delusions Of Candor,' slipped out on the b-side of Catherine's own Corgan-produced 'Songs About Girls' single in 1994.

'Isolation' itself was already featured in Starchildren's live set; as that band faded from view during 1995, the song then slipped into the Smashing Pumpkins' own repertoire – and that, of course, was a subject that was now very close to the band members' own hearts. *Mellon Collie and the Infinite Sadness* was scheduled for an October 1995 release, but the tour that would accompany it kicked off a full two months earlier, as the Smashing Pumpkins flew to Ireland for two nights at Dublin's SFX Centre, then across the sea to Britain, where they were to headline the Reading festival.

Billed over the likes of Neil Young, China Drum, Green Day, Tricky, Blind Melon and Bjork, the Smashing Pumpkins delivered an amazing set. No matter that the bulk of it comprised songs that none in the crowd had ever heard before, still the response was phenomenal, not only among the watching thousands, but also in the pages of the UK press, whose own denizens had surely attended the show with their doubts running amok. Smashing Pumpkins, after all, were not the only survivors of the grunge era to be appearing on the Reading bill. Dave Grohl's post-Nirvana Foo Fighters, Courtney Love's Hole, and grimly surviving Seattleites Soundgarden and Mudhoney were in town as well, all adding up to a veritable retro-fest of Last Year's Men.

Neither did the latter pair go out of their way to deviate from that pre-ordained script, turning in performances that even fans had to acknowledge were well past their sell-by date. The Foo Fighters and (perhaps unexpectedly) Hole were stronger, but it took the Smashing Pumpkins' set to confirm what they suggested, and demonstrate that the old-time Grunge scene was not the stark one-way street it had otherwise seemed to be. Indeed, compared to the far-after-the-fact drabness of the acts that preceded them, the contrast between the Smashing Pumpkins, bright and vital in their own latest guise, and the Ghosts of Grunge Fads Past elsewhere on the bill could not have been more pronounced.

Blistering through a set that shrugged off most of the band's earliest history, their Reading set included just one song from *Gish*, the acid 'Siva,' and a mere handful of snapshots from *Siamese Dream* – 'Cherub Rock,' 'Disarm,' 'Mayonaise' and 'Rocket.' But still the performance was a triumph, whipping an eager audience into a frenzy with a tantalizing taste of things to come from *Mellon Collie And The Infinite Sadness* – 'Jellybelly,' 'Zero,' 'Today,' 'Bullet With Butterfly Wings,' 'Porcelina Of The Vast Oceans' 'X.Y.U.' and 'Thru The Eyes Of Ruby' all proved that, whatever prophecies had been made for the forthcoming leviathan, the Smashing Pumpkins were looking to upset every single one of them.

CHAPTER FIFTEEN
NOT A STUPID RIP-OFF RIFF

The Smashing Pumpkins' greatest hopes for *Mellon Collie And The Infinite Sadness* were realized as soon as it was released in October, as the album shot to the top of the American charts. It was the first double album of all-new material to top the listings since Pink Floyd's *The Wall* back in 1980 – a coincidence, incidentally, that Corgan would soon have cause to relish even further, and the first purpose-built double CD ever to make that grade. In England, too, the band breached the UK top five immediately, placing the album at number four, matching *Siamese Dream*'s achievement.

A simultaneous single 'Bullet With Butterfly Wings' reached number twenty in Britain, while its stylish video spun off into heavy rotation in the US on MTV, effectively becoming a seasonal staple for the network. It was a well-chosen release in other ways as well, a wonderfully easy lead in to an album that would be rough going for many, even as it propelled the Smashing Pumpkins to their biggest success yet.

An unerringly ferocious slab of crunch guitar cut through by Corgan's biting lyrics, the song was a claustrophobic crash of pure post-Punk, Dark Wave, and Glam Rock that was as capable of thrilling the drowners as it was exhilarating for the head-bangers. The song had come together from the fragments of two separate incarnations, the first one dating from the *Siamese Dream* sessions, where Corgan first nailed down the main riff. The final puzzle piece was not schemed, he told *Guitar World,* 'until a year and a half later...writing the "rat in the cage" part on an acoustic guitar at the BBC studios in London on the same day that "Landslide" was recorded.' Together, they merged to become one of *Mellon Collie And The Infinite Sadness'* keynote songs. Bearing the Gen-X-er's favourite message, full of self-inflicted despair, nevertheless, it bristled with so much energy that it bred hope too. As personal as anyone wanted to make it, the song was a perfect dashboard confessional, and the public responded strongly.

Two further singles followed to similar success in January and May 1996. The first, '1979,' was another astute choice, but also a somewhat surprising one, as Iha's guitars again conjured up those My Bloody Valentine sentiments that seemed so out of place in the middle of the 1990s. 'Tonight, Tonight,' on the other hand, was a prime example of the new-style Smashing Pumpkins. Taking the strings to the front and backing them with the slowest heartbeat of a rhythm, the song packed an emotional punch that relied on beauty rather than the brat-beating snarl of earlier songs. It was understated and restrained, but urgent, and brought the band quietly into everyone's home, into everyone's childhood, but did so in such a way that the image felt like shadow, not nuclear flashpoint.

Despite such eminently tangible successes, reviews of *Mellon Collie And The Infinite Sadness* were, nevertheless, decidedly mixed, with the majority of critics falling firmly into the middle of the road – praising and damning in a single review the songs which had been so carefully crafted.

On the bright side, at least the critics were weighing in with opinions on the music, and not taking a personal lambaste at Corgan's personal life. That, if nothing else, was an improvement. But, from the British *Vox* magazine's assertion that Corgan 'only fizzles and occasionally crackles when a real explosion was so nearly of his making,' to *Rolling Stone*'s ying-yang punch which deemed the album '[a] career-suicide hybrid of Todd Rundgren's futurist-pop mischief on *Something/Anything* and Husker Du's Generation Angst opera, *Zen Arcade*;' many observers – those who had been so eager in the past to hang a grunge weight around the band's neck – simply didn't know what to do with such a huge undertaking; could not comprehend how a band they had so perfectly pigeon-holed had conceived of such a feast of pristine guitar-based pop.

They just didn't get it. And that was something that Billy Corgan hated most of all. He connected, he said, to people who 'got' the Smashing Pumpkins and, if you fell into one of those camps who *didn't*, well, then too bad for you. It was a feeling grabbed and so beautifully summed up in *Alterative Press*: 'In many interviews promoting *Siamese Dream*, Smashing Pump King Billy Corgan waved his open palms beside his ear, stuck his tongue out and taunted all the rock critics, vowing that if they hated that record, they were going to have a haemorrhage over the next one.'

They did, and in so doing, they confirmed the unspoken title that the Smashing Pumpkins had already been weighing for the last couple of years, of the band that everybody loves to hate. But still, *Mellon Collie And The Infinite Sadness* crowned any number of year end 'best of' polls, even turning up in the mainstream news weekly *Time*'s annual round-up of the entertainment world, The Album Of The Year, grasping the title for 1995.

It's interesting to note that, no matter how many hit 'em where it hurts critical snubs the band received, they still had no problems dominating the various year-end 'reader polls.' And the Smashing Pumpkins themselves knew

Early days touring by van

Smashing Pumpkins in the early '90s

Lying around in 1991

Blissed out at Reading

Our hero Zero

Catherine Wheel – sonic brothers on a parallel plane in the early '90s

Billy at Glastonbury 1997

D'Arcy & Billy – wicked in Belgium

Rocking with the Birthday Boy at Bowie's 50th Birthday Gig in 1997

The Pumpkins go New York minimalist on the David Letterman show

*Billy in 2000
– comfortable
in his skin*

Fountains Of Wayne in Toronto 1997

Courtney Love with Hole. Melissa Auf Der Maur, D'Arcy's replacement, is on the far left next to Eric Erlandson

D'Arcy in '97

that what they'd released was important, would be a show stopper, was not only an achievement for them, but would live on for future generations of listeners, an album that dovetailed ideally with Corgan's own description of the band 'as an anomaly. There's an audience for us which is beyond the influence of [all the] idiocy' of the music industry.'

Neither was the impact and beauty of *Mellon Collie And The Infinite Sadness* limited to its musical manifestation. Already renowned for their warp-speed musical shifts, the Smashing Pumpkins threw more seeds to the wind with some of the era's most innovative videos, each packed with a dreamy psychosis that was cinematographically flawless.

Of the six videos that accompanied the album, three remain among the finest videos of the entire decade, setting standards that the Smashing Pumpkins' peers could only aspire to emulate. The first of this charmed triptych, 'Bullet With Butterfly Wings,' was perhaps the most chilling, shot in grainy black and white, and showcasing the band's angst against a sweat-stained landscape that looked for all the world like a labour camp. With Corgan sporting his silver pants and that infamous Zero T-shirt, cowed with the rest of the band in the bottom of a pit by hordes of great unwashed youth, the microscopic, claustrophobic, slippery footage was a perfect visual echo of the song's directed rage.

'Tonight Tonight,' on the other hand, was gorgeous and exquisite in its detail. A mimic for the stars and moon motif of the *Mellon Collie And The Infinite Sadness* album art, the video was inspired by, and shot in homage to French cinematographer Georges Méliès and his groundbreaking 1902 film, *Le Voyage Dans La Lune* (A Trip to the Moon) – and, alongside White Town's similarly stylised 'Your Woman' video, later in the year, demonstrated that, for all the advances that have been made in cinematography and film, they really don't 'make 'em like they used to.'

Of all the videos that slammed the Smashing Pumpkins into rabidly heavy rotation on MTV, however, the one that accompanied '1979' was to prove the most fascinating, both in delivery and in its actual creation. The song itself was the last one written for the *Mellon Collie And The Infinite Sadness* album, although Corgan had been kicking its rudiments around for some time. He had just a few lines of lyric complete, but really wanted to include the song in the set. Flood laid down the law, telling Corgan 'you've got twenty-four hours to make it happen, so either come in here tomorrow and make this song happen, or it's not going to be on the album.' Corgan pulled it all out of his hat overnight.

The video shoot, however, did not go so well. The band shot most of the video in Los Angeles' Simi Valley during an eleven day stretch in February 1996. They were pleased with the effort, and felt that the images captured the song's back story of, Corgan explained, 'waiting for something to happen and not being quite there yet, but it's just around the corner.' However, all hell broke loose when a production assistant slapped the film cans on the roof of his car, forgot about them, and drove off. The reels of the video's party scene were lost.

The band were furious – as were directors Jonathan Dayton and Valerie Faris, who'd already effortlessly captured the budding sexuality and breathy, frenzied energy of the shoot's teens. The only hope was to reshoot the scene and the Pumpkins were hauled back to Los Angeles from New York to finally wrap it up.

Corgan put as much of himself into the visuals as he did into actually writing the songs. Of course, he'd always been exceedingly outspoken when it came to visual interpretation of his own written words – and why not? As author and instigator of some of the early 1990's most important songs, and an extremely creative personality on a myriad of levels, why wouldn't he be able to see how the video world should reflect the one inside his own mind?

For all Corgan's impact upon the entire process, however, *Mellon Collie And The Infinite Sadness* proved an equally remarkable outlet for the rest of the band. With Iha and Wretzky still smarting somewhat from the assertion that it was Corgan who'd played the lion's share of parts on *Siamese Dream*, the new album offered them the opportunity to really dig in and work together as a band, taking more equal shares in the recording process than ever before. Although Corgan again assumed the greatest bulk of the writing, Iha co-wrote the piano and guitar driven sleeper 'Farewell And Goodnight' with Corgan and was pleased as his own soft ballad 'Take Me Down' was slotted to close the first disc.

Iha also proved himself a grand spokesman when it came to defending the Smashing Pumpkins' open-minded acknowledgement of their 70s ideals. Readily admitting to the influences, but fiercely disputing the pigeonhole, he explained, 'I'm sure we've taken elements of that and brought it to the music. [But] if we have a riff, we make sure it's a good riff, not just some stupid rip-off riff.'

Although the band wouldn't be kicking off their monster tour in earnest until the New Year, the Smashing Pumpkins launched their next American journey with a handful of local, Chicago shows. It was the prelude to an eventful tour that would keep the Smashing Pumpkins on the road until the end of 1997.

Of this initial outburst, it was their 23 October gig at the Riviera Theater in Chicago that really took top honours. Billed as the official release party for *Mellon Collie And The Infinite Sadness*, the show was opened by another of Corgan's teenaged idols, Cheap Trick, as they re-launched their own career on the back of plaudits that oozed from every corner of the 90's Alternative scene. More than fifteen years had elapsed since the Rockford rockers hit the staggering peaks for which they are still best celebrated, the brace of well-received, but low-selling studio albums that first introduced them, and the *Live at Budokan* live album that, by late 1979, had half the planet dancing round to the punching power-pop of 'I Want You To Want Me.'

Unknown to America at large just a few months earlier, Cheap Trick entered the 1980s among the most popular groups in the world and, though the moment passed within, indeed, moments, as their next album disappointed, and successive ones simply passed muster, Cheap Trick retained their popularity. In spite of the prophets of doom, 1982's One On One album went platinum, while 1988's Lap Of Luxury reinvented the group as power balladeers par excellence, as they topped the American chart with 'The Flame,' and scored the first Top Ten Elvis Presley cover since Presley's own death eleven years before. And now the band was rising again.

For their own part, the Smashing Pumpkins cascaded through a set that was positively heaped with Mellon Collie And The Infinite Sadness nuggets, ranging from the album's lead single, 'Bullet With Butterfly Wings,' through 'Tonight, Tonight' and the keynote 'Zero,' before the quartet were joined on stage by Cheap Trick themselves, to close out the night with the Trick classics 'My Baby Loves To Rock,' 'If You Want My Love' and 'Auf Weidersehn.'

A fortnight later, on 11 November, the Smashing Pumpkins made their second appearance on television's Saturday Night Live, airing hard-hitting versions of 'Bullet With Butterfly Wings' and 'Zero'; the former would see another sharp reprise when the band returned to Europe the following month, for appearances on Britain's White Room television show, and French TV's Canal +.

It looked like everything was on the way up.

The New Year opened on a continuing high note, as Corgan was invited to help honour a band that, as much as Cheap Trick and the Electric Light Orchestra (or anybody else), ranked among his most sainted influences, and induct Pink Floyd into the Rock'n'Roll Hall Of Fame.

Staged on 17 January at the Waldorf Astoria Hotel in New York City, the event was remarkable among Pink Floyd's own fans from the absence of Roger Waters, the lyricist and vocalist who wrested control of the band following the enforced departure of their true muse, Syd Barrett. Band mates Dave Gilmour, Rick Wright and Nick Mason, however, did attend, to listen as Corgan introduced them with the promise to keep his comments 'to the length of an average Pink Floyd song.'

'I grew up in the 70s and 80s. I'm roughly twenty-eight years old. When people would say Pink Floyd, before I even heard a note, there was a certain reverence that surrounded this band. They were a strange anomaly in the 70s [which was] filled with this horrible, awful music, which some of you in this room are responsible for.'

His speech, eloquent and poignant, highlighted the manifold Floydian epics that were most important to him – the stereo demonstrator's delight of Dark Side Of The Moon, the chiming angered ambience of the epic 'Shine On You Crazy Diamond,' from 1975's Wish You Were Here, and the crowning conceit of, of course, *The Wall*.

All were appropriate touchstones for Corgan. *Dark Side of the Moon* was requisite fodder for American youth – more often than not, it was that album that introduced generation angst to the tripped out vibes of the venerable psychsters; 'Shine On You Crazy Diamond' represented an album that Corgan himself believed 'was completely un-commercial...a nine part ode to their former colleague Syd. It was a very, very brave record to make,' and one whose courage certainly resonated within Corgan's own awareness of the pressure to perform.

'Pink Floyd are the ultimate rock and roll anomaly. They sold massive amounts of records, have always been a popular live band, and they were never a singles driven band, a lesson forever needed to be learned in this particular business. Because they've always stood for, been about, music. And why? Because it is the people who listen to music that drive the business, not the other way around. They've always been a band that's thought about the fan first. And I have a lot of respect for them about that. They've always been everything that's great about Rock. Grandeur, pomposity, nihilism, humour and, of course, space.'

And, as for *The Wall*... well, in light of *Mellon Collie And The Infinite Sadness*, which itself was a concept album of sorts, Corgan's affinity for the sprawling diatribe is pretty much an open book. 'When I was fourteen years old, *The Wall* was beyond my conception. But at twenty-eight years old, it's one of the bravest records I've ever heard. And I really can't point to anything else that's ever summed up everything that's fucked up about life, everything that's fucked up about rock. It takes on politics, hero worship, rock and roll, and our desires to connect with the universe, all in one fell swoop. It really, truly is an amazing testament to how far they were willing to go to reach the outer limits of what's important.' As a child, he laughed, *The Wall* 'was too creepy, too intense, too nihilistic. And, of course, these are all the things that I believe in now.'

Indeed, he admitted that he thought a lot about *The Wall* as the Smashing Pumpkins' own new album came together, before acknowledging that he simply couldn't replicate that same level of societal psychosis, that he couldn't write an album like *The Wall* or a song about a teacher, the students, and the government. Instead, he turned those childhood memories into his adult mind, extrapolated some of the original album's intent and set about recording an album that was completely different, yet saw all those ghosts dance around the edges.

Pink Floyd were the last band to appear at the ceremony, taking the podium following a collage of old videos and film clips, to accept the award in almost total silence. Then, while Mason returned to his seat on the main floor, Gilmour, Wright and Corgan joined forces for an almost heartbreakingly gentle rendition of another of the songs that Corgan referenced in his speech, the spellbinding 'Wish You Were Here.'

'...When I was seventeen years old, my grandmother was diagnosed with cancer, and it was one of the most painful periods of my life, and the Pink Floyd song "Wish You Were Here" seemed to sum up everything that I was feeling. And when I couldn't take what was going on in my life with her dying, I listened to that song over and over, and it still makes me cry, it's such a beautiful song. You know, when you're seventeen, "Heaven From Hell," "Blue Skies From Pain," it means a lot.'

The collaboration had only been arranged a few hours earlier – according to Corgan, he received a call from Gilmour at 4:30 that afternoon, inviting him to join in. An hour later, the trio had their first and only rehearsal, and Corgan reflected, 'I learned it with this weird Chinese fingering. It was a little loosey-goosey.'

From the stage, the organisers intended for Pink Floyd and Corgan to go backstage, where the media waited for photographs and questions. The Floyd, however, refused to join such a circus, returning instead to their own seats and watching as the rest of the evening's inductees combined for a joyous jam session. Clearly, if Billy Corgan ever looked elsewhere in search of role models for his own occasionally bitter bouts with the media, the Pink Floyd on that evening must have provided him with all he could ever absorb.

CHAPTER SIXTEEN
THE LADDER TO LOATHSOME INFAMY

For their largest and most ambitious tour yet, the dates stretching almost *ad-infinitum* ahead of them, the Smashing Pumpkins planned a performance that would re-create as much as possible of the ambience and depth that they'd layered into the album. It was not a task they could accomplish single-handedly: much of the album's atmosphere was conjured with instrumentation far beyond the group's own traditional arsenal, a void that they determined to fill with the addition of a touring keyboardist.

They found a good match in Jonathan Melvoin, just weeks before the tour was scheduled to commence. A graduate of the world renowned Julliard Music School, Melvoin was also the brother of Prince cohorts Wendy and Susannah Melvoin, and had himself been a part of the Paisley Park family through the middle of the 1980s. There he contributed to the diminutive artist's 1985 hit album *Around The World In A Day*, before fleeing the brutal Minnesota winters for his own crack at stardom in the balmier climes of Los Angeles.

An accomplished multi-instrumentalist, Melvoin worked as a session player for a time, before joining the comically bent punk survivors, the Dickies, in 1991 – as drummer. 'It was his energy gig,' sister Wendy later explained. 'He needed to get up there and play 164 bpm.'

He had plenty of opportunity to do that. The Dickies formed in the American punk heyday of 1977 although, by the time Melvoin joined the party, they'd moved far, far away from the supersonic demolition of old rock classics that was their original calling card, to absorb themselves instead in the hardcore scene that, contrary to all expectations and predictions, had prospered through the 1980s and beyond, a brutal mix of speed and sex that kicked out the creaky strains of classic cock rock with all the agility and ferocity that its earliest icons – Fugazi, Minor Threat, Husker Du, Bad Brains – could muster.

It was an ethos that impacted across the American rock scene of the 1980s. Chicago was one of the many cities that found itself succumbing to Hardcore's snarling inferno. The Smashing Pumpkins' own musical upbringing was intuitively informed by what the Red Hot Chili Peppers' Anthony Kiedis once described as the music's 'emotionally potent impact on the connection between the heart and gut...if music can make me this sexually excited, this emotionally excited, and physically compelled to thrust my body back and forth across the floor, wouldn't that be a wonderful thing to make other people feel with your own music?'

It was a sentiment that obviously fuelled Kiedis's own Los Angeles-based career, and it was that same impetus, distilled (and slowed down) a decade later, that fuelled the be-flannelled Grungers whose own teenaged selves had knelt at Hardcore's diseased altar. It was that same sentiment, universal across era and genre, which echoed across Billy Corgan's words and music, that vision that fuelled the vision of all he wanted to accomplish within the Smashing Pumpkins' own world.

The addition of Melvoin, then, who'd left the Dickies in 1993 and settled in rural Conway, New Hampshire, in order to escape from beneath the hedonistic lifestyle that surrounded that band, closed another circle. All but retiring from music for a time, he trained and qualified as an EMT (Emergency Medical Technician), before re-emerging in the Midwest when he was sought out by former Fini Tribe frontman and Waxtrax! heavyweight Chris Connelly, and it was there that it all came together.

However, Melvoin brought more than his musical talent to the group. Even before the tour kicked off, it was becoming clear to his new band mates that Jimmy Chamberlin was again battling his old demons of drugs and alcohol – a problem that was so worrisome for the rest of the Smashing Pumpkins that it seemed almost providential that they should find a musician with medical training. What the band didn't know, however, was that Melvoin, too, remained at least passingly fascinated by some of those same vices.

'Jonathan dabbled, as almost everybody in our life did,' Wendy Melvoin said. 'We've all been around people who do drugs. We've all seen people go through programs.' But she was convinced that her brother was essentially clean. '[He] just didn't have, in our minds – in any sense – any of those classic symptoms.' The remainder of the Smashing Pumpkins, had they been asked the same question as they rehearsed with Melvoin through December, would have agreed wholeheartedly with that opinion.

After all, Melvoin was out on the road, doing what he loved. He had all the stability of an extended family cocooned around him, and he and his wife, Laura, were also eagerly anticipating the birth of his son, Joseph Arthur at the end of April.

After all the warm-ups and anticipatory previews, the Smashing Pumpkins' world tour finally kicked off with the first of two nights at the Toronto Phoenix on 2 January. Bundled up against the bitter cold weather, the band loaded into the venue, caught off-guard somewhat by the fans that waited outside. Corgan, too, was nursing a blasted cold, telling the *Toronto Star,* ' I'm on codeine, echinacea, cortisone, antibiotics...I don't even know what I'm taking. I'm just like Elvis.'

The band decided to warm-up slowly, to rev their jets across a handful of smaller seat venues before they jumped full-on into the stadiums that would take them across the globe and back again for the foreseeable future. Playing smallish theaters afforded the band an opportunity to work through any last minute kinks. Chamberlin explained to the *Star* that the upcoming shows were 'as much for us as it is for anybody else.' Corgan continued that part of the process was to '[satisfy] our own need to go out and fully enjoy the material that we worked so hard to present.'

Despite Corgan's cold, and any cobwebs the band were shaking off as they creaked their live machine into action, the shows marked a triumphant return to the live arena as the band performed the best of their *Mellon Collie And The Infinite Sadness* material. These earliest shows included electric and, always an audience favourite, acoustic songs. From the gorgeous 'Tonight Tonight' to the closing encore 'Farewell And Goodnight' it was apparent that the band hadn't lost their touch – and questions raised during their extended absence from the public eye were put to rest.

From Toronto, the band passed through Washington DC, spent five nights in New York and hit Brazil for two stadium shows before piling into Los Angeles' Shrine Auditorium at the end of the month, to perform their current single, '1979,' at the American Music Awards.

The American West Coast leg of the tour wrapped up in early February, with another triumphal return to Seattle – two nights at the downtown Moore Theater – before the group headed east across the Pacific, for a string of shows in Japan. By the end of the month, they were in Thailand, and it was there that things first began to go very wrong. In Bangkok for a show at the Dindeang Stadium, Chamberlin, who'd reportedly been on and off heroin since *Gish*, overdosed outside a hotel. He was hanging out with Melvoin at the time.

In an interview with *Details* magazine the following year, Corgan was quoted recalling, 'Jimmy overdoses, and because of the prior history, was told "you need some help"...he of course said everything was fine, that it was an isolated incident. Jonathan was told that if it happened again he would be fired.'

The incident was put behind the band and they travelled on. However, the following month, an increasingly shaky Chamberlin was dealt a horrific blow when he received the news that his father had passed away. Healing still from the Thai bobble, Chamberlin flew home from Australia to be with his family, and the band cancelled a handful of gigs.

With Chamberlin back on board following his father's funeral, April saw the Smashing Pumpkins launch into a dynamic sequence of shows, pounding through twelve European countries in less than a month. It was exhilarating, joyous, raucous and unbelievable as the Smashing Pumpkins crashed through

Mellon Collie and the Infinite Sadness songs; the album was selling by the bucket load (at the beginning of April, sales exceeded the six million dollar sales mark) and the entire continent seemed awash with Pumpkinmania. This is what you joined a band to experience, this was what made all those years of struggle and turmoil worthwhile. For four weeks, the Smashing Pumpkins weren't simply the biggest band in the world. They might also have been the happiest.

That joy was utterly quashed in Lisbon, Portugal at the beginning of May, when both Chamberlin and Melvoin overdosed. Rushed to hospital, the pair were revived with shots of adrenaline – 'real *Pulp Fiction* stuff,' as a horrified Corgan put it. Clearly, matters were coming to a head and, faced with a choice between Chamberlin's problems and, so far as his band mates could see, Melvoin's influence on those problems, Corgan, Iha and Wretzky could see just one way out. Melvoin was sacked almost as soon as he recovered, and Chamberlin himself was given another tough talking to – essentially a straight option of clean up or clear off. They prayed that he would take the former option but, for the sake of the band itself, were ready to act if he opted for the second.

For the moment, Chamberlin remained on track. However, with Melvoin out of the picture, still the band had to figure out a stopgap solution to their lack of keyboards – a sound that had become integral to their live performance. Neither Corgan nor Iha, who handled the instrument on the album, could abandon their own posts to fill the gap, but simply finding a replacement player could take days. Rehearsing him to the necessary level of expertise would take even longer – and the Smashing Pumpkins didn't have that much time.

'Jonathan was told he was fired,' Corgan told *Details* 'but was asked to complete the tour. It was the first successful European tour we'd ever had, and I felt he still owed us. We had to fly that day to Barcelona to do a live radio show and play, and it was like a black comedy, the two of them were so out of it.'

Wretzky continued, '[The heroin use] went on in secret behind our backs. We had already fired Jonathan. He came back crying, and begged for a second chance to prove himself. As far as we knew, he was clean. We liked him a lot, he was a very sweet guy, and we hired him back.'

There was no alternative. It had utterly disrupted the band's sound and their set when he left, and his return certainly ensured that the group would maintain its musical peak. Besides, said Corgan, when he spoke to the seemingly chastened, and certainly apologetic Melvoin, 'he assured me up and down that there would be [no more drug use] going on this tour, that playing with us was a completely great opportunity and he would do absolutely nothing to fuck that up. And, except for these [earlier] forays off the deep end, there was no evidence that he was ill intentioned.' Bound to the same agreement as Chamberlin, Melvoin was reinstated to the touring party.

Wendy Melvoin later admitted that news of her brother's own increasingly apparent habit was a shock to the family. 'He was having a fabulous life. He never had any problem with his friends or family. The only thing I can speculate is that somehow, some way, Jonathan developed this incredible jones with Jimmy on this tour. At the same time, we never heard of any of these episodes that had happened to Jonathan on the road. No one knew any of this.'

But the fates had yet to finish with the group. Arriving in Dublin, Ireland, for their 11 May appearance at the Point, the Smashing Pumpkins were about to encounter one of the most horrifying experiences they'd had to face. Anticipation for the gig was high, and the show was just packed. When the quintet took the stage, many of the fans left their seats and pushed forward to the empty space in front of the stage, forming a massive mosh pit. The energy was frantic, hot, claustrophobic.

According to eyewitness accounts, the crush at the front of the stage was horrible; with fan Caoimhe McCann recalling that 'it was hard to stand up.' From up on the stage, the band could feel their performance growing increasingly fraught as they watched the frenzied activity in the mosh pit, just feet from the lip of the stage. It was, Wretzky reflected, 'out of control, and we thought that kids were getting crushed in front.' Twice, then, the group stopped playing, halted the show, to plead for calm – or at least a modicum of restraint as security guards raced to keep the fans under control.

Their words were ignored, but when the Smashing Pumpkins were forced to halt the show for the third time, it was to be the last. The band were aware that something beyond a rough and tumble mosh was happening at their feet. As a stage hand delivered the dreadful news, Corgan pleaded for calm, telling the crowd as the band prepared to leave the stage, 'I'm sorry, we can't play on. The gig's over. There's a girl out there who's nearly dying. We as human beings cannot play up here while people are getting hurt.'

McCann remembered that Corgan 'looked really freaked when he told people to go home. People were booing until they were told a girl was dying.'

Caught in a surge of fans across the pit, a crowd was knocked over and trampled. Many were injured, some were unconscious and one, sixteen year old Bernadette O'Brien, from Ballymaloe Cottage, Shanagarry, Co. Cork, who had saved her hard-earned cash to buy her ticket, would die the following day from the massive internal injuries she sustained in that mad crush.

Devastated by the tragedy, the Smashing Pumpkins immediately cancelled their next show in Belfast. Corgan was especially shattered. He'd worked so hard and so painstakingly to present a good front to his fans, to follow the righteous path, to provide a show that was worth paying money to see. But it wasn't worth losing your life for; nothing in rock'n'roll was that important.

If there was anything to be gained from this horrible and senseless tragedy, it was that once again, people were taking a good hard look at live concert safety. Of course, the crush of the throngs, the sweaty airless thrust against barriers between masses and stage was nothing new. It was already a rich and rough history – indeed some seventy people had perished at the hands of rock and roll madness from 1992-2002, with a full twenty meeting their maker in 2002 alone. These statistics, however, only tell part of the story. According to the Crowdsafe website 'in addition to the twenty deaths...thirty-one concerts and festivals resulted in...4,567 injuries, 2,683 arrests/citations, and more than $542,000 in property damage.'

While people would rush to place blame on a band, or a genre, death by concert didn't discriminate. One of the earliest, and most famous tragedies dogged David Cassidy during his 1974 UK tour, when a girl was killed during his Wembley performance. The tally was pushed higher still during a 1979 concert by the Who, when the audience, making a mad dash to enter the Cincinnati venue, ran at the doors and bottlenecked themselves in their haste to get in for the show. By the time the bodies were peeled away from the horrible mess, ten people had perished. Later still, Pearl Jam reeled at Denmark's 2000 Roskilde Festival when the massive crush of fans at the front of the stage during their set resulted in eight deaths, with a further twenty-five people injured during the melée.

It wasn't anyone's fault, really, and certainly not any of the bands – all anyone ever wanted was to give people a good time, have a few laughs and walk happily to the bank and the beach at the end of it all.

But, of course, part of the backlash of the Dublin tragedy was directed straight back at the Smashing Pumpkins. Although no-one blamed the band for the death, when news of the crush hit the wires and raced back toward the States ahead of the commencement of the Pumpkins' next US tour leg, venues were edgy about having the band play. Worried about insurance, it was clear that extra steps needed to be taken. (Bernadette O'Brien's family were granted final closure when an inquest, held in 2000, awarded them ninety-five thousand dollars compensation.)

The band finally resumed their tour at London's Wembley Arena several days later, and the mood was subdued on both sides. The good groove of the London crowd was amiable, but hardly frenetic, while the Smashing Pumpkins were simply trying to recover from the shock of all they had witnessed, and ignore the padded barriers that had been erected around the mosh pit, in the hope of absorbing the kind of impacts that, in Dublin, had been dealt onto flesh alone.

In the midst of so much agony, there came one bright glimmering of humour, as the Smashing Pumpkins transcended mere mortal flesh and blood to attain geekdom's highest honour, portraying themselves in episode number seven hundred and twenty-four of Matt Groening's The Simpsons.

Broadcast on the 19 May, the episode unspooled all that transpired as Simpson patriarch Homer joined a Lollapalooza-like festival, Homerpalooza, as a sideshow performer. The Smashing Pumpkins, alongside Sonic Youth, Cypress Hill and, perhaps oddly, Peter Frampton provided the entertainment. The experience, Iha recalled, 'was really fun. We just read the script and it was really funny, and we went in there where they overdub all the voices...and we actually cut it live.' The highlight of the show, however – at least for Smashing Pumpkins' fans – was Homer's heartfelt tribute to the Smashing Pumpkins themselves: 'thanks to your gloomy music, my children have stopped dreaming about a future I can't provide.' It couldn't have been higher praise, or further from the mark.

If stellar sales and their rabid fans hadn't already driven the point home to anyone who had the slightest doubt left, then the Smashing Pumpkins' status elevation to a juicy role on America's longest-running prime-time cartoon should have tipped the scale. The Smashing Pumpkins were further immortalized – bigger than themselves, and nearly bigger than God.

Already out in England, the 'Tonight, Tonight' single made its appearance in the States in June, as the prodigal band returned to that county, to launch the next leg of the tour at the annual Tibetan Freedom Festival in San Francisco, California. Filling the city's heart with peace and good will nearly thirty years after the Summer of Love was not hard to do. Always maintaining a somewhat contrary cultural ambience in the midst of urban gentrification, San Francisco was still haunted by its musical past's ghostly presence and was, therefore, a natural venue for the Tibetan Freedom bash. With nearly one hundred thousand attendees converging on Golden Gate Park for the two-day festival, the city would be treated to good deeds, rocking sets by some of the year's hottest bands, and sufficient booty shaking fund-raising to elevate the year's proceeds above eight hundred thousand dollars.

It was about time. Although a group of Tibetan monks had taken the stage pre-concert during Lollapalooza 1994, awareness for their homeland's struggle for independence from the occupying Chinese was low. This two-day concert, masterminded by the Beastie Boys' Adam Yauch and underwritten by the Milarepa organization, brought awareness to a young generation with money in their pockets and looking for a radical cause to champion.

Like Lollapalooza, the Tibetan Freedom Festival prided itself on its musical eclecticism – the Smashing Pumpkins were joined on the bill by the Beastie Boys, Biz Markie, the Foo Fighters and Pavement. It was, however, an odd afternoon, its events unfolding in stark opposition to the peaceable mood that permeated the theme itself. Slipping onto the stage before the Beastie Boys' own set, the Smashing Pumpkins laid into their hits, searing through both 'Bullet With Butterfly Wings' and 'Zero' before the afternoon was suddenly laid to waste before their eyes.

One might have hoped that a festival promoting a just cause wouldn't become the occasion for over-agitated hormones to wing things up on stage.

But one would have been mistaken. The mosh pit was in full swing but, more alarmingly, so were the audience's arms, hurling whatever they could lay their hands on out of the depths of the pit and on to the stage. Finally, Corgan decided that the band had suffered enough. Recapturing all the snarling defiance of their earliest days, the quintet shifted from that apparently-not-so-crowd-pleasing set of hits and warm fuzzies, threw a big 'fuck you' to the object-throwing perpetrators, and launched into a vicious near twenty-minute version of 'Silverfuck.' Take that, unlovable audience!

With Butch Vig's very own Garbage booked as a welcome support band, everyone hoped that the next leg of shows would pass without trauma. Unfortunately, it would prove to be a very fragile peace. The band had worked their way up the American East Coast through Virginia and Maryland, playing sold out shows everywhere they stopped, before coming to rest in New York City on 11 July, on the eve of three solidly sold out nights at Madison Square Garden.

Chamberlin and Melvoin were sharing a room over at the swanky Park Avenue Regency Hotel. They'd been drinking, they'd gone out and scored, they were happy, dreamy in the city's sticky July heat. And, at 11:30 that evening, they shared a fix, the heroin that now coursed through their veins a particularly potent strain rejoicing under the creeped-out (for Stephen King fans) nickname of Redrum.

After they'd shot up, they both nodded off. Chamberlin awoke in the early hours of the morning, gathered his senses, and suddenly became aware of Melvoin lying motionless on the floor beside him.

Disquieted by his friend's still silence, Chamberlin tried to revive him; then, with all his own efforts in vain, he phoned the band's tour manager, Tim Lougee. But there was little he could do, either. The police were finally summoned to the hotel, and Jonathan Melvoin was pronounced dead at 4:15 am, on 12 July.

Forty-five minutes later, Corgan was awakened by the phone ringing in his room at the Four Seasons hotel – it was Lougee and the news was not good. In fact, it was devastating. The tour manager's message was short, it was blunt, and it didn't soften the blow one bit – 'Jimmy's OD'ed. Jonathan's dead. Cops are here.'

Summoned to the Nineteenth Precinct police station, the rest of the Smashing Pumpkins – Corgan, Wretzky and Iha – joined Chamberlin, but were quickly released. Chamberlin, however, wouldn't be so lucky. He was held, and charged with possession of heroin. Given a court date on 13 August, 1996, he was finally released a full five days after Melvoin's overdose.

The band were stunned. They immediately cancelled the three Madison Square Garden shows that were due to begin that night, left New York City and headed home to Chicago. They had a lot to figure out. With one member dead, another clearly in need of professional help, and the tour they'd worked so hard for on the very precipice of a spectacularly sordid, and very public collapse, it was time for some serious home truths.

Garbage, too, reeled from the blow. Being on tour with the Smashing Pumpkins was like taking an extended vacation with your very favourite family members, and the quartet were devastated. Butch Vig recalled, 'It leaves you feeling extremely numb, and it's a terrible tragedy. It's like we all got the wind punched out of us. I mean, the crew, the band, everybody has just been like hanging out the last couple of days. We're not quite sure what to do. It's just a horrible waste.'

With the *Mellon Collie* tour postponed indefinitely in the wake of the July tragedy, Garbage were left to move off on their own, to put together the remains of their shattered summer. By the time the Pumpkins' shows resumed later in the summer, Garbage had launched their own European festival circuit, leaving Los Angelino roots rockers Grant Lee Buffalo to fill their shoes until they rejoined the tour at the end of October, with a show at the Hilton Coliseum in Ames, Iowa.

In the days that followed Melvoin's death, as everyone struggled to come to terms with what had happened, Corgan found reality to be numbing, and, as he so succinctly told *Rolling Stone* later, 'You just refuse to accept that somebody is really dead. It's like they're on permanent vacation.'

But Melvoin wasn't on any kind of vacation. He was dead. And the Smashing Pumpkins had to deal with that fact. Initially, as Corgan put it, the feeling within the band's camp was, 'okay, Jimmy's got a court date, Jimmy's going into rehab – four weeks and we'll be back on tour. You just want everything to get back to the way it was. It wasn't until forty-eight hours later, that the bomb hit. The real weight of it was Jonathan's life, Jimmy's life. It was just completely devastating' – and it was devastating on so many really vital levels that, to worry about the mere business of rock and roll seemed completely crass. But, the Smashing Pumpkins knew that, no matter what had happened, no matter the turmoil that had ripped their universe apart, they had to gather their strength and go forward.

On 15 July, Chamberlin checked himself into drug rehab for another go-round, but this time, there was to be no warm applause from his band mates. Still shattered and angry, the remaining Smashing Pumpkins sacked him just three days later, on the 18th. The situation had finally reached the breaking point in Corgan's estimation. Never enamoured with Chamberlin's drug use, Melvoin's death and the ensuing agony was, for Corgan, the 'final straw'.

In an interview with KTBZ Radio, he explained 'it's been a very difficult situation for us. We love Jimmy very much but at some point, it was his life or the band's. And we chose him having a better life...as much as we love music, as much as we love our band, Jimmy's well-being is much more important to us than the band could ever be.'

The entire situation, sordid and sad as it was, generated – again – a backlash directed at the Smashing Pumpkins, and, as usual, at Corgan. The Smashing Pumpkins were criticized in the press and on the street for chucking Chamberlin out when he needed his friends the most. They were called callous, and worse. Even fellow musicians leapt aboard the Pumpkin-bashing bandwagon, with Black Crowes frontman Chris Robinson alleging that Chamberlin was fired not because of his drug addiction, but because he was a potential financial risk.

Talking to *Circus* magazine, Corgan exploded, 'we were in the middle of a tour. It is the most stupid accusation to claim there were "financial reasons." Seen strictly from a business view, the split was bad for the Pumpkins and harmed the band.' Of course such explanations fell on more or less deaf ears. The band that everyone loved to hate had just hitched themselves another few rungs up the ladder to loathsome infamy.

CHAPTER SEVENTEEN
THE PUMPKIN WALKS ON ROCK

Flashing back to the summer of 1996, it was obvious to all that there was a long, hard road ahead of everyone. The grim reality of the situation sunk in fast: Melvoin was dead, Chamberlin was out and, as if matters could get any worse, Corgan himself was devastated to learn that his mother, Martha, had been diagnosed with terminal cancer. She was, in Corgan's words 'totally healthy one day, dead five months later.'

Yet the Smashing Pumpkins were compelled to go on. They had decided that they would resume the *Mellon Collie* tour at the end of the summer, but still, they needed time to sort themselves, and the band, out. In order to accomplish that, the band needed not only to replace Melvoin's keyboards, but also, more importantly, urgently, and painfully, they needed to install Chamberlin's successor. That would prove to be difficult, not merely because, as Iha said not long after, 'Jimmy was probably the best musician in the band,' but because he'd been an integral part of the Smashing Pumpkins' family for the better part of a decade.

They were adamant that they couldn't put a new Chamberlin in the band, even if there was one to be found. There was no question of simply replacing one drummer with another and continuing on their merry way. Regrouping to figure out how to salvage the tour, they were pleasantly surprised to discover that, as a trio, they were infused with a spark that stood out separately from their existence as a quartet – and that sense of defiance that can only be born out of shared adversity. There was no question, then, of returning the group to 'full strength'; henceforth, Corgan, Iha and Wretzky alone were the Smashing Pumpkins, aided and abetted by whomever they required for the job at hand.

For their immediate requirements, fulfilling the shows that remained to be played, the group turned first to long-time friend and keyboard player Dennis Flemion, alongside his brother Jimmy, a founder of the Chicago Indie band the Frogs. Long championed by the Smashing Pumpkins, the Frogs had spent more than fifteen years foisting an eclectic brew of alternative politics, in-joke rock and roll and politically incorrect antics upon a completely unsuspecting public

– yet had waited almost a decade before releasing even their first album, 1989's *It's Only Right And Natural*. Picked up by the prestigious Homestead indie, the album raised more than a few eyebrows with its whimsically twisted collection of crazy songs needling homosexuality. (Jimmy Flemion, of course, had played alongside Jimmy Chamberlin in The Last Hard Men).

Unearthing a suitable drummer was less easily accomplished. Iha told the Chicago *Sun-Times* that 'anybody who played drums, or thought of playing drums…still offered to audition…we weren't just going to hire some kid or a person who hadn't toured before.'

With the clock ticking down, the band announced a series of auditions, offering both seasoned professionals and passing friends alike the same set of four songs to get to grips with, before finally settling on Matt Walker, at that time drumming with another Chicago band, Filter.

Formed by ex-Nine Inch Nails-er Richard Patrick and programmer Brain Leisegang, Filter was essentially a revolving door of accompanying musicians who came and went as the duo laboured together in their small Chicago studio, or stepped out to berate the masses with the results. Their latest live outing, the sprawling Short Bus Tour, was already underway at the time, but the opportunity to join the Smashing Pumpkins was one that Walker was not going to pass up on. Of all the players who took part in the auditions, he alone had proven capable of learning all of Chamberlin's parts; of keeping the Smashing Pumpkins' sound on track; and, perhaps, most importantly of all, standing proud in what were, by any drummer's standards, some fairly big shoes.

Corgan explained, 'We had a very special kind of relationship and language with Jimmy that we are finding impossible to achieve with anybody else.' Everyone agreed that the band would have been happier if 'the incident' hadn't happened, and the Smashing Pumpkins could have continued as they were – a quartet. But, in the end, the group just had to deal with the hand that Fate had dealt them, and move on. And Walker helped them do just that. Iha told the Chicago *Sun-Times* that 'it's tough to walk into anybody's shoes. Jimmy played with us for so long. What makes Matt really good is he's such a good musician that he is able to just sort of cop a lot of Jimmy's feel and his parts, but also put a little bit of himself into it, too.'

The auditions did not consume all of the band's time that month. There was an opportunity, too, for Corgan, Iha and Wretzky to sequester themselves in the studio to record a new set of demos towards their next album, embryonic versions of 'Ava Adore' and 'To Sheila,' while Corgan also spent time working on a commission that he had recently received, composing and recording material for the soundtrack to David Lynch's forthcoming movie *Lost Highway*. Of the two songs, 'Eye' and 'Tear,' the latter was discarded for the soundtrack, but would be reworked for the Smashing Pumpkins' own next album.

Corgan was also completing a number of instrumental compositions for the soundtrack to Mel Gibson's remake of *Ransom.* Working in tandem with conductor James Horner and drummer Walker, the sessions, at New York's Chung King Studio, had already been scheduled for September, a fierce, weeklong session that would see the team record half a dozen pieces: 'Rats,' 'Spiders,' 'Worms,' 'Lizards,' 'Worms pt. 2' and 'Squirrels With Tails.'

Although Corgan alone had made a tentative return to the stage when he joined Cheap Trick at Chicago's Park West on 21 July, accompanying the band through 'If You Want My Love' and 'Auf Weidersehn,' the new look Smashing Pumpkins themselves remained out of sight until the end of August when, still cocooned within the safe confines of their hometown, they debuted the new line up with a show at Cabaret Metro on the 23rd.

A hush-hush event, the Friday afternoon matinee saw the band playing to just one thousand witnesses. The gig was announced on the radio alone and was intended for fans only – no VIP, no press, no media – with the proceeds from the twelve dollar tickets going to the local Christmas Is For Kids charity. The Smashing Pumpkins played through a two hour set that saw them, according to the Chicago *Sun-Times,* treat the audience to alternate and unusual versions of their songs.

It was a time to stumble if they needed to, a time to warm up fingers, voices and souls, and it was cathartic. By the time they hit the Thomas & Mack Center in Las Vegas on 27 August, they were back on form and back on the arena circuit. On stage that night, Corgan talked a little about how the group's year had been, but kept that patter to a minimum, preferring to focus on the craziness of the Las Vegas scene rather than the craziness that followed the band.

With Walker and Flemion on board, 'just for the tour right now,' according to Iha, the band's own future plans were very much up in the air. 'We just want to get through the tour and see what happens,' the guitarist continued, while Wretzky acknowledged that she, too, was now doing her best simply to work through her feelings. 'Everything that happened, it was real sad, but it was also very stupid and very senseless. And we're very angry with Jimmy.'

Angry, certainly, but the three remaining Smashing Pumpkins would ultimately bear Chamberlin no real ill will. At the time they were all doubtful that he'd ever return to the band's fold but, at the same time, all hoped that he would be able to pull himself together, heal and come out whole on the other side of the horror that played out during the summer. In the meantime, though, rather than fold down and in, they channelled that anger, and all its attendant emotions, into renewing the group's own energy, groping for normalcy and placing themselves back out on the road, where – and how ironic was this – a life that had once seemed mundane, now offered them comfort and routine.

'Things...have just been getting better and better, and I think we're all learning to understand each other, especially after what happened with Jimmy, which is not taking things for granted anymore.' Wretzky sounded relieved. 'We just all were really badly scared. I didn't even really know it until we [went] back out on tour again. We never really used to hang out together that much. It was sort of a different chemistry in the band...it was kind of like Billy and Jimmy and myself and James. But now it's just brought me and James and Billy really much closer together.' She was adamant that the band had always been worth sacrifice, but all three members had suddenly discovered that it did not need to be so 'intense...heavy, almost unbearable sometimes. It's not like that anymore. I never thought it would be this way. I never thought it could be fun.'

On 4 September, the gloriously reinvigorated Smashing Pumpkins was unveiled for the first time on television, performing 'Tonight, Tonight' on the annual MTV Video Music Awards at New York's Radio City Music Hall (they would hit the MTV Europe Video Music Awards in London on 14 November, where they kicked through 'Bullet With Butterfly Wings'). The band finally played the rescheduled Madison Square Garden concerts toward the end of September, and, with the tour finally back on track, the Smashing Pumpkins continued gigging through the fall, criss-crossing the United States for a string of sold out stadium shows, before closing out the year in Los Angeles, at the great Western Forum on 18 December.

Neither was the demand for fresh Pumpkin product to be overlooked as the band finally prepared to put this grotesque year behind them. Following hard on the heels of November's 'Thirty Three' single, *The Aeroplane Flies High* was a boxed set collection that rounded up all the Smashing Pumpkins singles and b-sides of the *Mellon Collie And The Infinite Sadness* era, plus further unreleased material as compiled by Corgan during the summer. Now devilishly hard to find, the limited edition (two hundred thousand) discs were housed in a distinctive box that replicated a groovily-swirled 70's-style 45rpm carrying case, and between them boasted more tracks than *Mellon Collie And The Infinite Sadness* itself.

'Bullet,' of course, was just a simple two track single upon its initial release. For its re-emergence on *The Aeroplane Flies High* it now boasted an additional five tracks, and included some of the band's frequently-played-live, but damnably elusive cover versions. Kicking off that passel was an inspired take on the Cars' classic 'You're All I've Got Tonight,' Alice Cooper's 'Clones (We're All)' followed, alongside the Cure's 'A Night Like This,' Missing Persons' 'Destination Unknown' and Blondie's 'Dreaming.' It was an 80's fest replete with all the bells and whistles that informed that decade but, run through Corgan's crunch machine, the songs became something more than mere nostalgia, informed and infused by Corgan's twisted vision and spat out with an affection and aplomb that few others dared to bare.

Several of the performances stood out in the band's own recollections.

'Clones' for instance was rehearsed and recorded in little more than an hour, while 'Dreaming,' a rare up-front vocal excursion for Wretzky, was bedevilled, said Corgan, 'with all sorts of technical problems that made mixing it a technical nightmare – vocals with electrical noises, drums looped with scratch guitars recorded over them, etc.'

The electro/techno landscapes draped over the songs would also prove a surprising portent of the group's future ambitions, with Corgan explaining, 'the first grade techno vibe evolved out of boredom with some of the rock and roll-y things that we'd been working on.' It might be hard to perceive 'Destination Unknown' as a forebear of anything, but it would certainly emerge as a major stepping stone.

Indeed, as a document of what many outsiders insisted was a year of utter torture for the band, in which they'd been lucky to even hold themselves together, *The Aeroplane Flies High* revealed a wealth of material that was, Corgan said, recorded in starts and stops while the band were on tour. Furthermore, like *Pisces Iscariot*, the box gave fans a glimpse not only into some of the band's working songs – many of which were remarkably well-developed – but also allowed outsiders a decent look at some of James Iha's own Smashing Pumpkins' contributions.

The year of 1996 also saw the Smashing Pumpkins add their voice to the autumn release of *Sweet Relief II*. Sweet Relief was established in 1993 as a means of raising money for musicians unable, under the bizarrely prohibitive financial and bureaucratic strictures of the American health industry, to actually purchase health insurance. It was a plight first publicised when singer Victoria Williams was diagnosed with Multiple Sclerosis in 1992. Increasingly unable to cope with volley after volley of expensive medical bills, Williams was approaching her financial breaking point when a gathering of fellow musicians – Pearl Jam, Soul Asylum, Lou Reed and more – came together for the first Sweet Relief album, *Sweet Relief: A Benefit for Victoria Williams* the following July.

They followed through with a brace of sold out benefit concerts in Los Angeles and New York, at the same time as establishing the Sweet Relief Musicians Fund, set up solely to provide monetary assistance to musicians. Whether it was for health insurance, rehab costs, living assistance between jobs or a monthly top up for older, retired musicians, Sweet Relief was able to disburse money received from private donations and partial proceeds from album sales.

The Second Chapter, Sweet Relief II brought together Gravity Of The Situation, REM, Nanci Griffith, Hootie & The Blowfish, a returning Soul Asylum, Live and Garbage; for their part, the Smashing Pumpkins turned over one of two songs they recorded in fall, 1995, a version of the Vic Chestnutt chestnut 'Sad Peter Pan,' cut with the revamped Red Red Meat. The other, a collaboration with the Frogs, 'Medellia Of The Grey Skies,' would end up on the 'Tonight, Tonight' single.

The group recorded a second charity track in December, following the last of the year's concerts – flying back to New York they installed themselves at the new Hit Factory to cut a contribution for the following autumn's *A Very Special Christmas 3* benefit album, issued in aid of the Special Olympics. Amid the wealth of charity-themed albums that pockmarked the 90s, *A Very Special Christmas* was especially notable, explained mastermind Bobby Shriver, because 'everybody donates everything. The record company, the publishers, the artists, they all give one hundred percent.' The Smashing Pumpkins certainly did that – produced by Atlantic Records legend Arif Mardin, the Corgan-penned 'Christmastime' was a stripped down jewel that fell in between ballad and mid-tempo pop. Even more impressively, according to Shriver, the light-hearted and understated, piano, string and vocal driven song was written 'almost on the spot for us.'

Images of their nightmare summer were now dropping away like so many autumn leaves; at last, the Smashing Pumpkins were free to start looking ahead, towards their next projects – of which, it quickly transpired, there were lots, both a string of further one-offs, and several more lasting arrangements. Indeed, as if the new year, 1997, seemed determined to remedy all the ills that its predecessor had inflicted upon the band, January opened with the news that the Smashing Pumpkins had been nominated for a whopping seven Grammy awards, for Album of the Year and Best Alternative Performance (*Mellon Collie and the Infinite Sadness*), Record of the Year and Best Rock Performance ('1979'), Pop Instrumental ('Mellon Collie and the Infinite Sadness'), Hard Rock Performance ('Bullet With Butterfly Wings') and Best Video ('Tonight Tonight').

Ultimately, the band would take just one of those statuettes home the following month, for the Best Hard Rock Performance. But still, for anybody who continued to dream of pigeonholing the Smashing Pumpkins, such a spread must have seemed a living nightmare – indeed, one could think of few other bands who could ever have claimed a similar sweep through the alternative, pop and hard rock circles, and the days of Grunge and Glam surely seemed a long time ago.

January also saw Corgan step out on his own, as he joined the crème of rock iconography at Madison Square Garden on 9 January, for *David Bowie And Friends: A Very Special Birthday Concert*, a sold out show that marked both the Thin White Duke's half-century and a benefit concert for Save The Children. Across more than two hours, and a repertoire that stretched from Bowie's then-current album *Earthling*, back through a catalogue of almost thirty years duration, the star surrounded himself with a plethora of guest musicians, from Lou Reed and the Cure's Robert Smith, to Alternative *grand-peres* Sonic Youth and the Pixies' Frank Black.

It was a marvellous evening with a set list that was as odd as one would have expected, highlighted by Smith and Bowie's version of 'Quicksand'; a duet with Reed that wrapped up both 'Queen Bitch' and Reed's own 'Dirty Boulevard'; and the static crash of 'Hallo Spaceboy,' featuring the Foo Fighters and powered by no less than three massive drum kits.

For many onlookers, however, the evening's true peak arrived with Corgan's appearance onstage for the second encore, to let loose on two of the most powerful anthems in Bowie's entire repertoire, the guitar grind of 'Jean Genie,' and the all-encompassing rallying call of 'All The Young Dudes.' Looking both a little nervous to be on stage in such company, and overjoyed to be experiencing the time of his life, Corgan also appreciated the precise nature of a celebration that incorporated all of Bowie's worlds, from the early glam spangles to the most modern Electronica, from formative Folk ('Space Oddity' numbered among the other encores) to some good old-fashioned old rock'n'roll.

'He's celebrating his body of work tonight,' Corgan reflected. 'But he's also saying "Look, I'm still here. This isn't an oldies act" – a refusal to bow down to the forces of fossilisation that echoed so much of what Corgan himself had alluded to over the years, the driving force that lay behind the Smashing Pumpkins' own ability to shift; the reason why they didn't often resurrect songs from *Gish* and *Siamese Dream,* although they knew that the audience would go apeshit if they played them. You have to keep moving forward – because the moment you stop, you start sliding backwards. From the outset, the Smashing Pumpkins were adamant that they would never see themselves tottering around on stage doing some sad hits show. Or, as Wretzky used to quip, not until they were all in their eighties and needed the cold hard cash for rest homes!

Reconvening with his band mates, Corgan and the Smashing Pumpkins themselves returned to the road for one final burst of gigging, wrapping up the Infinite Sadness tour towards the end of February. Corgan stopped off in New York, sans band, to perform at the Tibet House Benefit concert on the nineteenth. Now in its fifth year, spearheaded by Patti Smith, it featured an eclectic assortment of musicians that ranged from Corgan to REM's Michael Stipe, Phish's Trey Anastasio, and composer Philip Glass.

Continuing the spirit of collaboration and creative jamming that had infused previous gatherings, Corgan teamed up with John Cale and Phillip Glass *and* beat poet Allen Ginsberg, picking out riffs on his guitar, while both Cale and Glass rock and rolled together on one piano to provide a backdrop as Ginsberg recited his anti-1990's themed 'Ballad Of The Skeletons.' While Corgan's inclusion at the Carnegie Hall performance probably caused old timers to scratch their heads, to anyone who was familiar with the towering singer's own rants at society, at life, at nothing in particular as he stalked the stages of venues worldwide, his sidestep into beat would have made perfect sense.

Further evidence that the Smashing Pumpkins continued to fire on all cylinders was delivered that same month when the band, with Matt Walker still sitting behind the drum kit, booked into Chicago Recording Company with the dual purpose of recording another clutch of demos for the next album, together with a renewed burst of soundtrack activity, this time for the next instalment in the on-going saga of *Batman* movies.

Productive on both counts, the band were able to work through early versions of 'Annie-Dog,' 'The Tale Of Dusty And Pistol Pete' and 'For Martha,' as well as nailing down a handful of songs for the soundtrack. Of these, two songs emerged the strongest, the circular notions of 'The Beginning Is the End Is The Beginning' and 'The End Is The Beginning Is The End.'

Re-recorded in March with Nellee Hooper and Chris Shepard, this pair would be released as a new Smashing Pumpkins' single in June, backed with multiple remixes as well as with two more songs, 'The Ether's Tragic' and 'The Guns Of Love Disastrous,' culled from the earlier sessions. But, though the single would score the band a number ten hit in the UK, the fickle mainstreamers of their homeland had moved onto newer, and in their eyes, tastier musical waters. Upon release, the single sank with barely a ripple on the radar, acknowledged in the USA only by the four nominations it earned at the MTV Video Music Awards.

The controversy and chatter that dogged the Smashing Pumpkins through 1996 was not to be dimmed by this early burst of calm activity; rather, it provoked a burgeoning hunger that Corgan finally acceded to on 19 February, when he agreed to appear on the nationally broadcast New York magazine program, *Regis & Kathie Lee*, to be grilled and stroked for an audience who wanted nothing less than celebrity skin for breakfast every morning. It was an odd place for a rock'n'roller to find himself, but Corgan carried the occasion with unexpected dignity, neither rising to the bait of his interrogator's questions, nor collapsing in dismay at the knowledge that his hosts probably had no more idea who he was than most of their show's traditional viewership.

Indeed, at a time when the music magazines of the day were loudly rumouring that the Smashing Pumpkins were on the verge of collapse, Regis and Kathy did not even move into such contentious territory. There again, that might have been because even they knew what a stale old tale it was to begin with. Of course, for the rumour-mongers and doomsayers themselves, there seemed to be ample evidence to point towards that end – everything from, of course, the events of the summer, through to the alacrity with which the group's most recent recordings had been stuffed onto the *Aeroplane Flies High* box set and a new single, rather than stockpiled towards another album.

Of course, Corgan himself had already stoked such speculation when, as reporters ramped up the endless barrage of questions regarding where the group could go in light of Melvoin's overdose and Chamberlin's sacking, he swore to *Live!* magazine in 1996, 'the Pumpkin has always walked on rock. I'm happy to not veer off in another direction, and to live or die by it.' Nevertheless, he also made it clear that there was more to music than feeding the need for a new Smashing Pumpkins album and, although he, Iha and Wretzky would continue beavering away behind the scenes, 1997 was also destined to be the first year in which all three members of the band would turn their attentions away from their day job.

CHAPTER EIGHTEEN
A SCRATCHIE INTERLUDE

Billy Corgan was first to stir outside of the confines of the Smashing Pumpkins, when he teamed up with former Cars maestro Ric Ocasek to co-produce and appear on the venerable New Waver's *Troublizing* solo album. The pair first met in New York in 1995, a meeting that the Smashing Pumpkins subsequently celebrated when they recorded 'You're All I've Got Tonight' for inclusion on the *Aeroplane Flies High* box. Now, when Ocasek asked Corgan to sift through some of the demos he'd been working on, the be-spectacled Bostonian was thrilled with the songs and instincts that the Pumpkin brought to the table.

It was very different to his customary style of working, Ocasek enthused. 'He's a great songwriter who knows how to get to the point, and he has a different style of writing [to me].' Ocasek also knew that he didn't want to use a producer for this album, and thought that 'since Billy is a songwriter and a leader of a band and a person who arranges and creates his own ideas, why not give it to someone who would be a little bit more like myself?'

With Corgan on board, the pair nailed down a set that took Ocasek back to the guitar driven waters that had characterised the Cars' very earliest strivings; Corgan also contributed a new song, 'Asia Minor,' to the album. The sessions themselves, meanwhile, saw the pair accompanied by what amounted to a supergroup of sorts, including Bad Religion's Brian Baker and *de facto* Pumpkin Matt Walker. In a deliciously prescient twist, Hole's bassist Melissa Auf Der Maur was also among the guests.

While Corgan busied himself with *Troublizing*, Iha, meanwhile, dabbled light-heartedly in the life of a runway model during the New York Fashion Week, modelling outfits created by his friend, designer Anna Sui; more importantly, however, he also began looking forward to the recording of his own first solo album, sketching what would become one of the lost classics of the age on his acoustic guitar, while taking further time out for singing lessons.

Working through summer 1997 in his basement Bugg Studios, demanding that 'the songs really stand out and the vocals be[come] the main driving force, instead of heavy-duty Alternative Rock drums and fuzz box guitar;' and intent on creating a sound that offered little more than the captivating image of Iha alone in an egg-crated cellar, the guitarist then put together a kick-ass band around the seemingly omnipresent Matt Walker on drums, the Fountains Of Wayne's Adam Schlesinger on piano, former Tribal Opera bassist Solomon Snyder, organist John Ginty and Matthew Sweet/k.d.Lang accompanist Greg Leisz on steel guitar.

The recruitment of producer Jim Scott confirmed the direction that Iha's initial demos had laid out. Recruited on the strength of his work with Tom Petty, Scott was a willing contributor as Iha filled the studio with the kind of instrumentation one would normally not expect to encounter outside of a photo of the Byrds. 'Everything I used...were used by bands in the 60s and 70s,' Iha boasted proudly. 'And I took kind of a 60's or 70's approach to arranging. Whatever style it's in, can always be redone, it can always be original, because no two people are the same.'

It simply iced an already delicious cake when Veruca Salt's Nina Gordon added backing vocals on 'Beauty,' while there was a rare vocal excursion for Wretzky. She, too, stepped up to sing on 'One And Two,' a song many people believe was written about their break-up.

The album itself was, on first inspection, seemingly the antithesis of everything that the Smashing Pumpkins' own energies embodied. Eschewing the roar of the guitar for the more restrained thrum of fingers across acoustic strings, thumped back drums, and lush pedal steel and sweet sweet harmonies, *Let It Come Down* wrapped James Iha up in a different dress altogether and delivered him, this new AOR sweetheart, onto fans' doorsteps, a retro throwback of simple love songs.

Completely natural and unerringly honest, Iha's album was a stripped catalogue of the states of the heart, a trip through love and loss of love, through the oceans of relationships cast in the glow of soft sonics. Undoubtedly autobiographical, the songs in his set are just as romantic lyrically as many of Billy Corgan's own lyrical twists; what made the songs on *Let It Come Down* pop out was the brutal openness of the lines – there were few hidden meanings and twists of the tongue to be found anywhere.

It was a brilliant release. By not playing into the hands of critics and, indeed, Smashing Pumpkins fans, James Iha took a huge personal risk with the content of his album. Always a little self conscious of his ability to carry the vocal line of a song, to release an album where he not only delivered every vocal line, but also did it in an arena where his voice was at the fore without any rough roar of instrumentation to bury mistakes, was a leap of unmitigated proportion.

Let It Come Down would be released the following February, a strumming guitars-in-the-country kind of an album that exploded every preconception of what the Guitarist With The Smashing Pumpkins would be getting up to on his own, but utterly fulfilling the brief that Iha himself sketched at the outset of the sessions, to pursue the roots of his own musical loves and fascinations.

Many of the songs were written during the 1996/1997 world tour as Iha reflected, 'there's only so many things you can do in a hotel.' The point of the album he told *Alternative Press* magazine was to create 'a whole record of my songs in my voice the way I wanted them to be. I generally co-write a couple of songs on Pumpkins' records. But...the only expectation I wanted to meet was to have good songs.' He was adamant however that this was not to be a 'typical side project: "I'm in this band, and I did this record in one day with my friends".' Elements of the end result were, he confessed, 'a gamble' for example, despite the singing lessons he was very self-conscious about his voice. '"Oh God" I would think..."I'd rather just play guitar".' In time, however, he came to appreciate his voice as simply another instrument at his disposal.

Although many outsiders were shocked (and perhaps underwhelmed) by the pastoral gentility of the songs, none of this should have come as a complete surprise, at least to those who'd paid close attention to Iha's work over much of the last decade. For them, the album was exactly what you'd expect the quiet guitarist to record, and, when journalist David Daley commented upon the album's overall sensitivity, Iha snapped back, 'Sue me. I'm sensitive.'

By the end of February, the album just barely cracked the US Billboard Two Hundred, coming to rest at a paltry number a hundred and seventy-one. Fans just didn't seem to want to ride Iha's train. Britain, too, usually more than willing to give something different a shake, all but ignored the album. Apparently Smashing Pumpkins' acolytes didn't want to explore the sensitive side of James Iha, they wanted the wailing rock and riffing spandex clad cat that caroused the stages across a thousand nights of glammed out Rock. And it was a shame really, because even today, as Pumpkins' fans still sniff their noses at James Iha's solo foray, the album remains completely underrated.

Let It Come Down would ultimately be released through the Smashing Pumpkins' regular contract with Virgin Records. Together with D'Arcy Wretzky, however, Iha was also throwing many of his energies into Scratchie Records, an independent label with whom the couple had been involved since its inception in 1995.

The brainchild of Wretzky's brother-in-law, and former Signet Records publicist Jeremy Freeman, together with graphic designer Jamie Stewart, Scratchie was launched following a series of soul-searching conversations about the state of the American music industry, as a renewed school of corporate piranhas emerged to further devour the field of functioning record labels. Freeman recalled, 'initially it was just Jamie and I talking about putting together Scratchie, asking what could we do on our own? We had some ideas – initially, we were going to start off distributing 7" records from Jamaica (the pair were involved both with Shaggy's Stateside breakthrough, plus a number of dancehall related compilations).

'Then, one day, D'Arcy and James came over, I think to watch basketball actually, and I told them we were starting this label blah, blah, blah, and D'Arcy said, "We've been really interested in starting a label, but none of us really have time." So I thought on that for a while, if we could put it together, and I decided "yeah, we definitely can." And then I brought in [Fountain Of Wayne's] Adam Schlesinger, just because he has the best pop mind in the entire world, he's almost frightening that way, and Scratchie Records was born.' Iha agreed. 'They told us what they wanted to do with this label. D'Arcy and I liked the idea and we started to get involved.'

The goal of Scratchie was, first and foremost, to embody the true spirit of the indie label – which, itself, was becoming an increasingly endangered species as the 1990s rolled on. Its ethic was certainly very much in keeping with the pioneers of past generations, the Wax Trax!, Homesteads, Blast Firsts and all, whose forward-thinking ideals had made the entire Alternative boom of the late 1980s possible in the first place. There would be no room for major stars, no budget for major campaigns, just an enterprising abode for interesting and worthwhile musicians who were well deserving of an outlet for their craft. Scratchie wouldn't screw their artists, nor would they sign anyone looking for a bandwagon to jump on.

The bands Ivy and Fulflej, and Chicago-born dancehall artist Pancho Kryztal were among Scratchie's first signings; Billy Corgan threw his weight into the fray when he took on production duties for the Frogs' *Starjob* EP; and the media jumped on board with the arrival of the highly-rated Fulflej. There was also a berth, perhaps inevitably, for Catherine – whose Kerry Brown quickly established himself as another vital component in the Scratchie chemistry.

In the years since he first entered the Smashing Pumpkins' family, Brown had proven an invaluable musical ally for the band members. More importantly, however, he and Wretzky started dating following her break-up with Iha and, two years later, were married. Freeman enthused, 'Kerry's really good on a nuts and bolts level. He ran a studio in Chicago for a long time; now he has his own studio, The Barn. He produced and co-mixed the Catherine record, and we did the Fulflej record at The Barn. We did all the guitar and vocals at James' studio, in his house, then all the drum tracks at Kerry's studio, and then we cut four different songs at The Place in NY, which is the studio that Adam works out of. It's a good thing for the band, because they didn't have to pay for any studio time!'

Recruiting acts to the label was very much a co-operative venture. Freeman explained, 'what we've done with all of the stuff that we've signed is, we play tracks for each other and say, "What do you think?" There's some things that I'll give the benefit of the doubt to, like James, D'Arcy or Adam will bring in something and, if they're really adamant that this is a great indie rock record, I'll believe them, and I'll listen to it and if I like it, and they're saying it's really great, my belief is that this makes sense.

'Now, if they brought in something, and I absolutely hated it, and Jamie and Adam absolutely hated it, then we'd have a problem with it. The same goes for the dancehall stuff, that's not James and D'Arcy's forte, but when they heard Pancho's stuff, they said, "This is really good, whether or not I understand the music or not, the songs are really well written, musically it's good." We've been fortunate that, everything we've released, all the owners have agreed it's really good.'

Neither was the involvement of Iha and Wretzky some kind of 'friends in high places' trip that would hopefully draw in a few extra listeners for the Smashing Pumpkins' connection – although Freeman confessed that he didn't mind if people did hatch that opinion.

'I think they represent the company incredibly well; they are the company, they're part owners, and they have just as much to do with it as anyone else. [But] my basic feeling is that it's a good thing for people to have that reaction, there's certain things that help out. The Pumpkins have a lot of fans; the only thing that bothers me about it is when that starts overwhelming the music that we're doing. I'm excessively proud of the music that we do; I think we've put together a good, strong list of people.'

'James and D'Arcy are fantastic on an ear level, they'll hear things that I don't hear on a record. They're also very wise on the running of bands' careers, they have a lot of experience on good choices and bad choices. If [a band] just got added to a radio station [playlist], James will call and thank them for playing the record. They're obviously not going to be the people in the office answering the phones, but they get a lot of good music and they have the best connections in the world from producers on down.'

The label's early months were fraught. Freeman continued, '[that was] the hardest I ever had to go through in my entire life, that was true desperation. When we were starting out, we had a small bank loan (thirty thousand dollars), we did the 7"s, [dancehall artist] Lenky Don's 12", and the EPs, and all those first vinyl pieces pretty much sold out immediately.' However, it was simply too difficult to maintain the label as a purely self-distributed entity, even though the profits from one record would automatically finance the recording of the next. 'We were able to get a bunch of money back on [the first 7-inchers], and that's how we funded the EPs. But then our independent distribution started not ever paying us. It became suddenly really awful.'

Even after the Mercury major stepped in with the offer of a three year mainstream distribution deal in early 1996, the situation was difficult. Arranging a deal whereby Scratchie would be able to pick and choose which releases went through the major, and which would remain fully independent 'took a long time, so there was this horrible period before we were signed with Mercury, where our independent distributors were pissed because we wouldn't confirm them getting any more records. It was a total Catch 22, but we ended up with me totally starving for about two months, hand to mouth, I hated that, it sucked. But now, that part of it is better.'

Fulflej, Phoenix Thunderstorm and the Smashing Pumpkins' old touring buddies, the Chainsaw Kittens, were the first beneficiaries of the new deal, with the latter falling into the handful of bands that Iha enthused over who, through no fault of their own, 'had been bumped... by the majors.'

Having developed over the years into glam-tinged extravaganza that *Alternative Press* deliriously described as the missing link between Nirvana and Gary Holton's Heavy Metal Kids, the Chainsaw Kittens had become 'really good friends' with the Smashing Pumpkins. But while they certainly found many admirers in the media, their mainstream career had never exploded in the direction that their press clippings were convinced they were destined to take.

Vocalist Tyson Meade recalled, 'when we left [our first label] we didn't have a deal, [so] I called D'Arcy.' His call came just as she alone was first getting involved with Scratchie, and the timing couldn't have been better.

'She was like, "Tyson, wow, it's so weird, because I've been talking to Jeremy about starting a label. But there was nobody I wanted to sign except for you guys, but you were already on a label. Don't do anything, and I'll call you back soon." Three or four days later, she called back and said, "Tyson, we're going to start this label, and we'd really like for you guys to sign to it." It started as just D'Arcy who became interested; D'Arcy said "it would be a lot better for everybody if I got James into this too." A month later he was.'

Meade continued, 'the thing that was really appealing was that we were the emphasis for James and D'Arcy to be involved with the label to begin with and, we knew that, if we signed to them, they wouldn't want our first born child. They gave us total artistic freedom all along the way. They just let us do the record [1996's *Chainsaw Kittens*]. We didn't even have to send demos in.'

Scratchie announced its existence to the world with a label showcase at the Cabaret Metro. 'That night was pretty strange,' laughed Meade. 'Definitely kind of a strange bill, for sure. It seemed to work, though; there were a lot of people there, and we got really great reviews afterwards. James [Iha] coming up [on stage] helped too. He'd said right before we played, "Hey, want me to come up and play?" We're like, "Yeah, sure, that would be fun," because it kind of took some of the pressure off too, because it wasn't a real serious thing, it was a fun thing. He did "Connie I've Found The Door," from *Flipped Out In Singapore*, he'd learned it a while ago, so he came up and played it, and then played a bunch of crazy, Hendrix solos. And I just screamed a lot.'

For all its high hopes, Scratchie never truly established a presence on the American market and would wind down somewhat towards the end of the decade. Early in the new Millennium the label drifted away from distributors Mercury and contented itself instead with a small roster of bands that includes

the Fountains Of Wayne, Chicago's Blank Theory and Sweden's The Sounds –
at the time of writing, James Iha's most recent bequest to the label. Today
Scratchie continues to percolate, pushing their bands to the surface with the
same attention to detail that characterised the label's heyday.

CHAPTER NINETEEN
WE HAD JOY, WE HAD FUN

In the midst of so much extra-curricular activity and, though they remained tantalisingly elusive Stateside for much of the year, the Smashing Pumpkins did make time for the European Festival circuit during the early summer. They were home by the beginning of July 1997, though, waiting while Iha wrapped up *Let It Come Down* before grabbing some more time to work on demos during the early fall.

They broke away for a handful more shows, including two that found them opening for the Rolling Stones, as their *Bridges To Babylon* extravaganza got underway in late September. The Smashing Pumpkins were one of several top-rated bands to join the Stones on the outing – other dates saw Sheryl Crow, Blues Traveler, the Foo Fighters and the Dave Matthews Band called up to open the show, although there would be little opportunity to fraternise with the stars, as Iha reflected.

'At the level they're at, there's no camaraderie. You're not hanging out with Keith, throwing TV sets out of the window. They're off sheltered in their own little world. They came out to do a photo opportunity. We shook hands with them and that was it. It's not like they were being jerks. They're the Rolling Stones, you know.'

And they had a Rolling Stones audience, a prospect that had, on more than one past occasion, turned the mightiest support acts to jelly. The Smashing Pumpkins, however, felt comfortable – maybe the audience picked up on the Jagger-esque sneer that occasionally flickers through Corgan's vocal; maybe they got off on a riff machine that was as resolute in the 1990s as the Stones themselves were thirty years before. Or maybe, they just liked what they heard. "It was cool," Iha affirmed. "Surprisingly, a lot of people were into it."

There was another high-profile engagement waiting in mid-October, in the form of a two day stint at the Bridge Benefit Concert in Mountain View, California. Like so many of the Smashing Pumpkins' recent outings, it was a wholly charitable affair, raising funds for an establishment founded by Neil Young's own wife, Peggy; the Bridge School offered a safe and sympathetic environment within which to school children with severe physical and speech problems – a predicament from which one of the Youngs' own children suffered.

The line-up for this eleventh year of benefit concerts was as star-studded as ever, bringing together a high-spirited mixture of genres and eras, from Lou Reed and Blues Traveler to Metallica and Young himself. But perhaps the most exciting part of the 1997 event hinged on the Smashing Pumpkins' own first night set. The last act of the evening, the group took the stage to perform acoustic versions of 'To Sheila,' '1979,' 'Bullet With Butterfly Wings,' the seldom-heard *Aeroplane Flies High*-era b-side 'Set The Ray To Jerry' and more.

From there, however, the timbre of the evening changed dramatically. Introduced by Wretzky as 'Billy the Space Cowboy,' none other than Marilyn Manson sashayed on stage to lead the band through a tempestuous 'Eye,' and his own 'The Beautiful People,' a song scheduled for the shock rocker's next album. Manson's appearance horrified many fans, yet Corgan was, in fact, in occasional attendance throughout the recording of what would become Manson's landmark *Mechanical Animals* album, and later acknowledged 'I put my two cents in here and there, but my involvement was pretty minimal.' He was, after all, somewhat busy elsewhere.

Behind the apparent façade of calm that now enveloped the group, the Smashing Pumpkins were again approaching turmoil. With his temporary tenure with the band having turned into a year or more, drummer Matt Walker was growing restless, eager to get going on his own gestating new band, Cupcakes – formed out of the wreckage of another Chicago group, Tribal Opera, whose Preston Graves, Greg Suran and Solomon Snyder were numbered among Walker's band mates. (Cupcakes would finally release their debut album in 2000.)

To compound the Smashing Pumpkins' discomfort, his decision to depart coincided almost perfectly with their own scheduled return to action, as they locked into the recording sessions for their next album in November.

Inevitably, news of Walker's departure aroused the already intermittent buzzing of those observers who confidently predicted an imminent return for Jimmy Chamberlin; the Smashing Pumpkins, however, silenced such chatter by turning instead to a string of guest drummers, including ex-Soundgardener Matt Cameron and Beck's Joey Waronker.

Opting for a completely fresh start in their now preferred base of the Chicago Trax Recording studio, the Smashing Pumpkins' first choice for producer was Brad Wood, veteran of sessions with band favourites Veruca Salt and Red Red Meat, as well as with Liz Phair, and Sunny Day Real Estate. It took only a few of the earliest autumn sessions, however, for all to agree that the fit was not as comfortable as they had hoped.

A number of tracks were finished, including no fewer than six of the songs that made the final cut when *Adore* was complete. But, as the band developed more fully the sound they required, Wood departed and Corgan decided to produce the album by himself, before bringing in the big guns – old hand Flood among them – for the mixing process. No blame was laid – Corgan acknowledged that the Smashing Pumpkins had long ago found their own pace in the studio and it was difficult for any newcomer to match their own capacity for work.

Shuffling drummers in and out of the studio; shuffling studios, as the sessions drifted to Chicago's Hinge and Battery Studios, and LA's Sunset Sound, juggling single track recordings with live work and pulling in snippets from both Sadlands and Bugg Studios, the *Adore* sessions were just three months old and the group already had twenty songs in the can – all of which marked another gallantly deviant turn for the band, shifting ever further from their *Gish*-era thrusting and, in so doing, fulfilling at least part of Corgan's dream of someday 'doing just a totally beautiful album.'

And, indeed, there are moments on *Adore* that are so quiet that they truly encapsulated the spirit of the 'soft shit' that Corgan has always insisted he loves as much as fiery rock and metal. The final cut of the album would indeed shift the band another significant notch on their own measuring stick, but the songs that were etched to groove were as fresh as anything they'd attempted on *Gish*, just different.

'We didn't invent the loud-quiet rock thing, but we helped popularise it,' explained Corgan. 'Now there are so many bands imitating the Smashing Pumpkins sound, it gets to the point where you're competing not only with yourself, but with other people doing yourself, and it just becomes redundant. Bush, for instance, are one of many Nirvana junior bands who are highly irritating to me at this point in time. They all jumped the train, so we're gonna build another train.'

Reiterating his own reasons for loving REM, he told TV's Charlie Rose, 'We always kind of [thought], in the back of our heads, if we ever had the kind of success that people only dream of, would we, in essence, cave in to what people expect of us when you have big success, which is to continue what we're supposed to be doing? We broke completely from our past as much as one could, and made an album that we think is a bold step in a new direction, a direction that no one's really going in yet. Because in our minds, it's got to do with continuity, what we're attempting to do in the long run, which is influence and be progressive and stay on very much the cutting edge of music. It's strange, because we find ourselves in the position we were in seven years ago, when people were saying "you guys are crazy, you don't know what you're doing," which is what was said about our first album, so we've gone completely full circle.'

Of course, it was a calculated move, as Wretzky acknowledged when she was asked about...or perhaps reminded of...the Smashing Pumpkins' early adherence to at least some strain of Grunge. 'People [are] moving away from [Grunge]. We've been talking about it…since when we did *Mellon Collie* and it was just vital for our own sanity.' Indeed as far back as May 1996, the group had been discussing change, with Jimmy Chamberlin, oblivious of course to what the future held, telling *Modern Drummer* magazine that the Pumpkins had recorded their final rock album. 'We don't want to [become] a parody of ourselves. I'm thirty-one now, and I don't see myself playing 'Jellybelly' at forty.'

But it was also a case, Iha said, of the band *having* to change. 'We'd been playing together for so long, it was hard to get a new, original rock Smashing Pumpkins song out each time. So, the change in sound just seemed to make sense.'

So did the shift away from any other sound with which the group had hitherto been associated – even though the critics would bite hard into the band over the perceived incongruity of adding *Adore* in their canon, following its appearance later in 1998. The success of *Mellon Collie And The Infinite Sadness*, after all, had already liberated the Smashing Pumpkins from the necessity to churn through another rock'n'roll album and, with those constraints lifted, the musicians were able to finally explore whichever avenues they wished, without the push of anyone behind them, urging them on to fuzz and frenzy.

Those avenues would take them into a whole new arena of both stylistic and emotional imagery. Visually they were spellbinding. Corgan had never been afraid to dress for the occasion. Indeed, following a show where he cavorted in a dress, his mother told him to be careful in case people thought he was gay. Corgan responded that it didn't matter. 'They already think I'm an asshole.' Now he was to step even further in the realms of fantasy as the supreme circus master, decked out in full Max Von Shrek-as-Nosferatu drag, cast out of silent cinematic hell and spat up in modern day America, with Iha and Wretzky his ghoulishly stylish cohorts.

Not necessarily a hit 'em over the head album, the music that tangled together on *Adore* was deeply personal, especially for Corgan, who unabashedly wove the grief he felt following his mother Martha's death in 1997 into the songs – the penultimate 'For Martha' was only the most pronounced of these offerings. But, even as sundry observers patted him on the back for baring that side of his soul, they were sniping at him anyway, as they picked over the bones of the rest of the album, in search of songs that might reflect those other turbulent losses he had suffered since *Melon Collie And The Infinite Silence*… the death of Jonathan Melvoin, the departure of Jimmy Chamberlin and, hot off the gossip-rag headlines, the break-up of his marriage to Chris Fabian, and even a dispute with Virgin Records over the terms of their contract.

Corgan would not play ball. 'I think people have tried to put this album in context of my mother passing away, our former drummer leaving the band, my divorce, but I think you can look at loss, and see the cup's half empty, or you can look at loss and see someone who's decided to live and take the memories they have and empower them to move on.' The door on that part of his life was closed to all discussion and that was exactly as it ought to be.

A public figure in the world of his work, once Corgan unstrapped his guitar and turned off the microphone, he expected to be treated with the same respect as any other private citizen – a vain request, of course, but one that he himself stuck rigidly to. 'My mother was close to me, passes away…early, you go "well, do I really care what this magazine says about me, or do I care about fulfilling happiness in my life?" I looked at those things and I learned those lessons because I feel that's the greatest respect I can pay my mother…to take her courage in dying and the fact that she lived her life the way she wanted, and use that strength and energy to do what I want to do in my life.'

He did not rub his personal business in the world's face; the least the world could do was stop asking him if he'd start, and he was no less resolute when he reminded the most persistent investigators that lyrics taken out of context, and ascribed meaning by those who didn't write them, are false. Deep meaning to one is gobbledygook to another, and it's a shame really, that he needed to continue to flog that rotten old donkey as late as 1998, to have someone get the point. One would have thought he'd reinforced that often enough in the past.

As threatened, *Adore* shifted more perceptibly away from the rock arena than anything that the Smashing Pumpkins had released before. Adhering to what Iha described as 'more of a hybrid of acoustic and some electronic elements'; adding, indeed, a wealth of pure electronic trappings to the already eclectic mix. It transformed the Smashing Pumpkins' sound completely, causing it to resonate in an entirely fresh way, one that highlighted the band without brick-beating the obvious absence of Chamberlin's' sticks. 'Rock is dead,' Corgan belligerently pronounced, 'and you'll be dancing on its grave to our music.'

With Flood working on the project, it would be easy enough to see where some of the electronic impetus came from. However, there were other, lesser-known hands at work on *Adore*, among them former Nitzer Ebb mastermind Bon Harris. A long time acquaintance of Flood, Harris had relocated to Los Angeles and was enjoying a complete revival of his talents and creativity due to the late 1990's boom in electronic music. Planning a new project, Maven, Harris met Corgan at a party and fell into a conversation that revolved around building up and tearing down musical walls. That led, in turn, to talk about a collaboration, and, with that idea still very much in mind, Harris was set up in a Los Angeles studio towards the end of *Adore*, to see what he could come up with.

His work was subtle, adding a bit here, taking a bit away there, and layering drum programming throughout. The songs lent themselves well to Harris' own ideals. Some of his work survived – 'Daphne Descends,' 'Once Upon A Time,' 'Crestfallen,' 'Appels And Oranjes,' 'Pug' and 'Behold! The Night Mare' all bear Harris' imprimatur – some didn't, but it all came together well as Harris recalled, 'It's quite a testament to the mix job that nothing really jumps out at you as being super-different, which was some of the craft of Billy and Flood getting together for the mixes.'

He also complimented the Smashing Pumpkins' open-minded decision to allow him his own space when they chose to marry their sonics to the electronic revolution. 'So many artists have suddenly decided they're going to "go electronic". But it's not really an integration, it's them singing over the top of an electronic track. That's one of the reasons why the new Smashing Pumpkins thing is so good, because it's not like that.' Indeed, far from the slim smoke and mirrors and a puff of bandwagon that was the late 1990's rule in such endeavours, the Smashing Pumpkins instead followed the direction laid down by David Bowie across his own most recent albums (*Outside*, *Earthling*) to bend the proffered elements of electronica to their own whim, without once compromising or undermining their original intention.

As the *Adore* sessions moved into their final stretch, February brought Iha's own album to the stores. A triumph for the guitarist, *Let It Come Down* quickly became a cult classic with an audience that was only partially drawn from the Smashing Pumpkin faithful, although it failed to make any substantial waves on the mainstream American or British charts. One single, 'Be Strong Now' appeared alongside the album release and, like its parent disc, didn't cause quite a stir. But that was fitting, really, for such a quiet, beautiful album. It was an exquisite achievement nonetheless.

To promote the album, Iha managed to squeak out a handful of nearly-acoustic shows, kicking off a little tour in January that would continue through February, and include one memorable night where he appeared as the unannounced opener for a surprisingly solo Corgan at Los Angeles' Viper room on the fifteenth. Iha ran through a clutch of songs off the album, while Corgan concentrated on acoustic versions of songs from the forthcoming *Adore*. The audience, which included Wretzky, producer Rick Ruben and Hole's Erik Erlandsen who'd come to cheer Iha on, mostly talked their way through his set, until the opening notes of the closing '1979' sounded, at which point there was an extra big hoot at the familiar song, and the audience chimed in all beery.

Erlandsen's presence would not have come as a surprise to Corgan either. This same period of time saw Corgan renew an acquaintance that had long become an intrinsic part not simply of his own mythology, but of 90's Rock in general, as he teamed up with Courtney Love and Hole as they prepared to record their first all-new album since the death of Kurt Cobain, *Celebrity Skin*. Much water had passed under the bridge since that last public pairing, the night that Love met Cobain; and a great deal of worthless tittle-tattle too.

As recently as 1995, Corgan hissed 'I have nothing to say to her anymore. I will have nothing to do with her. I won't talk to her.' Now, however, he was recruited to the proceedings under the official title of 'consultant.'

Corgan's input to the finished album included co-writing five of the songs, but far more interesting for watching tongue-wagglers was the opportunity for a fresh go-round of rumour and supposition, all the more so after Corgan's involvement in the album degenerated into a public battle with Love. Of course it was fought in the music press, as the pair determinedly added an entire new chapter to the continuing story of their involvement.

From the moment Corgan's involvement was announced, the suggestion that Hole (or, more properly, Love) required some kind of outside inspiration and assistance ricocheted around the music industry, a supposition that only took on further impetus when Corgan himself told *Select*, 'there would not be a new Hole album without me,' and described himself as a 'svengali.'

Love immediately retaliated via a statement despatched to *USA Today*, in which she railed furiously less at Corgan's words, than at the climate that those words had fed. 'Eric (Erlandson) and I co-wrote five songs of the twelve...with Billy Corgan. Billy does not have a majority of publishing percentage on any one of those songs....' She acknowledged that Corgan did 'spend quality time mentoring and teaching me a craft that I really needed to learn in order to make the record I wanted to make,' but she understandably and accurately complained, 'I feel it's silly and somewhat sexist to credit Billy Corgan with things Billy Corgan did not do, based, on the assumption that accomplished male musicians are somehow superior to accomplished female musicians.'

Of course, such attitudes were nothing new in the music industry; it would, in fact, have been more shocking had they not raised their spiteful little heads over the critical parapet. How many journalists, after all, had credited Kurt Cobain as the silent songwriting partner on the past two Hole albums, without once considering that, not only were the group themselves readily capable of writing their own songs, but had been doing so for close to a year before the Grungemeister even arrived on their scene?

So it was in this case, and Eric Erlandsen, at least, seems to have foreseen such problems even before the sessions commenced. He told *Rolling Stone*, 'I was really against [Corgan producing] right away. In fact, when Courtney suggested it, I said, "Courtney, I'll never talk to you again if Billy produces this album." I was really strong about it...but then I caved.'

Neither would he allow the self-styled Svengali any more control than was necessary. When others thought the band had reached the end of the sessions, Erlandsen continued working on the tapes, adamant that the album would not be released 'until it was right, until I felt it was done...that's all I cared about. Everyone thought I was losing my perspective, and on some things, I did. But, for the most part, I think I was pretty objective. I wanted to make sure that every song fit in with the record, all sounding good together.'

He succeeded. Although *Celebrity Skin* would never share the impact of the preceding *Live Through This*, still Hole turned in an album that confirmed their own status among the upper echelon of 90's American Alternative acts and, if no-nothing outsiders still needed to distort the credit away from the group that actually made the album, then Hole could nevertheless take a twisted compliment away from their jibes. How many other bands, after all, ever maintained close to a decade at the top of the pile, doing nothing more strenuous than letting other people jerk their strings?

It was now April 1998 and, as the snow shook off the branches and the biting northern winds receded, the Smashing Pumpkins reconvened and geared up for a whirlwind spring tour, slated to kick off in Europe in May, following a warm-up show at the Cabaret Metro on the second, as special guests of the headlining Cheap Trick. The continuing search for a drummer was closed when long time sessioneer and occasional John Mellencamp collaborator Kenny Aronoff, was publicly confirmed for the upcoming tour. 'He's just a great drummer,' Corgan enthused, 'he's amazing, he's fantastic. And he's a really great groove drummer and that really suits this particular record.' The band also intended fleshing out their touring retinue with the addition of underground diva Lisa Germano, who would play violin.

Another veteran of Mellencamp's camp, Germano had since released a string of highly-regarded albums under her own name, amassing a devoted cult following as she did so. Her hopes that she herself might break news of her latest engagement to her audience were dashed, however, when the MTV networks picked up the story and blared it from the rooftops.

Shaken both by the surprise announcement and by the dismay that arose from her own core following, Germano grew increasingly uncomfortable with the situation, a discomfort that led, in turn, to her entire relationship with the Smashing Pumpkins deteriorating to breaking point before the tour even started. Having already made her way to London for the first shows, Germano then travelled back to the United States without even playing a concert – but adding an entire new dimension to the belligerent baggage that the Smashing Pumpkins seemed capable of amassing every time they set foot in public.

The Smashing Pumpkins themselves were not deterred by that affair. Dropping the violin altogether from their musical plans, the group launched the *Adore* tour with an appearance on BBC TV's *Later...With Jools Holland*, where they ripped through the album tracks 'Ava Adore,' 'Daphne Descends,' and 'Once Upon A Time,' and disrupted the programme's traditional filming techniques by stuffing the studio with so much gear that Simply Red's Mick Hucknall, a fellow guest on the show that week, later described the experience as 'gladiatorial.' *Later...* producer Mark Cooper explained, 'the [Smashing Pumpkins]...brought so much equipment into the studio that we couldn't film the bands on either side of them.'

The group's appearance on *Later...* also marked the arrival of a new face in the touring party, as the Smashing Pumpkins welcomed pianist Mike Garson aboard. A classically trained pianist from the age of seven; leader of a jazz group that ranked among the most respected combos in early 1970's New York; Mike Garson came to international prominence when he was recruited to David Bowie's band for the recording sessions that produced 1973's *Aladdin Sane* album. He remained by Bowie's side for the next two years, moved onto a career as both a solo artist and a sessioneer (recent years had placed him alongside acts as disparate as Seal and Nine Inch Nails), then rejoined Bowie as the singer commenced his critical and commercial rejuvenation in the mid-1990s.

He and Corgan had more likely than not been introduced when Corgan encored with Bowie at his 50th birthday party concert in 1997, but Garson remembered only that he first truly connected with Corgan later that year, when the Smashing Pumpkins and David Bowie's own latest tours crossed paths on the European festival circuit. A year later, Garson recalled, he happened to hear that 'Billy was auditioning keyboard players,' so he went along. Inevitably, not another player in the land had a look in after that.

Later... aside, the Smashing Pumpkins were constantly in front of the cameras during 1998, making television appearances in London, Madrid, Toronto and Paris, before returning to the US and, on 30 July, adding their first ever appearance on *The Late Show With David Letterman* to their itinerary.

The band also arranged for cameras to attend various shows around Europe and the United States, with an eye towards filming a tour documentary. MTV producer Jesse Ignjatovic was keyed in to direct, taking a leave of absence from his regular work to tour with the Smashing Pumpkins throughout their May-September outing. Shooting performance, rehearsal, and behind the scenes life, the intention was for the Smashing Pumpkins to emerge with a *cinema verité* document to rival any of the greatest epics of rock cine-journalism – Dylan's *Don't Look Back*, the Stones' *Gimme Shelter* and so forth. Sadly, however, the *Adore* film was not to be; Ignjatovic's work languishes, unreleased, in the archive and the greatest opportunity to capture the magic of the live Smashing Pumpkins was abandoned.

There were, indeed, some memorable nights for the director to have preserved, beginning with the Smashing Pumpkins' 25 May appearance at the Shepherd's Bush Empire in London, where they were joined onstage by Duran Duran frontman Simon le Bon, to roar first through a tremendous version of his own band's 'Nightboat,' followed by a show-capping 'Transmission.' Once upon a time, a watching veteran journalist was heard to muse, the idea of Simon le Bon singing one of Joy Division's most sacred songs would have been sufficient to transform the watching rabble into a veritable lynch mob. Today, they simply cheered and sang along. How times have changed....

The UK dates were followed by journeys through Europe and the Far East, with the band purposefully stretching the traditional reality of such jaunts by eschewing the usual circuit of venues, and dabbling instead in a host of new locations. The band settled in to Tivoli Gardens in Copenhagen, Brussels' Botanique Gardens, and the Guggenheim Museum in Bilbao, Spain, before heading to Germany for another stint at the Rock Am Ring Festival, their first since 1994. They then wrapped up with two shows in Tokyo, including one that allowed them to walk the very same Budokan boards that had transformed Cheap Trick into American superstars, almost exactly twenty years before.

Adore was finally released in the States on 2 June 1998, where it seemed, upon first inspection, that it would be met with only lukewarm response at best. The band were derided for creating an electronic album, and slammed for appearing to have cut a record that was little more than an updated Cure clone. Fair-weather fans mourned the loss of the band's early in-your-face thunderstorms, while the electronic hipsters dismissed the album with barely anything other than a cursory glance.

Once again, the Smashing Pumpkins had carved a niche that was forward thinking, but close enough to jockey with genres in such a way that *Adore* was cast aside without any real examination of what the band had actually achieved. All those who pooh-poohed the album never really allowed the veil of haute-hip to be lowered enough to see what was in front of them.

Adore could be taken as a deliberate experiment in sound, a sonic shift born out of the need to compensate for Chamberlin's departure. It could also have been a well-finessed play to break a musical market far removed from the gutter-worn knees of Grunge. Or, just perhaps, the music was simply the sound of a long-together band growing out of their old skins and stretching out in new ones.

New skins on tight, the Smashing Pumpkins still seeded the songs with the blueprint that had propelled them to fame in the first place. In and amongst the big electronic beats of 'Ava Adore' lie guitar riffs that are equal to any on the first two albums, while the play of Corgan's vocals beating against the music sounded as glorious in '98 as it did in '88.

Everything anyone could want from the Smashing Pumpkins was there, it was not even a matter of knowing *where* to look – it was understanding *how* to look. What *had* changed, however, was the pure sophistication of the songs themselves. Corgan's lyrics had become sublime – had become poetry, had become lines which stood on their own. Even stripped of the cadence and rhythm of guitar, bass and drums, these words kept their metre and shape.

The hints of his comfort in writing that blazed across *Mellon Collie And The Infinite Sadness* exploded on *Adore*. From the brutal and enigmatic 'Annie Dog' to the perfect 'Blank Page', the band demonstrated how they'd grown. And although both these songs swung into the softer part of the band's oeuvre, it was the latter particularly which allowed Corgan's lyrics, sung simply in duet with Wretzky, to meander in between piano keys.

These were the moments that proved this band were so very much more than a pile of flannel and glitter. The hooks were there, hooky as ever, but just shuffled out of the spotlight a little. Ultimately, what pushed *Adore* to the next level was the Smashing Pumpkins' ability to just let the songs be what they were, to exist as they were – to allow them to fulfil their own promise.

Certainly, critics had valid points in rants and raves about his new breed of toned down, AOR-oriented Smashing Pumpkins. And sure, the songs on *Adore* didn't harbour any great smash and grab antics to grate on ears not accustomed to the times. Although many would call the album a disappointment, it was anything but. The hordes who screwed up their eyes and punched fists at the heavens for allowing their guitar gods to create this *electronic* album were more fit to lie in the grave they'd dug the band than the band themselves were.

Change can be good. What does it say about an individual who wants nothing more than to hear the same album over and over, re-created ceaselessly? The Smashing Pumpkins' fans, those who knew what they wanted, embraced *Adore* in the same way as they'd loved every other of the group's albums. They kept it close.

The Smashing Pumpkins returned to the United States at the end of June, just three weeks after the launch of the album, hoping to launch a tour of free concerts. Unfortunately this particular scheme was doomed to failure, but not wanting to 'let go of the idea of doing something different,' the outing was re-aligned as a series of benefits, raising funds for a hornet's nest of different charities, from New York's Hale House to the Make-A-Wish Foundation, a cause that seemed especially close to Corgan's heart.

Dedicated to fulfilling terminally-ill children's wishes, Make-A-Wish, Corgan explained to KTBZ Radio, 'helps them achieve some wish in their life that they would never get a chance to...whether it's meeting Michael Jordan or meeting the Pumpkins, or anything like that.... We just want to say "it's not so hard to do good." You know, things are not like what you see on the *Jerry Springer Show*. That's not the world. The world is a lot better place than it's made out on TV.'

Again, the initial intention for these magnanimous dates would quickly change. Originally the Smashing Pumpkins intended to concentrate their energies on the theatre circuit, in an attempt, as Corgan put it, to 'stick with the vibe of *Adore* through thick and thin.' Demand for tickets, however, remained as strong as it had ever been and, long before the first show, the larger stadia and arenas began popping up like mushrooms all across the band's itinerary. Nor could the various beneficiaries of such largesse have had much of a problem with the revision. Between the opening night in San Francisco on 30 June, and the final date in Miami Florida on 8 August, the Smashing Pumpkins raised over two and a half million dollars for the various charities they'd chosen to support.

Not all of the plans for the outing were shunted aside. The live set was totally overhauled for the occasion, with the band serving up very few 'old songs,' preferring instead to keep the material fresh across *Adore* – there was even a handful of shows where, according to Corgan, 'we did the whole *Adore* album.' Other nights saw the group relax so much that audiences simply had no idea what might happen next – such as the night at New York's Radio City Music Hall, when the Smashing Pumpkins themselves capped the closing 'Transmission' by hauling a handful of fans onto the stage, handing off their instruments and departing to the wings, allowing the novice rock and rollers to finish the song.

It was an amazing thing to watch, for fans and band alike...so much so that the routine was quickly incorporated into several other shows – if a gig went well, and the audience got the vibe, they were rewarded with Joy Division and a cacophony.

On 2 August, the night after that Radio City Music Hall epiphany, Corgan made an eagerly anticipated appearance on another of American television's most lauded (and, occasionally, controversial) talk programs, *the Charlie Rose Show.* Broadcast journalist Rose had carved a bright spotlight for himself and cast and even brighter spotlight in the American media with his hour-long show. With a format that focused on in-depth one-on-one interviews and the occasional round table discussion, he asked the hard questions of politicos and authors, of socialites and musicians, without discrimination or bias. Broadcast on 3 August, Corgan spoke candidly with Rose about the newly released *Adore* and about the state of alternative music in the late 1990s.

He did not paint a pretty picture. Early sales of *Adore*, Corgan candidly admitted, were 'not what we hoped,' a consequence of what he called 'a general backlash against...our stance that rock music has reached a finite point and it's time to assess what it means and what it's about and what it's for. It's become so commercial and certainly the music that we came from, Alternative music, which was supposed to be anti-Rock...it's become very conservative.'

The Smashing Pumpkins set out to shatter a cliché and, in so doing, created – and became – a new one. 'And so...it's time for us to push the plunger and blow it all up again, [and] I think there's been a kind of knee-jerk reaction, not only cos we're attempting to change, but also because people are sad that the era has come to a conclusion' – the era, that was, of 'rawk-alternative bands that redefined rock'n'roll when people thought there was nothing left to define.' Groups like Nirvana, Pearl Jam, Soundgarden, Alice In Chains, the Smashing Pumpkins themselves, took 'something that was supposed to be dead' and reinvigorated it with a passion and, more importantly, a commercial impact unseen since the heyday of Punk.

But where were those bands today? 'Kurt Cobain killed himself, Pearl Jam made a conscious decision not to play the game of music…Alice In Chains is not really a functioning band right now…Soundgarden's broken up.' All the 'leading lights of the movement' had come to some kind of bitter end, and the Smashing Pumpkins…Corgan's words were muffled on the broadcast, but it sounded very much as though he was saying, 'we're being punished for that.'

It was a theme to which Corgan would return, of course, and with increasing vehemence as the Smashing Pumpkins' own career moved towards its conclusion. They, and the bands who grew up alongside them, had been offered the world on a plate. They dropped the plate.

The US shows at an end, the Smashing Pumpkins next headed south for a handful of South American gigs, wrapping the tour with two shows in Buenos Aires, Argentina. (Plans to continue on from there, and close the outing with four shows in Johannesburg and Cape Town, South Africa were abandoned.)

Back in the States, the Smashing Pumpkins made yet another appearance on *Saturday Night Live*, performing 'Perfect' on the show's 26 September season premiere; stepping completely out of the mould, but reawakening memories of *The Simpsons* regardless, Corgan and the band also made a brief appearance as themselves in a comedy skit with that evening's host, actress Cameron Diaz, and show regulars Chris Kattan and Will Ferrell. October then brought further high profile ventures, first when the band hit the VH1 Fashion Awards on the twenty-fifth; then when they turned out in front of a packed Dodgers Stadium in Los Angeles, to open KISS's Halloween party.

It was another odd pairing. However Corgan and KISS actually dated their friendship back several years. Gene Simmons was one of the few musical associates who was able to offer Corgan some solace and advice around the time of the Jimmy Chamberlin/Jonathan Melvoin tragedy. At lunch the very day the Smashing Pumpkins fired Chamberlin, Simmons told Corgan, 'it may seem like a heavy thing right now, but when you get out from under this black cloud and the air clears you'll feel better.'

To people who were not aware of this history, putting The Smashing Pumpkins next to KISS only revived ghosts of their Guns 'n' Roses stadium shows. How two bands, so seemingly out of step with one other could rock an audience only there for one of them, has always been a puzzle, and the Smashing Pumpkins must have felt a little wobbly as they walked into Dodgers Stadium on the eve of KISS' *Psycho Circus* world tour. That band's fans, rabid at the best of times, were on a high amp not seen since the early 1980s.

Nevertheless, the Smashing Pumpkins entered in their usual, inimitable style, dressed as the Beatles, to open with a cover of 'Money (That's What I Want)', before driving into a hard rocking set handcrafted to melt the makeup off the onlookers' faces.

Corgan alone then stepped out in December, to appear at the KROQ *Almost*

Acoustic Christmas concert at Shrine Auditorium. The LA radio station's ninth annual charity concert was always sure to pull in a wide variety of Alternative artists, and the 1998 show was no exception. From Soul Coughing and Cake, to the Brian Setzer Orchestra and Garbage, there was more than a little something for everyone, with the event's traditional affection for the so-called unplugged format proving the ideal environment for the clutch of songs that were to be Corgan's gift to the audience.

Turning in the only wholly acoustic performance of the entire evening, Corgan also offered up what many onlookers claim to have been one of his most memorable shows ever. Accompanying himself on either guitar or piano, his set was custom-designed to highlight the sheer poetry that he was now writing, stripping the songs of percussion and scything guitar; stripping, too, the electronic jiggery and orchestral sweeps, to allow them to stand completely alone and naked.

It was a varied set, inevitably heavy on *Adore* material, but unafraid to hunt both backwards and, to the joy of many, forward in search of further material. Premiered that evening were two new songs, 'If There is A God' and 'One Less Moment' (later recorded as 'Lover'), previewing the earliest of the numbers written for what would become the Smashing Pumpkins' final album. For fans the entire set was a crystalline moment of pure beauty and, for those who professed to really hate Corgan's voice, it was a torture that did not end once Corgan's own spot was finished. He reappeared later in the evening to join Depeche Mode for a shimmering rendition of 'Never Let Me Down Again' – the song, of course, that Smashing Pumpkins donated all those years before to the *Music For The Masses* Depeche tribute album.

As 1998 disappeared into history, the Smashing Pumpkins were left to look back on a year that had both reconfirmed and reinvigorated the band's status among the most popular acts in the world – at the same time as confirming the bleak picture that Corgan had acknowledged on the *Charlie Rose Show*, as disappointing early sales for Adore signally failed to pick up.

Two singles, 'Ave Adore' and "Perfect' had dipped outside of the British Top Ten (beyond the Top Twenty in the latter instance), at a time when bands of the Smashing Pumpkins' stature were more likely to enter the chart at number one; while *Adore* itself bottomed out at number five, one place lower than either of its predecessors. American audiences, meanwhile, sent the album no higher than number two, where it hung for just one week before spiralling down the chart. The album would be awarded a single platinum disc for its troubles, a mere drop in the ocean compared to the four that *Siamese Dream* notched up, and the staggering nine earned by *Mellon Collie And The Infinite Sadness*.

Yet, when the media trotted out to quiz Corgan on his 'failure,' he seemed remarkably unperturbed by any suggestion that the Smashing Pumpkins' season in the sun was nearing its end. 'My definitions of success have changed,' he told *Rolling Stone.* 'If you'd asked me that question a year and a half ago...I would say it was a failure, definitely. [But] you're talking to a guy who, in a two year span, lost his mother, lost his drummer – the person he was closest to in the band – and got divorced. To have gone through that tunnel and come out the other side, I'm happy.' And he remained equally unperturbed by the more perceptive of critics who might have sensed that Corgan himself was aware that a crisis point had been reached. No matter what the future held, after all, he was secure in the knowledge that, to the people who cared, *Adore* still mattered. And, though their days *were* numbered, though that fact had not yet been revealed, so did the Smashing Pumpkins.

CHAPTER TWENTY

AND WHERE DO WE GO FROM HERE?

Corgan, or course, wasn't nearly finished. He'd already recorded a handful of acoustic demos for the final Smashing Pumpkins album at Sadlands; had already vowed to himself that the band was going to pull out all the stops, record something that would set fans' hair on fire and test the loyalty of anyone who'd been around since *Gish*. And there would be no apologies.

Throughout their career...that itself had now, incredibly, passed the ten-year mark...the Smashing Pumpkins had placed themselves in the unique position of being able to do whatever they wanted to do, following a path that they'd mapped in a very deliberate manner, and working their way from one sound to another, knowing that even if they weren't sure where they were going, they'd like it when they finally arrived there.

No one had anticipated the frightful events of summer 1996 and, once all was said and done, no one, except the band, perhaps, expected the Smashing Pumpkins to continue, let alone record again. What would have happened had Melvoin not died, had Chamberlin remained in the band through the end of the *Mellon Collie* tour, and into the recording of *Adore*?

Would that album have emerged so electronically-inclined as it did, had it been built around the bigger beats that Chamberlin nailed down, rather than the softer sonics? And, would the Smashing Pumpkins have set themselves up for the cracked wickedness of what became *Machina/The Machines Of God*, its aftermath? It's impossible to say. But the course that the Smashing Pumpkins embarked upon post-the infinite sadness of the *Mellon Collie* era could never have been predicted by any observer; including the Smashing Pumpkins themselves.

By the end of 1998, with the bulk of his intended demos already in place, Corgan had utterly laid to waste the aura of *Adore* and was itching to get to work on the next album. Flood was slated to work in the studio during recording and, as the band tramped into Pumpkinland in November for their first go round, they already had more than a dozen songs in progress. Yet songs were not to be the issue on *Machina/The Machines Of God*. It was moods, textures and sensations that the band sought, a process that would keep them locked into the studio almost permanently for the next ten months. And, when they did finally re-emerge, blinking into the sunlight, it was in considerably altered state. The dying season was beginning – although, in typical Smashing Pumpkins style, it first commenced with a rebirth.

In February 1999, the *L.A. Times* ran a story claiming that Jimmy Chamberlin was on the verge of returning to the band. The drummer had remained completely off both the band and the fans' radar for almost three years now, a period during which he had finally conquered every one of the demons that assailed him during his years with the Smashing Pumpkins.

But was the story – which itself arose from rumours that had been circulating since the release of *Adore* – true? Nobody could pin it down. Certainly there was a large dose of wishful thinking bound up in the allegations – no matter how artistically delicious *Adore* had emerged, there were many listeners who were convinced that it missed Chamberlin; that the Smashing Pumpkins missed Chamberlin, and that much of their latter-day eclecticism was simply a form of over-compensation, an attempt to convince themselves, even more than their fans, that they did not miss the drummer's outstanding style and preternatural sense of timing; that the jive between his sticks and the rest of the band could be replaced with lush orchestration.

Balanced against that, however, was the ferocity with which the Smashing Pumpkins themselves had pledged that they wanted no further dealings with the drummer, and the single-mindedness with which they remained silent now, still sequestered in the studio even when Iha himself emerged to put the finishing touches to his own latest extra-curricular venture, the Stratosphere Sound studio.

Located in New York's hip Chelsea district, Stratosphere Sound was a partnership formed by Iha, Adam Schlesinger and Andy Chase, one of Schlesinger's band mates in Scratchie label heroes, Ivy. It was originally envisioned as a cool and comfortably gear-loaded place in which they could record both their own projects, and work with various Scratchie artists. Quickly, however, the studio threw its doors open to other performers – as Iha put it, 'we say unto thee, come record. We welcome any artist.'

The studio got off to a rocky start when a fire in the restaurant downstairs damaged the space. Undeterred, the trio packed up bands, gear and tapes and relocated a few blocks, from West 14th Street to 239 11th Ave. and a completely re-invented three thousand square foot space that was designed by New York based designer Francis Manzella, and boasted two complete studios and more equipment to play with than anyone could ever want. As Iha put it, 'it just feels like a very homey, cool, grown-up version of the old place' and, in the years since Stratosphere Sound first opened its doors, acts ranging from Ivy and Arto Lindsay to Me'Shell Ndegéocello have taken advantage of its cosiness, while Smashing Pumpkins' cohorts Fountains Of Wayne, and Melissa Auf Der Maur have also made good use of the studio.

While Iha was occupied with setting up Stratosphere Sound, Corgan took the opportunity to fulfil an ambition that surely dated back to his childhood, when he was invited to contribute to the latest album by Tony Iommi, the doom laden guitar god who once ground Black Sabbath through their majestic paces.

Black Sabbath themselves had long since been transformed into little more than a museum piece, a slumbering beast that arose periodically for a sell-out tour of the arenas, but was more frequently sighted in no place more challenging than the reissue racks. Iommi himself, however, operated a solo career that was at least as dynamic (if not, perhaps, so commercially bankable) as former vocalist Ozzy Osbourne's, with his latest project delighting not only in mining his own musical past, but also in recruiting the cream of modern musicianship to accompany him on the journey.

And so Foo Fighters' frontman Dave Grohl rubbed shoulders with Ozzy Osbourne, Pantera's Phil Anselmo stood alongside the Cult's Ian Astbury, as Iommi sought a middle ground that would prove 'an amalgamation of it all.' Both writing and recording with his guests, Iommi visualised an album that offered something for everyone, 'a selection of old to new. The only [person] I couldn't get was Tom Jones. I wanted to get him on, but he was doing his own project.' Corgan, on the other hand, would have moved heaven and earth to make his appearance, arriving at the studio alongside the Smashing Pumpkins' *Adore*-era drummer Kenny Aronoff, and settling instantly into the relaxed groove that Iommi required from the outset. 'In the morning we came up with a riff,' enthused Iommi. By lunchtime they had a title, 'Black Oblivion,' 'and in the afternoon, we were putting it to tape,' It really was that simple.

Corgan took another step outside of the Smashing Pumpkins on 25 March, when he joined his father on stage in Chicago, to take part in the Neon Street Program For Homeless Youth's First Waltz benefit. Performing alongside an impressive line-up that included Rick Danko of the Band, the Mekons' Jon Langford and Cheap Trick's Rick Nelson, all ballbusting their way through an impressive blues revue, Corgans Sr and Jr played just two songs, the tributary 'Muddy Waters' and a rocked out version of the Robert Johnson Delta Blues classic 'If I Had Possession Over Judgement Day.'

The Smashing Pumpkins swung back into action little more than a week later. With the California based Queens Of The Stone Age in tow, they launched the *Arising* tour on 10 April at St. Andrew's in Detroit, Michigan. It was a purposefully low-key outing; determined, this time, to return to basics, the band insisted that they play no venue with a capacity beyond a couple of thousand fans, and do so without any of the rigmarole of a heavily promoted outing. Several of the gigs existed as little more than word-of-mouth exercises, but that mattered little – every venue sold out well in advance of the show itself; and well in advance of the first night's confirmation of the speculation that had sprung to such thrilling light a few months previous. Quietly and unobtrusively, Jimmy Chamberlin had slipped back behind the drum kit. For once, the rumours were right.

The drummer admitted, later, that the return to action was intimidating. In the years since he slipped from the limelight, he had turned completely away from the life he'd known since he was a teenager, throwing himself into a passion that he had never had time to cultivate in the past, as a licensed car racer. He did keep his drumming hand in trim, of course, working as a music teacher in Chicago, and that seemed to be enough for the time being. It loosened him up, put his mind back on track, and that, he said later, was 'so rewarding. I think it's really important to share what you've got.'

The nature of this return to the Smashing Pumpkins' spotlight was itself designed to help Chamberlin ease back into his old role – small clubs, intimate atmospheres, and a relaxed schedule that saw the group play just nine shows in a month. Then it was back to the studio, to continue piecing together the new album. It was as though the last three years had never happened.

Machina/The Machines Of God was falling nicely into place. Ethereal and heavy, dreamy, hypnotic and full to overflowing with all the electronic twists and bells that Corgan had long admired, the album was set to fulfil a promise he had made around the time of *Siamese Dream* when he'd expressed an interest in creating 'something pretty heavily technological…turn to One Inch Nails.' The pretty pastures of *Adore* could not have been further from the landscape and, when Corgan was quizzed by *Rolling Stone* as to what might be expected, and whether he was drawing any influence from the current state of rock'n' roll, he reflected that he hadn't heard a single record all year that he enjoyed. Instead, he was turning once again back to his halcyon 70s and further still.

'You don't want to know what's in my CD changer,' he counselled, and then proceeded to map out a landscape that stretched from Maria Callas and Phillip Glass to Lynyrd Skynyrd and Rainbow. 'I'm reluctant to talk about what the next Pumpkins record is going to sound like,' he said. 'But I will tell you, it's going to sound a lot like Mountain.'

Among the other musicians brought in to flesh out the *Machina/The Machines Of God* soundscapes was, perhaps inevitably, Mike Garson. His own commitments ensured he would appear on just one track, the superlative 'Light,' but around the Smashing Pumpkins' sessions, he and Corgan did find time to collaborate on another project, as they teamed up to score the Rupert Wainwright movie thriller, *Stigmata*.

The pair had been talking for some time about trying to do something 'different,' about creating something that fell far from their traditional stamping grounds – the invitation to compose the score, then, brought these ambitions to swift fruition; allowed them, in fact, to raise the bar even further and, as

Corgan put it, 'set about [making] music that would hopefully stand up on its own, without the movie.'

Bearing in mind that it is almost impossible for anyone to create an instrumental swathe for the screen that retains compete meaning when divorced from the visuals, they came very close to succeeding. Sparse, electronic and contemporary, the score does stand on its own across songs that exist and come to closure in their own right, but the entire performance does better when matched to the film – for that, after all, was how it was crafted in the first place. The pair paid exquisite detail to the celluloid frames, matching moods and moments to the film and its characters. 'The music for "Identify" [for example] came from one of the love scenes in the movie,' Corgan explained. 'Mike…and I decided to make that cue the title song, and the words were written from Patricia Arquette's character, Frankie's perspective.'

The soundtrack was delivered to stores in two separate formats, one comprising a vocal soundtrack disc alone, packed with contributions from David Bowie, Massive Attack and Remy Zero, together with 'Identify,' as performed by Natalie Imbruglia; the other a double CD, added on Corgan and Garson's instrumental score.

Such activity both within and without the Smashing Pumpkins camp very much gave the impression that it was business as usual for the band. A new album was imminent, a fresh tour was being scheduled, and the classic line-up had been reconstituted. Yet there was one niggling doubt that continued simmering just beneath the surface – a doubt that would, when confirmed, see the nature of the group changed forever.

The *Adore* tour was still underway when the first rumours began drifting around the music industry that relations within the Smashing Pumpkins were souring; that Wretzky and Corgan, in particular, were clashing on a regular basis. The group themselves kept their own counsel – they were experienced enough to know that the bitterest rifts were part and parcel of the touring life, as minds tired and tempers frayed, and bodies wanted nothing more than to collapse exhaustedly into bed and not be disturbed for a month.

The Smashing Pumpkins themselves seemed impervious to the story-telling; they had, of course, continued on exactly as before. But the rumours wouldn't quit and neither, as the summer passed, would the insistence that something major was about to unfurl. And, in September 1999, it did. Wretzky was quitting the band.

Of course, there had been rumours swirling forever, it seemed, and the air was rife with whispers that Corgan and Wretzky were clashing over everything and nothing. There were reports that Wretzky was angry that Jimmy Chamberlin had been given another chance with the band, there were voices that swore Wretzky just wanted to do her own thing – solo projects, movie acting, just finding herself alone, without what had become the bitter spectre of the band hanging over her head, and apparently, around her neck.

There had been more firm allusions to Wretzky's departure too, in the weeks leading up to the early September break, but only if you knew where and how to look. Corgan himself, giving an interview to the *Chicago Tribune* newspaper in August, revealed that he was glad that the band was 'back together for the moment. How long that is going to last I don't know.'

Much later, in early 2004, Corgan expounded on the long, convoluted dissolution of the Smashing Pumpkins on his web-site, alleging that it was not so much that Wretzky quit, but that '[she] was fired for being a mean spirited drug addict, who refused to get help'. But Corgan also admitted that, while her departure 'didn't help keep the band together...it made it very hard to go on, but we soldiered through it even though our hearts were broken.'

For Wretzky, though, the break was a move that was long overdue. She said at the time that, for her, the experience of being with the band was 'like being married to three other people. Imagine being on a tour bus with them, living with them and working with them,' she says. 'People you didn't pick. It's like people you didn't want to date.' The straw had snapped, shattered. The implosion was beginning.

And fired, quit, shattered, imploded – whatever – the fact remained true that Wretzky's autumn departure left a wide wound in the band, a raw and gaping hole that would have to be filled, and quickly if the tour wasn't to be completely derailed. She seemed to slip out of the band's memory with a rapidity that was incongruous to a collective that had spent the better part of a decade in each other's company. And, probably thankfully, what transpired behind the scenes remained private, and the band stuck together, shaky, but together – for the time being.

Dropping out of the band's radar, Wretzky would move on, to feature films, she hoped. She was slated to star with bad boy Mickey Rourke in a project titled *Pieces Of Ronnie* but, when that film was abandoned, she returned from Los Angeles to Chicago. There, she hit the headlines again when she was arrested on 25 January 2000 for possession of crack cocaine – a charge that she maintained was false. And, indeed, all charges were dropped, and she was sentenced to probation and a three month drug awareness course at a court hearing in February. She continued to percolate through the musical ether, in between long sojourns at the normal life she'd not had during her tenure with the Smashing Pumpkins – a span of years that had occupied nearly one third of her life.

She guested on Filter's 'Cancer', from their *Title Of Record* album, and that band's Richard Patrick remembers that 'it's a thing I really enjoyed. We're good friends and she was kind of hanging out, so she told me to sound more boyish...and I thought "Why don't you just do it?" So she pushed me aside and sang the song over these bombastic drums and big loud guitar and her beautiful voice on top of it.'

Wretzky's abrupt departure could have left the Smashing Pumpkins in chaos. However, with a new tour scheduled to start at the Cabaret Metro in December, before the band headed to Europe to close out the millennium and ring in a new era, they had a little breathing room available in which to regain their bearings. Wretzky's departure would shift their sound; that was inevitable. Her rolling, roiling bass had evolved into the beat that beat back Corgan's and Iha's dual guitar assault and, no matter who the Smashing Pumpkins found to fill her shoes, there would be a change. However, the group had already proved they could go with the flow when they replaced Chamberlin. And, as it turned out, a replacement bassist was right around the corner...and closer to home as well.

Almost from the moment that Wretzky's departure was announced, mutterings abounded that Hole's Melissa Auf Der Maur would be replacing her on tour. It would, after all, be an easy extrication – like the Smashing Pumpkins' post-Chamberlin array of drummers, Auf Der Maur had never formally joined Hole, operating instead as a contract musician

Of course the rumours were furiously denied by both her band and by their record company, Universal. But, as is so often the case, they could deny, deny, deny all they wanted. It still didn't alter the truth. At the end of September, Auf Der Maur bowed out of the band she'd been with since 1994, announcing she intended moving on to 'solo projects.'

Now the only question was, would she, or wouldn't she join the Smashing Pumpkins? It would be close to a full month before Billy Corgan finally answered the question.

Taking time out from buffing the last remaining rough edges from the album, both Corgan and Iha were invited to perform at the latest Bridge Benefit concerts on October 30 and 31 1999. Walking onstage, Corgan announced that they'd hoped to have their new bassist, Melissa Auf Der Maur indeed, join them. Unfortunately, she wasn't able to, so they'd be performing as a duo instead. It was about as official as it could get – Melissa Auf Der Maur was a Pumpkin.

Corgan and Iha, meanwhile, muddled through a set that included 'Stand Inside Your Love' and 'Glass + The Ghost Children' from the forthcoming Machina/The Machines Of God album (at that time still going under the title Desolation), alongside covers of Tom Waits' 'ol' 55' and U2's 'Stay'. Later in the show Jimmy Chamberlin joined Corgan and Iha on stage and, with such a public re-introduction in the wake of the low-key Arising tour dates earlier that summer, he resoundingly reclaimed his rightful place in the band's line up.

By the end of November, all the waiting was over for good, as the Smashing Pumpkins finally revealed the correct title of the album and formally announced the addition of Auf Der Maur. After all the build up, she finally made her live debut with the Smashing Pumpkins as the band rounded out the year with a pair of shows at the Cabaret Metro on 20 and 21 December, treating the packed house to a set that focused on songs from the upcoming album, (now slated, after several delays, for release at the end of February 2000), alongside a clutch of old favourites – '1979,' 'Bullet With Butterfly Wings' and a surprising reappearance for the now elderly 'I Am One,' together with a rollicking version of the David Essex classic 'Rock On,' itself destined to become both a live staple and, from the joyous demeanour of the band as they rattled through their set, a mantra that would take the Smashing Pumpkins firmly into the new millennium. They would, indeed, rock on.

CHAPTER TWENTY ONE
THE MEN WHO FELL TO EARTH

With their latest World Tour kicking off in Stockholm, Sweden on 7 January 2000, it seemed that once again, the band were riding an up-current. Even a brief hiccup in the Smashing Pumpkins' management could not derail the sense of optimism that swirled around them – back in October, the group had signed with Sharon Osbourne's management company, but just three months later, on 11 January, the future star of reality television and the talk show circuit (not to mention the mastermind behind husband Ozzy's continuing career) was publicly walking out on the job. Uttering the now famous statement in which she insisted 'I must resign…due to medical reasons. Billy Corgan was making me sick,' Osbourne was out, and the band were on their own.

Osbourne delved deeper into the problem in a now-legendary interview with *Q* magazine that March. Referring to Corgan's still-favoured Nosferatu look, the man she described as 'a six foot baldy twat in a dress,' she growled, had 'an ego bigger than my arse,' admitting that the final straws came via Corgan's already fractious relationship with the media. First, he demanded that both control over, and the copyright in any interviews he granted be surrendered to him – a condition that was never going to fly; then, preparing for an interview with another *Q* reporter, convincing himself that, 'by trying to humiliate [the] writer, he would earn respect. I bet him a thousand dollars that it wouldn't lead to a wonderful arse-licking story' – and she was right.

'The sad thing is, he's a nice person underneath all the bullshit. Unfortunately…he's extremely competitive and that's a bit sad. *Adore* was a great record, but as soon as it wasn't a major success, he blamed the record company, sacked his…management' and completely overlooked the fact that 'it wasn't a particularly commercial record.'

In light of all that the band had endured over the last few years, of course, such turbulence was little more than a minor inconvenience, and the Smashing Pumpkins continued to tear up Europe throughout January, providing a sharp preview for the album's ever-looming release on the last day of February. Back home, they turned in an appearance on political satirist and comedian Bill

Maher's *Politically Incorrect* television programme on 30 January, performing 'The Everlasting Gaze' and 'Stand Inside Your Love'; at the same time, American radio began gearing up for the group's re-emergence when it, too, received the first play copies of 'The Everlasting Gaze.' And the following evening, 31 January, the Smashing Pumpkins embarked upon the wryly titled Resume The Pose tour of the US.

Machina / The Machines Of God was a miraculous piece of work. It brought spit-biting hatred from many, and adoration for a job well done from others. It was divisive and demonized, and it was utterly unlike anything that the Smashing Pumpkins had ever released in the past. It sparked controversy, it sparked rabid debate among fans, and its content, musical and otherwise, led more than one person to wonder if Billy Corgan had finally gone off his rocker.

The first thing one encountered upon opening the CD was an expansive booklet that was printed to look like rough-hewn wood, and contained a mightily abstract array of religious iconography from a host of belief systems. Indeed, the booklet was as much a work of art as the album itself. The paintings and etchings printed onto aged vellum was majestic, a prelude and a postscript to a short, two page piece of prose that, buried deep within the package, purported to be an excerpt from *Glass And The Machines Of God* – a story, a mythology, a Corgan-penned epic that, disguised as an oddly written stream of consciousness, clashed Patti Smith's rambling prose with John Bunyan's cautionary *Pilgrim's Process* to produce…what? Corgan's own views on the meaning of his life? Or a complete and utter put on? Or maybe even a combination of them both?

The narrative was continued on an insert included in the vinyl release of *Machina/The Machines Of God*, while Corgan seeded further speculation as he tapped into the internet with his online tour diary, *Chards Of Glass*. Therein, he disseminated whatever information and ramblings he felt like – unfettered by the censorship of listening journalists or watching cameras, he held forth on the state of the band, the state of the world and the state of his head. He also began leaking songs to his public, drawing from the stockpile of unreleased demos and live material that had been floating around the tape traders forever, but had always eluded the mainstream fan.

It was also an early taste of a major treat that the band were planning for fall – a full internet-only collection of *Machina/The Machines Of God* out-takes and offcuts that would be freely available to anyone with download and MP3 capabilities. *Machina II/ The Friends And Enemies Of Modern Music* would be neither the first album to be released in that format, nor were the Smashing Pumpkins any longer the biggest band to have done so. But, amid the continued unravelling of the parent album's inner meanings, it was certainly among the most eagerly anticipated. The only black spot on the entire horizon was the one that hung over Virgin Records, as they were faced with trying to figure out what to do about an album that was released for the sole purpose of being bootlegged.

As it transpired, the true meaning of the *Machines Of God* fable would never be satisfactorily deciphered, not even after the entire tale was finally posted on the internet in January 2001. In the lead up to that anti-climactic publication, however, fans had a whale of a time puzzling over the symbolism of the words, how they related to the album and what exactly it all meant. Of course, it gave the press another glib field day as well – and Corgan must have loved every minute of it, for whatever the actual meaning of the essay, whatever *Glass And The Machines Of God* was designed to reveal, it was a delightful accompaniment to the music on both *Machina/The Machines Of God* and *Machina II/ The Friends And Enemies Of Modern Music*. And the end result was a bloated, beautiful, tribute to every modern concept album ever released.

Corgan warmed to that theme in period interviews, although he continued to be purposefully obtuse. 'The concept is part of the mythology of the band,' he teased, explaining that as the *Machina/The Machines Of God* project came to fruition, the Smashing Pumpkins found themselves with two options – to tell the *Machina* story straight up, and include a cheat sheet that keyed into the deeper meanings (assuming there were any), or draw the whole experience out into one long, torturous tease, to 'create a mystery reverse energy where people were sucked into it' and draw, from their own understanding of the words and music, all the symbolism and meaning that they themselves required from the experience. In other words, a concept album where the concept itself was the listener's own imagination. Brilliant.

All of that, of course, was dropped into the expectant listener's lap before the album even hit the machine – there to spit out the oddest, and some of the most oddly beautiful songs the Smashing Pumpkins had ever recorded. Deep, heavy, lush, dreamy, drugged – these adjectives all described the package the Corgan and his reunited band had put together, an achievement that was soured only in that Wretzky, one quarter of the most creative quartet the new millennium had to offer, was not there to share in the limelight that now devoured her erstwhile band mates.

From the feedback fuzz of 'Blue Skies Bring Tears,' that pinned listeners to the ground, to the full frontal dark rock assault of 'Stand Inside Your Love' which Corgan initially 'envisioned as a New Wave song,' the Smashing Pumpkins hadn't simply departed from their usual style and sound, they had allowed the entire circus to turn full circle, and posit the music they might have made had *Machina/The Machines Of God* been their first album…and not their last. Same inputs, same influences, same players. But their mood was based now on the experience of the worldly-wise, not the excitement of the virginal ingénues, and the ensuing blaze of deteriorating stars sparked with every sound they'd ever recorded, with every nuance they'd ever cupped. It was the most triumphant statement they could make.

Following on from the radio-only thrust of 'The Everlasting Gaze,' which wasn't only awash in feedback and fuzz, but drowned in it, the first single, 'Stand Inside Your Love,' was an obvious choice to break the album to the masses. Opening with a deep drum beat and the now-classic Smashing Pumpkins guitar, the song suckered listeners in to what could easily have been mistaken for a return to the days of *Mellon Collie and the Infinite Sadness*.and 'Tonight, Tonight' era balladeering.

And, truly, while both songs straddled the sonic dichotomy that now epitomized the Smashing Pumpkins, the magic of *Machina/The Machines of God* lay strewn amongst the other songs on the album. What the band had once only dreamed they'd grasp, they now recorded effortlessly. 'Raindrops and Sunshowers,' in particular, would emerge a glorious rendition of every tide the band had ever tempered. With a snappy pace and an all-enveloping beat that thrummed in heartbeat time, 'Raindrops and Sunshowers' was poignantly happy, a love song for the sappy everyman with enough brainpan clatter to chase the cobwebs out.

There was indeed a little something for everyone on this album. Feedback lovers could happily bang heads to 'The Impending Voice' or 'Heavy Metal Machine', while both 'Try Try Try' and 'With Every Light' emerged sing-along smoothies for a mellower crowd. But, with all these *classic* Smashing Pumpkins' sounds in abundance, it would have been easy to overlook several moments on *Machina/The Machines of God* that took the Smashing Pumpkins and Billy Corgan especially, into another realm entirely.

Both the bittersweet, and presumably personal 'The Crying Tree Of Mercury' and the pure Cure meets Bauhaus goth grind of the unyielding 'Glass And The Ghost Children' were so wildly skewed from any anticipation, that any comparisons to what the band had done previously seemed less than worthless. And, while the latter, in particular, would spark debate as to exactly how sane Corgan was, both songs were illustrative of just how far he'd come.

Clocking in at a whisper under ten minutes, 'Glass And The Ghost Children' ensured that Corgan would be the recipient of an awful lot of flak; from critics, from fans and from people who wondered just what the hell he was getting at. Lushly electronic, awash with patient noodly bits, it was the meat of the song, the warped tape confessions that Corgan included in the heart, which caused people to stop, listen, and then begin backing away slowly.

Nobody knew exactly what this minute and a half spoken word interlude meant. Was it a small excerpt from his religious vision? His personal manifesto? Or simply the story of 'Glass'? Was Corgan laying bare those things that rested most heavily on his heart, or was it fictional meandering? Had the writer left behind the veiled biography of past song lyrics for an in-your-face confession of what was in his brain, or was this just the tortured artiste stroking an already massive ego? Did he really think God was speaking through him – or was God *really* speaking through him?

No matter, whether you believed that Corgan had gone off the rails completely, or that he'd just taken his music to another level, or even if you felt that the hand of God Himself reached down through the heavens to puppet Corgan, and indeed had been doing so since the band formed, it was moments like these that brought the Smashing Pumpkins to a halt. It was moments like these that made people inordinately uncomfortable. It was moments like these that caused strong reaction.

But, as far as the band were concerned, that was all another level of smoke and mirrors, another seed to plant, another row to sow. They had other things on their minds, and live shows to tend to. As the end of the Resume The Pose tour wound into view, and the group abandoned stage work for a series of in store appearances and record-signing sessions around the US and Canada, *Machina/The Machines Of God* shot into the Billboard charts at number three, before commencing the slow downward turn that, in the modern age, is the apparent fate of every new release. Again, it was a poor performance when compared to the heights that the Smashing Pumpkins once scaled, but such criticism is, surely, subject to so many caveats that, to analyse a band's popularity based upon the fickle frailties of the mainstream audience is pointless. History states that *Machina/The Machines Of God* spent just thirteen weeks on the American chart, and qualified for a gold disc alone – their lowest-selling album ever. But history will also bear out its brilliance, and remind us that a lot of classic albums started life as bombs. Ask the Velvet Underground about that.

The next leg of the band's journey kicked off on 8 April, as they launched the Sacred And Profane Tour in Kansas. And, again, any sense that all things were smooth in the Pumpkin camp, was swiftly to be shattered. At the end of May, Corgan resurrected the comment he had made once before, years before, when he insisted that the Smashing Pumpkins would be destroyed and defunct by the end of the year. This time, however, few listeners were inclined to call his bluff.

Fans were stunned, but probably not surprised. The rumour mill had never ceased churning out stories about this rift and that since the band had formed. Detractors did little more than sneer – great grunge gods always imploded in the end, didn't they?

But did they? Or was there another meaning to the band's graceful collapse...the fulfilment of some dark prophecy that Corgan made to himself years before, perhaps, or even an acknowledgement of one of rock'n'roll's own most potent truisms, brought back to screaming life at a time when the very opposite seemed to be the rule...*live fast, die young, leave a beautiful corpse*.

Too many of Rock's previous gods had thrown that law into the garbage years ago, as they trotted out onto the revival circuit one more time, to hope they grew old, rich and fat before they died, and not care a hoot for the memories and dreams that they trampled on in the process.

The Smashing Pumpkins, of course, still have time to make that same mistake themselves. Ten years, twenty years, can heal a lot of rifts; can cause any number of bold intentions to evaporate with the wind. That is their decision... that is their right. But it would also be their mistake. For what would be the point? By the time the Smashing Pumpkins released *Machina/The Machines of God*, they'd come so far from where they started that one wondered, exactly where they could go next. Had they wrapped themselves up in such a tangle that there was no alternative but to depart? Or had they simply done what they'd set out to do all along, and now chose to bow out gracefully rather than flogging the donkey for another half decade?

Corgan himself opted for the former. It was not the Smashing Pumpkins alone who had failed in their quest. Alternative Rock itself was finished, crushed beneath the welter of 'new' 'talent' that rushed to stand in the first wave of bands' already-crowded footsteps, to dilute and diminish even the greatest past accomplishments in the name of increasing financial returns.

'I use the analogy of being given the keys to the car,' Corgan sighed. 'But instead of driving the car, establishing our corner of the market, our parameters, our sense of what the music business should be, we kinda said "we don't want 'em": and dropped the keys. And somebody else came along and picked them up. Now bands like us are suffering in an environment more suited to a band that's willing to do whatever, to get wherever.'

It was a betrayal of all that the original movement of the 1990s had stood for, of course, but it was an wholly self-inflicted betrayal. 'We had a chance to control, to have more say, more interest in what actually goes on within the music business...[an] opportunity to redefine what the music business is about, like baseball players with free agency. But, in order to do that, you have to be in a commanding position...and we just didn't take it.'

For the time being it was business as usual. In August, the Smashing Pumpkins recorded a show for VH1's sometimes-spectacular *Storytellers* series, at New York's Hammerstein Ballroom. Set for broadcast on 4 November, the event featured an extraordinarily garrulous Corgan spinning a wealth of entertaining yarns as the band dove in and out of *Machina/Machines Of God*, although the lucky audience were treated to earlier favourites '1979' and 'Today'.

Corgan waxed poetic on the genesis of 'Try Try Try', written while on a James Iha sanctioned vacation to New York's Long Island, and delved into prophecy before playing 'Thirty-Three,' explaining to the audience that 'I have a friend read my tarot cards and the person said that "when you're thirty-three years old" – this is when I was twenty-seven – "when you're thirty-three years old, your life is going to completely change." So, as I sit here today at thirty-three years old, my life is going to completely change at thirty-three.'

Corgan and the rest of the Pumpkins appeared to enjoy themselves, although Corgan, who was known for his many, many rants and raves and diatribes in between and even during songs at Pumpkins' gigs, did admit that 'it's very strange talking so much, I'm not used to it.' It was hard to be in the spotlight, to expound on songs, to talk about their genesis, to delve deep into the muck and haul out thoughts, dreams and histories often better left behind. And, for someone like Corgan, who'd been notoriously private about his lyrics, who felt that they should just be taken as they were, it must have been doubly tough. He pulled it off, however, as he had pulled off everything else over the last decade. But now, it was time to pull away.

In September, the Smashing Pumpkins 'released' *Machina II/The Friends And Enemies Of Modern Music*. Printed as an enduring farewell and lasting gift to all who'd been so supportive, this last album was pressed out over two full LPs and three ten inch records, totalling five discs. Packed with all new music, a paltry twenty-five copies were pressed and carefully disbursed by the band, with the instructions to put the music further afield.

There was a sense of closure bound up within such an eclectic issue, an eccentric gesture, a symbolic return to the miniscule distribution of those first cassettes that the band manufactured back before they had even released a record. They too, had since been widely disseminated via the ingenuity of the internet; they too, are a preciously guarded secret among the faithful. The difference is, wheras those cassettes bespoke a bold beginning, this latest release merely signalled the end.

By the end of the summer it was apparent that the band was winding down and, by the time autumn had closed around them, the Sacred And Profane tour had metamorphosed into an unashamed Farewell Tour. It was official. The band toured through Japan and Canada and then went on to Europe. The end was so close you could touch it.

During the few months left to them, the Smashing Pumpkins concentrated upon regaling saddened audiences with huge sets that rewound the band's entire history, then spooled it out across nearly a decade of hits. Rubbing shoulders with a patiently poignant take on the Talking Heads' 'Once In A Lifetime,' 'Rock On' was still a regular in the set, but it hung far from the affirmation that it had once appeared; far from the promise of great times to come that its first performances seemed to evince. Rather, Corgan's ever-sharpened appreciation of the importance of myth to rock'n'roll music brought to the song a saddened edge, an ironic shrug, a weary farewell. The kids could rock on forever. But their elders had other things to accomplish.

Bidding a final *adieu* to the UK and Europe, the Smashing Pumpkins were home by mid-November, to premier 'Cash, Car, Star' on TV's *Tonight Show With Jay Leno* on the eighteenth. Originally recorded during the sessions for

Adore, a redrawn rendition of the song now graced *Machina II* – the album, of course, that wasn't an album. It was the Smashing Pumpkins' first ever appearance on America's top-rated late night talk show – and it was the last broadcast they would ever make.

On 29 November, the Smashing Pumpkins performed their penultimate concert, at Chicago's United Center. It was an emotional, raucous affair that lasted some three and a half hours as the band regaled the sold out crowd with three solid sets, digging all the way back to 'Rhinoceros' in search of material, then bringing things up to date with numbers that was still fresh on the group's internet website. Mike Garson and Chris Holmes, the Chicago based founder of both the *Dr. Who* inspired Sabalon Glitz and Yum-Yum, both appeared on stage as the concert wore on, but perhaps the most the most poignant moment of all occurred near the end of the show, when William Corgan Sr appeared on stage to join his son on a heartfelt version of 'For Martha'.

Three nights later, it was all over – appropriately enough, in the same hallowed halls that it all began, as the Smashing Pumpkins returned once again to the Cabaret Metro on 2 December. A thousand people crammed into the club – but still it felt like a private party; or, perhaps, a private wake.

The night went on forever; checking watches as they finally left the venue at the end of the evening, exhausted onlookers realised that the Smashing Pumpkins had played for over four hours, with the stage a constant blur of action as guest after special guest poured on to share in the bands' final moment of glory – Cheap Trick's Rick Nelson, ex- touring drummer Matt Walker, the Frogs' Dennis and Jimmy Flemion – all stood alongside Corgan, Iha, Chamberlin and Auf Der Maur as they pulled the curtain down on a career that played itself out to the last note with grace.

Tears flowed at that final show – fans who'd won tickets inside were matched in emotion by the throngs who hung on the sidewalks outside, straining to hear their Alternative god speak just a few words more. And there were crocodile tears shed, too, by the masses who'd derided the band for nearly their entire existence, and now proclaimed that the world would be a whole lot emptier without the Smashing Pumpkins to fill the void.

And as the strains of the last song died down, and the band packed their gear for the last time and left the building, Corgan finally did what he said he would. He called it quits on the Smashing Pumpkins, and never looked back. Neither would there be any further explanations.

Drawing on the ancient fable that had so informed the band's iconography in the past, he merely acknowledged, 'based on where we began,' the Smashing Pumpkins had fulfilled all they could have ever hoped to. But 'based on the potential we had,' they could have flown much higher. 'We got pretty close to the sun,' he said, '[but then] we Icarused.'

CHAPTER TWENTY TWO
POST MORTEM

Billy Corgan did not look back, and neither did the rest of the band, as they swaggered off into the sunset, the colors of the Alternative revolution bleeding down to darkness behind them. But that doesn't mean that the band were dead, buried, forgotten and rotting in eternity. Their very afterlife was a rebirth of sorts, one that commenced almost as soon as the lights were extinguished on their decade-long show.

A little over a year after the break-up, Virgin released the band's first, and only, greatest hits album, *(Rotten Apples) Greatest Hits*, a career-spanning tribute that peaked on the fringe of the Top Thirty on both sides of the Atlantic. It was an inevitable gesture, of course, and could easily have proven as sour-tasting as its title. Yet *(Rotten Apples)* was a welcome surprise. Packaged as both a single and double CD, the first disc collected the band's hits, leaving the second, more delicious, *Judas O* set to follow in the footsteps of *Pisces Iscariot* by corralling a generous helping of previously unreleased material. From 'Winterlong' and 'Lucky 13' to the live staple 'Rock On', *Judas O* laid to rest many of the legends that the band had laid to waste.

A video hits package and the long-awaited upgrade of *Vieuphoria* followed, but Corgan, at least, was not prepared to rest back on the laurels of his past. The self-described workaholic leapt gleefully back into the fray.

Although he'd sidestepped the Pumpkins' threads, no one believed for a moment that Corgan's face would remain in the shadows for long. Indeed, that same summer, another circle from so many years ago was closed as Corgan accepted an invitation from Peter Hook to work with New Order on their forthcoming comeback album, *Get Ready*. Corgan added vocals to one song, 'Turn My Way' and, by July, he was gearing up to join the band as a guest guitarist as they hit several warm up shows in England before joining Moby's *Area: One* festival in the United States at the end of the month.

Corgan debuted on stage with the band in Liverpool for a preview show and New Order leader Peter Hook was thrilled. For him and his bandmates, the group's revival represented a new era, a new start with a new crowd; for

Corgan, it was a chance to get up on stage and play with some of his idols. Hook said of the experience, 'Billy enjoyed it, which was amazing, because he was absolutely terrified...more nervous than me, which I didn't think was possible.' Corgan did enjoy it. It was, he told *Kerrang!* magazine, 'just a bloody fucking fantastic experience.'

Corgan would continue to rub shoulders with blasts from the past, as he also turned up among the supporting cast on 1960s doyenne Marianne Faithfull's latest album, August 2002's *Kissin' Time*. The most recent in a series of collaborations that linked Faithfull with well-chosen musicians from beyond her own immediate peer group, *Kissin' Time* also commissioned the talents of Pulp's Jarvis Cocker, Beck, the Eurythmics' Dave Stewart and Blur; for his part, Corgan would co-write and appear on two tracks recorded during the spring of 2001, 'I'm On Fire' and 'Wherever I Go,' plus a masterful rendition of the Herman's Hermits' chestnut 'I'm Into Something Good.' Later, following the album's release, he appeared alongside Faithfull for her 11 September 2002 appearance on the *Late Show With David Letterman*.

If outside projects were going well, Corgan's inside track was going even better. In March 2001, he joined a host of musicians, including Faithfull and Wilco's Jeff Tweedy at the Cabaret Metro for a blow-out charity show for the Third Waltz benefit to help local homeless youth. Clad in black and bald, Corgan blistered through an eclectic assortment of songs, taking the lead on a cover of Roxy Music's 'Out Of The Blue' with Cheap Trick drummer Bun E. Carlos, backing Faithfull on her cover of the Bob Dylan gospel classic 'Gotta Serve Somebody' and duetting with her later on the Beatles' 'Norwegian Wood (This Bird Has Flown).'

Bob Dylan's sonic soul continued rattling around Corgan's head six months later. When the Smashing Pumpkins splintered, and the members each moseyed off on their own merry ways, Corgan and Chamberlin found themselves still to be beating the same path and the pair were instantly reunited when Corgan was invited to participate in a televised tribute to Chicago childrens' favourite Bozo The Clown, *Bozo: 40 Years Of Fun*, alongside guitarist Chris Holmes from Yum Yum, Urge Overkill bassist Eddie Roeser, and keyboardist Linda Strawberry.

Bozo the Clown was a local, and national television favourite, a character that inspired love or fear (or both!) among children from 1960 onward. It was a show Corgan especially remembered from his youth...one that had helped inspire his own decision to appear onstage as a clown in London. The Smashing Pumpkins had even talked from time to time about making a guest appearance on the show, although it had never come to pass. Now, when Corgan found out that Bozo would be taping his very final episode in June, he jumped at the chance to be a part of the celebration. With the impromptu band behind them, Corgan and Chamberlin worked up a poignantly appropriate cover of Bob

Dylan's 'Forever Young' to perform at the studio.

Such extra-curricular activities could not help but inflame rumours of a full-fledged return to action for Corgan and, with the Bozo show now behind him, the singer was ready to unveil his immediate future – a new band called Zwan. With Chamberlin cemented behind the drum kit, Corgan and Chavez guitarist Matt Sweeney began rehearsing in mid-summer; by September, they were joined by Slint bassist David Pajo; and, in November 2001, a new era began for Corgan, a 'happy' Corgan, a Corgan seemingly without angst or despair.

The band played a handful of shows in the Los Angeles area that month, kicking off in Pamona, California, where they blistered through a set that boasted more than a handful of the songs that would end up on Zwan's January 2003 *Mary Star Of The Sea* debut, as well as a cover of Velvet Underground's street-smart 'Waiting For The Man'. The following month, Zwan were in the Midwest, peppering Missouri and Indiana with what Corgan was already enthusiastically proclaiming a new breed of rock'n'roll.

Taking a brief step away from the thrill of launching a new band, 22 March 2002 saw Corgan and Chamberlin alone appear at the Cabaret Metro for the Fourth Waltz Benefit, regaling the audience with a clutch of songs that including a mini Ramones covers set that sopped up 'Blitzkrieg Bop', 'I Don't Care' and 'Teenage Lobotomy.' But they were back to business a week later, as Zwan poached Paz Lenchantin from the Tool spin off, A Perfect Circle. The group was complete.

Corgan appeared more at ease with the press, with the public and with his band than he had in years. Although many observers were surprised that he'd chosen to launch an all-new band with an untried line-up, rather than bank on his own star as a solo artist, it was, he felt, more natural, and ultimately more satisfying.

'I love being in a band,' he told *Kerrang!* magazine. 'It's a lot more fun...I can do the solo thing any time I want. I prefer working with people I'm close to. The best music is made by bands. I think eighty per cent of the greatest music is made by bands, and fifteen per cent done by the singer-songwriter types. But ego-driven solo "projects", they're neither here nor there.'

Corgan was in his comfort area, then, blasting ideas and ideals at fellow musicians who shared his grooves – which themselves were now snugly wrapped in warm guitars and awash in a neo-psychedelic thrum. That summer saw Zwan ink with Reprise Records; November 2002 then brought their first UK single, 'Honestly.' That was followed, of course, by the rabidly anticipated *Mary Star Of The Sea* album the following January.

Of course the album generated a buzz, in the pages of the music press and in the hearts and hopes of the old Smashing Pumpkins faithful. But, despite their already blustering renown, Zwan remained very much an unknown quantity – the 'Honestly' single scarcely set the world ablaze, while gigs remained at a premium. For many of the people hanging on to hear Corgan's next move, the release of the album would be their very first taste of the group. And many would profess themselves disappointed by what they found there.

Though the album debuted at number three on the US chart, its lifespan was short; sales were lukewarm. Promotion, such an important vehicle for any new release in an age when records are peddled like hamburgers, was shockingly minimal. Sales of a mere quarter of a million units wasn't simply paler than a ghost's cheeks in comparison to anything the Pumpkins had released, it was almost insultingly low for any so-called superstar's return to action.

Especially damaging to the cause was Corgan's refusal to grant more than a very select handful of interviews. Fans wanted to know what he was doing, wanted to get to grips with theis latest manifestation of his musical psyche. They did not, however, want to be railroaded into purchasing the appropriate issues of whichever 'high profile' magazines that Corgan and his marketing team deemed he ought to grace. He talked to *Kerrang!*, but if a kid hates heavy metal more than he loved the Smashing Pumpkins, he's not only going to ignore the magazine, he'd probably be ignoring Zwan as well. After all, if that's the market they're catering for now....

Live reaction to Zwan continue to be strong but, again, it never took off as the band had hoped. Zwan continued to tour throughout the spring, but signs that the project was going seriously awry came in June, when they cut their European tour short to return to the States, following their 10 June show in Velleurbanne, France. The curtailment was blamed upon unspecified 'family matters,' but even impartial observers were not slow to detect the first dark clangs of Zwan's death knell.

If Zwan appeared to be running away from the spotlight, James Iha was running right toward it. The guitarist had maintained a very low profile in the wake of the Smashing Pumpkins' dissolution, all but abandoning the public side of the rock'n'roll circus to concentrate instead on Stratosphere in New York, and to breathe new life into the Scratchie Records revival, working in the studio with that label's most recent signing, the Sounds.

Even before Zwan got underway, of course, there had been much anticipation about the various former Pumpkins' future plans. Like Iha, Melissa Auf Der Maur had already announced that she intended to 'take 2001 off, so I could figure out who I was, what I wanted to do with music, and if I wanted to do anything at all with music,' but rumours were already circulating that the pair, Auf Der Maur and Iha, were planning a supergroup of sorts, the Virgins... in November 2001, VH-1 proudly announced that 'Ex-Members Of Pumpkins, Hole, Whiskeytown, Lemonheads Are Virgins.' They spoke too soon. The project never took off, instead, Auf Der Maur stepped out with a new, if somewhat light-hearted project, the Black Sabbath tribute band Hand of Doom. And, although that particular endeavour didn't endure, Auf Der Maur kept her hand in, returning with her self-funded and long, long promised solo album, *Auf Der Maur*. With a staggered launch that would see the album pepper Europe in the beginning of February 2004, England on 1 March and the United States later that same month, *Auf Der Maur* emerged a funky six-degrees-of-separation type reunion, with James Iha and Eric Erlandson scything alongside Queens Of The Stone Age's Josh Homme and Nick Oliveri, while Helmet's John Stanier joined the roster of drummers, and A Perfect Circle's Jeordie White and Paz Lenchantin also stepped up.

Iha, meanwhile, continued his New York sabbatical.

And then A Perfect Circle came calling. Iha and A Perfect Circle's Billy Howerdel had been acquainted for a couple of years now (Howerdel, in fact, was the Smashing Pumpkins' guitar tech on their last tours); and, of course, he had looked on admiringly as A Perfect Circle gracefully overcame the loss of Paz Lenchantin, a year before. So, when he was invited into the group, he at least agreed to think about it. Other offers might well have been turned down flat.

He had imposed some very firm limits for himself, he later told the *Winnipeg-Sun* newspaper, determining not to play 'in another band unless it was something really good. It had to be of a certain quality level. It would be weird to play in a lame band after being in a really good band.' A Perfect Circle met all the criteria that he demanded; in mid-September 2003, Iha was confirmed as A Perfect Circle's latest member.

With one ex-Pumpkins' door opening, though, another was slamming shut. That same middle of September, Corgan announced that Zwan had disbanded, putting the experience into context when he told Chicago's WGN Television that 'our attitude in the Pumpkins was, it was a do or die proposition, and that got us through all the hard times we went through, particularly with the Pumpkins where we had two members with serious drug problems. I really enjoyed my experience with Zwan but, at the end of the day, without that sense of deeper family loyalty, it just becomes like anything else'. At the time of writing, his future plans remain shrouded in secrecy.

EPILOGUE

ICARUS REDUX

'We Icarused,' Corgan said of the demise of the Smashing Pumpkins. But did they? Did the band fly too close to the sun, did they reach the pinnacle of heaven only to be burned up and cast down in ashes on the wind? Perhaps.

The band's path did follow the way of that greatest Greek myth. And, as Corgan grappled and danced around the self-fulfilling prophecy of band destruction, it became by that very fact reality. But, take that end out of the equation, out of the history and look back – the Pumpkins were placed well outside the constraints of the castle. Those walls would be built up later.

They were there *before* – with a mythology of their own creation. Remember, in the beginning, to re-iterate the time of the Smashing Pumpkins' very inception: there was no form to these ragged insurgents, no single sold shape into which their disparate brands of aural terrorism could be scooped up to say, 'now, here is a scene.'

The Smashing Pumpkins, by their very existence and their fortitude to push the envelope of popular music, helped to *create* a scene, an environment where not only was there a cascade of new sounds, but a place where the very fabric of what those sounds were became thin enough that this new breed of music was accepted into the mainstream. The walls were truly broken between the Alternative underground and the everyday folks in a way that hadn't happened before. And yes, that happened alongside Nivarna and Mudhoney, alongside Pearl Jam and the Pixies, alongside a flannel flag that spired up to circle the globe.

But, as those other bands stayed firmly in the shadow cast by that flag; indeed, as they continued to wear the very essence of what it represented on the their breasts, the Smashing Pumpkins were pushing at the confines of the keep, looking for a loose brick through which they could push, taking the lessons learned at the dawn of Grunge, and incorporating everything they were into a new sonic dimension.

In always looking forward, in being unafraid to explore new avenues, to tear down the assumptions of what Alternative was, the group were able to bring the genre into a limelight that, admittedly, was not completely of their own doing, but let people re-invent Hard Rock in startling new ways.

However, with every rich new vein tapped, with each foray higher up the musical charts, with each arena show conquered, the Smashing Pumpkins took themselves ever closer to the sun. There is only so far you can go before the top of the stars turns to become a pit at the bottom from which you must crawl.

Corgan realized that, and even as the band burned, they were shot through with glitter and spangles until the end. They went out on a high note, missed falling, like Icarus, into the water at all. Scattered to all corners, Billy Corgan, James Iha, Jimmy Chamberlin, D'Arcy Wretzky, Melissa Auf Der Maur each continue to shine, to glimmer just out of reach, just beyond the range of clear sight.

And, as the Smashing Pumpkins' members move in ever widening circles, rippling away from the strong centre core that bound them together in the first place, it's not unlikely that somehow, someday, they'll collide with their future selves rippling out from another mythos altogether. And, perhaps, we will discover that it's not that the Smashing Pumpkins Icarused, so much as, like another Greek legend, that they will Phoenix instead.

ACKNOWLEDGEMENTS

The Smashing Pumpkins were a band who grasped at, received and deserved not only the greatest success that any group of musicians can have, but also faced the challenges of finding a path to walk in a musical climate that was building itself up, only to tear itself asunder like a great volcano. That they were able to keep their course, and continue to create albums like no other with all this ash and grit and water and crash around them, is testament both to the vision that Billy Corgan and his band mates held firmly in hand, but also to the very essence of the music they were making.

For me, that is one of the great fascinations held by the Smashing Pumpkins – not only that their place in the rise and demise of the American Grunge scene firmly cemented their own crown down, but also that, at the same time, their style and verve ensured they remained proudly out of step with all that transpired around them.

The Smashing Pumpkins, by their very nature and within their very distinct sound, have built up a glorious, murky mythology that picks apart like panels of an ancient tapestry. There is the thread that holds the mysteries of their music, of their chemistry in creation and of the musical essence that is the Smashing Pumpkins distilled. There are the threads that are pulled through in the shape of the band's many fans, supporters and bearers of accolades. And, right next to them, lies the thread that holds the bite and spit of detractors and nay-sayers and the ghosts who whispered 'grunge sell-out' from beginning to end, at the periphery of sight and reason.

And then there are those threads that hold the secrets of Billy Corgan, James Iha, Jimmy Chamberlin and D'Arcy Wretzky. Those are not for display, for public consumption and regurgitation; rather they lurk behind – the backbone of the warp and weft that allows everything else to fall into place. Those lives, those stories, gossip and grim flaying open of privacy are not to be found here. Those things are for the band members alone to have.

There are times when incidents and personal moments will dance, when they affect the Smashing Pumpkins and their course in sonic history. There are many ways to pick apart a celebrity, his life, his very lifeblood. This book, though, is about the band, their music, and their place in time. The astute reader, listener, dreamer can create his own mythology of who the Smashing

Pumpkins were, between the opening downstroke of *Gish,* through the massive cacophony of *Machina/The Machines Of God.* Both truth and beauty lie in the eyes of the beholder, but there is plenty packed into Corgan's lyrics, in the Smashing Pumpkins melodies and into the course they plotted as they shifted their sound time and time again, while setting a precedent with a distinctive style that would shape the 1990s and are certain to endure long after as well. The band's life, then, is seen through their work, as perhaps Billy Corgan intended it all along. There are pictures, shots, montages that wind their way through, there are the threads that are pulled taut to create the finished pieces, and others that snap off, to trail away.

For my own attempts to weave these strands and untangle these skeins there are many people to thank. Especial acknowledgements must go to Dale Griffin, Dave Hawes and Bob Nolan, who so gracefully shared their memories of their own early encounters with the group; and to Lilli Thillet, Lauren Nixon and Steve Miller, for their observations on the various scenes within which the story is set; and to all the people who agreed to talk to me off the record. Jo-Ann Greene and Dave Thompson generously shared their own interviews with members of the Smashing Pumpkins, Pearl Jam, Nirvana, Jonathan Poneman, Tyson Meade and many other of the era's greatest movers and shakers; and Neville Viking provided a number of introductions I may never have otherwise been granted. And thanks to Sean Body and Helter Skelter for helping me bring the book to life.

Finally, to... Ella and Sprocket, The Shecklers four, Dad & Jane, Marcia, The Possum, The Pants, Jugs, the ladies of COS who listened, and Anne Smith who faithfully provided Wednesday night libations. Thanks, especially, to my Mom Joey, who, although she isn't able to see this book come to fruition, cheered me on all the way while she could.

BIBLIOGRAPHY

Aside from sources cited elsewhere, the following publications were consulted:

MAGAZINES AND PERIODICALS

Alternative Press (US); *B-Side* (US); *Big O* (Singapore); *Chicago Insider* (US); *Chicago Sun-Times* (US); *Circus* (US); *Creem* (US); *Details* (US); *Goldmine* (US); *Guitar Player* (US); *huH* (US); *Kerrang!*; *LA Times* (US); *Live!* (US); *Live! Music Review* (US); *Melody Maker*; *Modern Drummer* (US); *Mojo, Musician* (US); *New Musical Express*; *The Onion* (US); *Q*; *Record Collector*; *The Rocket* (US); *Rolling Stone, Sounds*; *Spin* (US); *Spiral Scratch*; *Uncut, Vox.*

WEBSITES

www.netphoria.org
www.spfc.org
www.blamo.org/sp/
www.starla.org
www.zwan.com

REFERENCE BOOKS & BIOGRAPHIES

Guinness Book of Hit Singles, Hit Albums (various editions)
Martin C Strong: _Great Alternative Discography_ (Canongate)
Joel Whitburn: _Top Pop Singles, Top Pop Albums_ (various editions: Record Research)
Rees/Crampton: _VH-1 Book of Rock Stars_
Dave Thompson: _Better To Burn Out_ (Thunder's Mouth)
Jim DeRogatis: _Milk It_ (Da Capo)
Michael Azerrad: _Come As You Are_ (Doubleday)
Joel Selvin: _Summer Of Love_ (Dutton)
Ken Garner: _In Session Tonight_ (BBC)

ABOUT THE AUTHOR

Amy Hanson is a freelance journalist/author. She lives in Seattle.

DISCOGRAPHY

The Smashing Pumpkins have a rich recorded history. Included here are US and UK discographies as well as selected international releases, compilation albums and solo discographies of note.

Selected Worldwide Discography

7" Singles
US

Limited Potential	(Limp 006)	I Am One/Not Worth Asking	04/90
Sub Pop	(SP 90)	Tristessa/La Dolly Vita	
		(black + pink vinyl)	12/90
Reflex	–	Daughter (flexi give away with	
		Reflex magazine)	02/92
Virgin	(7243 8 38522 7 7)	1979/Bullet With Butterfly Wings	07/96

UK

Hut	(HUT 31)	Cherub Rock/Purr Snickety	
		(clear vinyl)	06/93
Hut	(HUT 37)	Today/Apathy's Last Kiss	
		(red vinyl)	09/93
Hut	(HUT 43)	Disarm/Siamese Dream	
		(purple vinyl)	02/94
Hut	(HUTL 48)	Rocket/Never Let Me Down	
		(peach vinyl)	12/94
Hut	(SPBOX 1)	Siamese Singles (4 x 7" singles in	
		a box – Cherub Rock/Today/	
		Disarm/Rocket	12/94
Hut	(HUT 101)	Ava Adore/Czarina	05/98

10" Singles
UK

Hut/Strange Fruit	(SFPCD 214)	Siva/A Girl Named Sandoz/	
		Smiley	??/92
Hut	(HUTTEN 18)	I Am One/Terrapin(live)/	
		Bullet Train To Osaka	08/92

12" Singles/EPs
US

Caroline	(CAROL 1465-2)	Lull EP – Rhinoceros/Blue/Slunk	
		Bye June	11/91
Virgin	(7234 8 38541 1 0)	1979 Mixes – Vocal/Instrumental	
		Moby/Cement	03/96

UK

SubPopUK	(SP10/137)	Tristessa/La Dolly Vita/Honeyspider	
		(UK single from Germany)	12/90
Hut	(HUTT 6)	Siva/Window Paine	08/91
Hut	(HUTT 10)	Lull EP – Rhinoceros/Blue/Slunk	
		Bye June (demo)	02/92
Hut	(HUTT 17)	Peel Sessions EP – Siva	
		A Girl Named Sandoz/Smiley	06/92
Hut	(HUTT 18)	I Am One/Plume/Starla	08/92
Hut	(HUTT 31)	Cherub Rock/Pissant/French Movie	
		Theme/Star Spangled Banner	06/93
Hut	(HUTT 37)	Today/Hello Kitty Kat/Obscured	09/93
Hut	(HUTT 43)	Disarm/Soothe(demo)/Blew Away	02/94
Hut	(HUTT 67)	1979/Ugly/Believe/Cherry	01/96
Hut	(HUTTX 67)	1979 Remixes – Vocal/Instrumental	
		Moby/Clement	03/96

CD Singles
US

Caroline	(CAROL 1465-2)	Lull EP – Rhinoceros/Blue/Slunk	
		Bye June	11/91
Virgin/Hut	(HUT 2080 18 2)	I Am One/Plume/Starla	06/94
Virgin/Hut	(HUT 1700 43 2)	Today/Hello Kitty Kat/Obscured	08/94
Virgin/Hut	(HUT 1700 31 2)	Cherub Rock/Pissant/French Movie	
		Theme/Star Spangled Banner	11/94
Virgin	(8 38522 2)	Bullet With Butterfly Wings/	
		…Said Sadly	10/95
Virgin	(8 38534 2)	1979/Ugly/Believe/Cherry	01/96
Virgin	(8 38545 2)	Zero EP – Zero/God/Mouths Of	
		Babes/Tribute To Johnny/Marquis	
		In Spades/Pennies/Pastichio Medley	05/96
Virgin	(8 38547 2)	Tonight, Tonight/Meladori Magpie/	
		Rotten Apples/Medellia Of The	
		Grey Skies	06/96
Virgin	(38574)	Thirty-Three/The Last Song/The	
		Aeroplane Flies High (Turns Left,	
		Looks Right)/Transformer	11/96

Virgin	(SPBOX 2)	The Aeroplane Flies High box – Bullet With Butterfly Wings/1979/ Tonight, Tonight/Thirty Three/Zero	11/96
Warner Brothers	(W 0404C)	The End Is The Beginning Is The End/The Beginning Is The End Is The Beginning/The Ethers Tragic/ The Guns Of Love Disastrous	06/97
Warner Brothers	(W 0410C)	The End Is The Beginning Is The End remixes – 2 Fluke mixes/Rabbit In The Moon mixes/Hallucination Gotham Mix	06/97
Virgin	(38647)	Ava Adore/Czarina	06/98
Virgin	(72438 38650 24)	Perfect/Summer/Daphne Descends (Kerry B. Mix)	10/98

UK

Hut	(HUTCD 10)	Lull EP – Rhinoceros/Blue/Slunk Bye June (demo)	02/92
Hut	(HUTCD 17)	Peel Sessions EP – Siva A Girl Named Sandoz/Smiley	06/92
Hut	(HUTCD 18)	I Am One/Plume/Starla	08/92
Hut	(HUTCD 31)	Cherub Rock/Pissant/French Movie Theme/Star Spangled Banner	06/93
Hut	(HUTCD 37)	Today/Hello Kitty Kat/Obscured	07/93
Hut	(HUTCD 43)	Disarm/Soothe(demo)/Blew Away	02/94
Hut	(HUTDX 43)	Disarm/Dancing In The Moonlight/ Landslide	02/94
Hut	(HUTCD 63)	Bullet With Butterfly Wings/ ...Said Sadly	10/95
Hut	(HUTCD 67)	1979/Ugly/Believe/Cherry	01/96
Hut	(HUTCDX 67)	1979 Remixes – Vocal/Instrumental Moby/Clement	03/96
Hut	(HUTCDXE 67)	1979 Mixes – Vocal/Instrumental	03/96
Hut	(HUTCD 69)	Tonight, Tonight/Meladori Magpie/ Rotten Apples/Medellia Of The Grey Skies	05/96
Hut	(HUT CDX 69)	Tonight, Tonight/Jupiter's Lament/ Blank/Tonite(reprise)	05/96
Hut	(HUT CD 73)	Zero EP – Zero/God/Mouths Of Babes/Tribute To Johnny/Marquis In Spades/Pennies/Pastichio Medley	09/96
Hut	(HUT CD 78)	Thirty -Three/The Last Song/The Aeroplane Flies High (Turns Left, Looks Right)/Transformer	11/96

Hut	(HUT CDX 78)	Thirty-Three/The Bells/My Blue Heaven	11/96
Hut	(HUT CD 101)	Ava Adore/Czarina/Once In A While 05/98	
Hut	(HUT CD 106)	Perfect/Summer/Perfect (Nellee Hooper mix)	09/98
Hut	(HUT DX 106)	Perfect/Daphne Descends (Oakenfold Perfecto mix)/Daphne Descends (Kerry B mix)	09/98
Hut	(HUT CD 127)	Stand Inside Your Love/Speed Kills	02/00
Hut	(HUT CD 140)	Try,Try,Try/Here's To The Atom Bomb	09/00

JAPAN

| Toshiba/EMI | (VJCP-14047) | Today/Hello Kitty Kat/Obscured Apathy's Last Kiss/French Movie Theme | 01/94 |

GERMANY

| Hut | (H170439) | 1979/Ugly/Believe/Cherry/The Boy/Set The Ray To Jerry | 01/96 |

Vinyl LPs

US

Caroline	(CAROL 39834)	Pisces Iscariot (gold-lp)	10/94
Caroline	(CAROL 1767-7)	Pisces Iscariot (w/free gold 7" single – Not Worth Asking/Honeyspider)	10/94
Virgin	(7243 8 39663 2 5)	Gish (reissue)	10/94
Caroline	(CAROL 17401)	Siamese Dream (double vinyl reissue)	12/99
Caroline	(CAR 48936 / 7243 8)	Machina/The Machines Of God	05/00
Constantinople	(CR 01 04)	Machina II/The Friends And Enemies Of Modern Music (2LP plus 3 10" set)	09/00

UK

Hut	(HUT LP 002)	Gish	02/92
Hut	(HUT LP 011)	Siamese Dream	07/93
Hut	(HUT LPX 002)	Gish (reissue)	05/94
Hut	(HUT LP 41)	Pisces Iscariot	10/96
Hut	(HUTT LP 30)	Mellon Collie And The Infinite Sadness (triple vinyl reissue)	04/96
Hut	(HUT DLP 51)	Adore	05/98
Hut	(HUT DLP 59)	Machina/The Machines Of God	02/00

CD Albums

US

Caroline	(CAROL 1705)	Gish		08/91
Caroline	(CAROL 88267)	Siamese Dream		07/93
Virgin	(7243 8 39834 2 1)	Pisces Iscariot		10/94
Virgin	(7243 8 39663 2 5)	Gish (reissue)		10/94
Virgin	(40861)	Mellon Collie And The Infinite Sadness		10/95
Virgin	(45879)	Adore		06/98
Virgin	(48936)	Machina/The Machines Of God		02/00
Virgin	(11316)	(Rotten Apples) Greatest Hits		11/01
Virgin	(11318)	(Rotten Apples) Greatest Hits with bonus Judas O disc		11/01
Virgin	(724354270628)	Vieuphoria		11/02

UK

Hut	(HUT CD 002)	Gish	02/92
Hut	(HUT CD 011)	Siamese Dream	07/93
Hut	(HUT CDX 002)	Gish (reissue)	05/94
Hut	(HUT CD 041)	Pisces Iscariot	10/96
Hut	(HUT CD 30)	Mellon Collie And The Infinite Sadness	10/95
Hut	(HUT CD 51)	Adore	06/98
Hut	(HUT CD 59)	Machina/The Machines Of God	02/00
Hut	(HUT CD 70)	(Rotten Apples) Greatest Hits	11/01

JAPAN

EMI/Virgin	(VJCP-28179)	Siamese Dream (JP CD has one bonus track – Pissant)	08/93
Toshiba/EMI	(VJCP-25203/4)	Mellon Collie And The Infinite Sadness (JP CD has two bonus tracks – Tonite Reprise/Infinite Sadness)	10/95
Virgin/EMI	(VJCP-25396)	Adore (JP CD has one bonus track – Once In A While)	05/98

NOTABLE COMPILATION ALBUMS
US

Halo	(Halo 001)	LP	Light Into Dark inc. My Dahlia/Sun	04/88
Pravda	(PR 6338)	CD	20 Explosive Dynamic Super Smash Hit Explosions inc. Jackie Blue	—/91
Epic	(EK 52476)	CD	Singles OST inc. Drown	06/92
Sup Pop	(SP 0153)	CD	Afternoon Delight inc. La Dolly Vita	07/92
Arista	(07822 18737 2)	CD	No Alternative inc. Glynis	10/93
KROQ FM	(no cat)	Cass	Kevin And Bean (No Toys For OJ) Inc. Rudolph The Red Nosed Reindeer (live)	—/94

ONxrt	(3)	CD	Live From The Archives Vol 3 – WXRT radio compilation inc. Rocket	04/96
Columbia	(CK 67573)	CD	Sweet Relief II: The Gravity Of The Situation inc. Sad Peter Pan	07/96
Warner Brothers	(46620)	CD	Batman And Robin Motion Picture inc. The End Is The Beginning Is The End/The Beginning Is The End Is The Beginning	06/97
A&M	(31454 0764 2)	CD	A Very Special Christmas 3 Inc. Christmastime	02/98
Nothing/Interscope	(INTD-90090)	CD	Lost Highway OST inc. Eye	
A&M	(31454 0919 2)	CD	For The Masses: A Tribute To Depeche Mode inc. Never Let Me Down Again	08/98

UK

NME	(NME BRAT94)	CS	NME Brat Pack 1994 inc. Space Boy (acoustic)	01/94

BILLY CORGAN
Starchildren
US

TVT	(TVT 462-7)	7"	Split single w/Catherine inc. Delusions Of Candor	06/94
A&M	(7243 8 40660 2 4)	CD/LP	A Means To An End: The Music Of Joy Division inc. Isolation	09/95

UK

Hut	(HUTCD29)	CD	A Means To An End The Music Of Joy Division inc. Isolation	09/95
Hut	(HUTLP29)	LP	A Means To An End The Music Of Joy Division inc. Isolation	09/95

SOLO
US

Hollywood	(HR 62086-2)	CD	Ransom OST (Rats/Worms/ Spiders/Lizards/Worms Pt 2/ Squirrels With Tails	11/96
Virgin	(7243 8 47753 2 2)	CD	Stigmata score	08/98

JAMES IHA SOLO
US

Virgin	(7243 8 45411 2 5)	CD	Let It Come Down	02/98

UK

Hut/Virgin	(CDHÜT 47)	CD	Let It Come Down	02/98
Hut/Virgin	(HUTLP 47)	LP	Let It Come Down	02/98
Hut/Virgin	(HUTCD 99)	CD	single (Be Strong Now/ My Advice/Take Care/ Falling	02/98

ZWAN
US

Warner Brothers Star Of The Sea	(9362-48436-27) 01/03		CD	Mary
Warner Brothers Star Of The Sea	(9362-48425-21)		CD/DVD	Mary
			(Bonus DVD titled For Your Love)	01/03

UK

Reprise	(9362-48436-2)	CD	Mary Star Of The Sea	01/03
Warner Brothers	(W600CD)	CD	single (Honestly/The Number Of The Beast/ Freedom Ain't What It Used To Be)	02/03
Warner Brothers	(W600)	7"	single (Honestly/The Number Of The Beast)	02/03
Warner Brothers	(W607CD)	CD	single (Lyric/Nobody 'Cept You/Autumn Leaves)	06/03
Warner Brothers	(W607)	7"	single (Lyric/Nobody ('Cept You)	06/03

NOTABLE SCRATCHIE RELEASES

Belltower: Underwatertown/Orbit
Blank Theory: *Beyond The Calm Of The Corridor* (2002)
Chainsaw Kittens: *Candy For You* EP (1996)
Chainsaw Kittens: *Chainsaw Kittens* (1996)
Chainsaw Kittens: Grandaddy's Candy/Bones In My Teeth (1996)
Dan Bryk: *Lovers Leap* (2000)
Eszter Balint: *Flicker* (1999)
Fondly: *F Is For...* (1997)
Fountains Of Wayne: *Utopia Parkway* (1999)
Freak Magnet: Clean Shave/Looks Familiar (1996)
Frogs: *Hopscotch Lollipop Sunday Surprise* (2001)
Frogs: *Starjob* EP (1997)
Fulflej: *Mircrowave* EP (1995)
Fulflej: *Wack-ass Tuba Riff* (1996)

Fulflej: Work In This Universe/Parallel To Gravity (1996)
Ivy: *I Hate December* EP (1996)
Ivy: I Hate December EP (1995)
Mike Ladd: *Easy Listening 4 Armageddon* (1996)
Pancho Kryztal: *Pancho Kryztal*
Phoenix Thunderstorm: *Ride Of The Lawless* (1996)
Phoenix Thunderstorm: *Stained Glass Trash* (1997)
Sounds: *Living In America* (2003)

Other Titles available from Helter Skelter

Coming Soon

Everybody Dance
Chic and the Politics of Disco
By Daryl Easlea

Everybody Dance puts the rise and fall of Bernard Edwards and Nile Rodgers, the emblematic disco duo behind era-defining records 'Le Freak', 'Good Times' and 'Lost In Music', at the heart of a changing landscape, taking in socio-political and cultural events such as the Civil Rights struggle, the Black Panthers and the US oil crisis. There are drugs, bankruptcy, up-tight artists, fights, and Muppets but, most importantly an in-depth appraisal of a group whose legacy remains hugely underrated.
ISBN 1-900924-56-0   256pp   £14.00

Currently Available from Helter Skelter

Be Glad: An Incredible String Band Compendium
Edited by Adrian Whittaker

The ISB pioneered 'world music' on '60s albums like *The Hangman's Beautiful Daughter* – Paul McCartney's favourite album of 1967! – experimented with theatre, film and lifestyle and inspired Led Zeppelin. 'Be Glad' features interviews with all the ISB key players, as well as a wealth of background information, reminiscence, critical evaluations and arcane trivia, this is a book that will delight any reader with more than a passing interest in the ISB.
ISBN 1-900924-64-1   288pp   £14.99

Waiting for the Man: The Story of Drugs and Popular Music
Harry Shapiro

From Marijuana and Jazz, through acid-rock and speed-fuelled punk, to crack-driven rap and Ecstasy and the Dance Generation, this is the definitive history of drugs and pop. It also features in-depth portraits of music's most famous drug addicts: from Charlie Parker to Sid Vicious and from Jim Morrison to Kurt Cobain. Chosen by the BBC as one of the Top Twenty Music Books of All Time.
"Wise and witty." *The Guardian*
ISBN 1-900924-58-7   320pp   £12.99

The Clash: Return of the Last Gang in Town
Marcus Gray

Exhaustively researched definitive biography of the last great rock band that traces their progress from pubs and punk clubs to US stadiums and the Top Ten. This edition is further updated to cover the band's induction into the Rock 'n' Roll Hall of Fame and the tragic death of iconic frontman Joe Strummer.
"A must-have for Clash fans [and] a valuable document for anyone interested in the punk era." *Billboard*
"It's important you read this book." *Record Collector*
ISBN 1-900924-62-5   448pp   £14.99

Steve Marriott: All Too Beautiful
by Paolo Hewitt and John Hellier £20.00

Marriott was the prime mover behind 60s chart-toppers The Small Faces. Longing to be treated as a serious musician he formed Humble Pie with Peter Frampton, where his blistering rock 'n' blues guitar playing soon saw him take centre stage in the US live favourites. After years in seclusion, Marriott's plans for a comeback in 1991 were tragically cut short when he died in a housefire. He continues to be a key influence for generations of musicians from Paul Weller to Oasis and Blur.

Love: Behind The Scenes
By Michael Stuart-Ware

LOVE were one of the legendary bands of the late 60s US West Coast scene. Their masterpiece *Forever Changes* still regularly appears in critics' polls of top albums, while a new-line up of the band has recently toured to mass acclaim. Michael Stuart-Ware was LOVE's drummer during their heyday and shares his inside perspective on the band's recording and performing career and tells how drugs and egos thwarted the potential of one of the great groups of the burgeoning psychedelic era.

ISBN 1-900924-59-5   256pp   £14.00

A Secret Liverpool: In Search of the La's
By MW Macefield

With timeless single "There She Goes", Lee Mavers' La's overtook The Stone Roses and paved the way for Britpop. However, since 1991, The La's have been silent, while rumours of studio-perfectionism, madness and drug addiction have abounded. The author sets out to discover the truth behind Mavers' lost decade and eventually gains a revelatory audience with Mavers himself.

ISBN 1-900924-63-3   192pp   £11.00

The Fall: A User's Guide
Dave Thompson

Amelodic, cacophonic and magnificent, The Fall remain the most enduring and prolific of the late-'70s punk and post-punk iconoclasts. A User's Guide chronicles the historical and musical background to more than 70 different LPs (plus reissues) and as many singles. The band's history is also documented year-by-year, filling in the gaps between the record releases.

ISBN 1-900924-57-9   256pp   £12.99

Pink Floyd: A Saucerful of Secrets
by Nicholas Schaffner   £14.99

Long overdue reissue of the authoritative and detailed account of one of the most important and popular bands in rock history. From the psychedelic explorations of the Syd Barrett-era to 70s superstardom with *Dark Side of the Moon*, and on to triumph of *The Wall*, before internecine strife tore the group apart. Schaffner's definitive history also covers the improbable return of Pink Floyd without Roger Waters, and the hugely successful *Momentary Lapse of Reason* album and tour.

The Big Wheel
by Bruce Thomas   £10.99

Thomas was bassist with Elvis Costello at the height of his success. Though names are never named, The Big Wheel paints a vivid and hilarious picture of life touring with Costello and co, sharing your life 24-7 with a moody egotistical singer, a crazed drummer and a host of hangers-on. Costello sacked Thomas on its initial publication.

"A top notch anecdotalist who can time a twist to make you laugh out loud." Q

Hit Men: Powerbrokers and Fast Money Inside The Music Business
By Fredric Dannen   £14.99

Hit Men exposes the seamy and sleazy dealings of America's glitziest record companies: payola, corruption, drugs, Mafia involvement, and excess.

"So heavily awash with cocaine, corruption and unethical behaviour that it makes the occasional examples of chart-rigging and playlist tampering in Britain during the same period seem charmingly inept." *The Guardian*.

I'm With The Band: Confessions of A Groupie
By Pamela Des Barres   £14.99

Frank and engaging memoir of affairs with Keith Moon, Noel Redding and Jim Morrison, travels with Led Zeppelin as Jimmy Page's girlfriend, and friendships with Robert Plant, Gram Parsons, and Frank Zappa.

"Miss Pamela, the most beautiful and famous of the groupies. Her memoir of her life with rock stars is funny, bittersweet, and tender-hearted."
    Stephen Davis, author of *Hammer of the Gods*

Psychedelic Furs: Beautiful Chaos
by Dave Thompson £12.99

Psychedelic Furs were the ultimate post-punk band – combining the chaos and vocal rasp of the Sex Pistols with a Bowie-esque glamour. The Furs hit the big time when John Hughes wrote a movie based on their early single "Pretty in Pink". Poised to join U2 and Simple Minds in the premier league, they withdrew behind their shades, remaining a cult act, but one with a hugely devoted following.

Bob Dylan: Like The Night (Revisited)
by CP Lee   £9.99

Fully revised and updated B-format edition of the hugely acclaimed document of Dylan's pivotal 1966 show at the Manchester Free Trade Hall where fans called him Judas for turning his back on folk music in favour of rock 'n' roll.

Marillion: Separated Out
by Jon Collins   £14.99

From the chart hit days of Fish and "Kayleigh" to the Steve Hogarth incarnation, Marillion have continued to make groundbreaking rock music. Collins tells the full story, drawing on interviews with band members, associates, and the experiences of some of the band's most dedicated fans.

Rainbow Rising
by Roy Davies   £14.99

The full story of guitar legend Ritchie Blackmore's post-Purple progress with one of the great 70s rock bands. After quitting Deep Purple at the height of their success, Blackmore combined with Ronnie James Dio to make epic rock albums like *Rising* and *Long Live Rock 'n' Roll* before streamlining the sound and enjoying hit singles like "Since You've Been Gone" and "All Night Long." Rainbow were less celebrated than Deep Purple, but they feature much of Blackmore's finest writing and playing, and were one of *the* best live acts of the era. They are much missed.

Back to the Beach: A Brian Wilson and the Beach Boys Reader REVISED EDITION
Ed Kingsley Abbott   £14.00

Revised and expanded edition of the Beach Boys compendium *Mojo* magazine deemed an "essential purchase." This collection includes all of the best articles, interviews and reviews from the Beach Boys' four decades of music, including definitive pieces by Timothy White, Nick Kent and David Leaf. New material reflects on the tragic death of Carl Wilson and documents the rejuvenated Brian's return to the boards. "Rivetting!" **** *Q* "An essential purchase." *Mojo*

Harmony in My Head
The Original Buzzcock Steve Diggle's Rock 'n' Roll Odyssey
by Steve Diggle and Terry Rawlings £14.99

First-hand account of the punk wars from guitarist and one half of the songwriting duo that gave the world three chord punk-pop classics like "Ever Fallen In Love" and "Promises". Diggle dishes the dirt on punk contemporaries like The Sex Pistols, The Clash and The Jam, as well as sharing poignant memories of his friendship with Kurt Cobain, on whose last ever tour, The Buzzcocks were support act.

Serge Gainsbourg: A Fistful of Gitanes
by Sylvie Simmons £9.99

Rock press legend Simmons' hugely acclaimed biography of the French genius.

"I would recommend *A Fistful of Gitanes* [as summer reading] which is a highly entertaining biography of the French singer-songwriter and all-round scallywag" – JG Ballard

"A wonderful introduction to one of the most overlooked songwriters of the 20th century" (Number 3, top music books of 2001) *The Times*

"The most intriguing music-biz biography of the year" *The Independent*

"Wonderful. Serge would have been so happy" – Jane Birkin

Blues: The British Connection
by Bob Brunning £14.99

Former Fleetwood Mac member Bob Brunning's classic account of the impact of Blues in Britain, from its beginnings as the underground music of 50s teenagers like Mick Jagger, Keith Richards and Eric Clapton, to the explosion in the 60s, right through to the vibrant scene of the present day.

"An invaluable reference book and an engaging personal memoir" – *Charles Shaar Murray*

On The Road With Bob Dylan
by Larry Sloman £12.99

In 1975, as Bob Dylan emerged from 8 years of seclusion, he dreamed of putting together a travelling music show that would trek across the country like a psychedelic carnival. The dream became a reality, and *On The Road With Bob Dylan* is the ultimate behind-the-scenes look at what happened. When Dylan and the Rolling Thunder Revue took to the streets of America, Larry "Ratso" Sloman was with them every step of the way.

"The *War and Peace* of Rock and Roll." – Bob Dylan

Gram Parsons: God's Own Singer
By Jason Walker £12.99

Brand new biography of the man who pushed The Byrds into country-rock territory on *Sweethearts of The Rodeo*, and quit to form the Flying Burrito Brothers. Gram lived hard, drank hard, took every drug going and somehow invented country rock, paving the way for Crosby, Stills & Nash, The Eagles and Neil Young. Parsons' second solo LP, *Grievous Angel*, is a haunting masterpiece of country soul. By the time it was released, he had been dead for 4 months. He was 26 years old.

"Walker has done an admirable job in taking us as close to the heart and soul of Gram Parsons as any author could." **** *Uncut* book of the month

Ashley Hutchings: The Guvnor and the Rise of Folk Rock – Fairport Convention, Steeleye Span and the Albion Band
by Geoff Wall and Brian Hinton £14.99

As founder of Fairport Convention and Steeleye Span, Ashley Hutchings is the pivotal figure in the history of folk rock. This book draws on hundreds of hours of interviews with Hutchings and other folk-rock artists and paints a vivid picture of the scene that also produced Sandy Denny, Richard Thompson, Nick Drake, John Martyn and Al Stewart.

The Beach Boys' Pet Sounds: The Greatest Album of the Twentieth Century
by Kingsley Abbott   £11.95

Pet Sounds is the 1966 album that saw The Beach Boys graduate from lightweight pop like "Surfin' USA", et al, into a vehicle for the mature compositional genius of Brian Wilson. The album was hugely influential, not least on The Beatles. This the full story of the album's background, its composition and recording, its contemporary reception and its enduring legacy.

King Crimson: In The Court of King Crimson
by Sid Smith   £14.99

King Crimson's 1969 masterpiece *In The Court Of The Crimson King*, was a huge U.S. chart hit. The band followed it with 40 further albums of consistently challenging, distinctive and innovative music. Drawing on hours of new interviews, and encouraged by Crimson supremo Robert Fripp, the author traces the band's turbulent history year by year, track by track.

A Journey Through America with the Rolling Stones
by Robert Greenfield   UK Price £9.99
Featuring a new foreword by Ian Rankin

This is the definitive account of their legendary '72 tour.

"Filled with finely-rendered detail ... a fascinating tale of times we shall never see again" *Mojo*

The Sharper Word: A Mod Reader
Ed Paolo Hewitt

Hewitt's hugely readable collection documents the clothes, the music, the clubs, the drugs and the faces behind one of the most misunderstood and enduring cultural movements and includes hard to find pieces by Tom Wolfe, bestselling novelist Tony Parsons, poet laureate Andrew Motion, disgraced Tory grandee Jonathan Aitken, Nik Cohn, Colin MacInnes, Mary Quant, and Irish Jack.

"An unparalleled view of the world-conquering British youth cult." *The Guardian*

"An excellent account of the sharpest-dressed subculture." *Loaded*, Book of the Month

ISBN 1-900924-34-X   192pp   £9.99

Backlist

The Nice: Hang On To A Dream
by Martyn Hanson   1900924439   256pp   £13.99

Al Stewart: Adventures of a Folk Troubadour
by Neville Judd   1900924366   320pp   £25.00

Marc Bolan and T Rex: A Chronology
by Cliff McLenahan   1900924420   256pp   £13.99

ISIS: A Bob Dylan Anthology
Ed Derek Barker   1900924293   256pp   £14.99

Razor Edge: Bob Dylan and The Never-ending Tour
by Andrew Muir   1900924137   256pp   £12.99

Calling Out Around the World: A Motown Reader
Edited by Kingsley Abbott   1900924145   256pp   £13.99

I've Been Everywhere: A Johnny Cash Chronicle
by Peter Lewry   1900924226   256pp   £14.99

Sandy Denny: No More Sad Refrains
by Clinton Heylin £13.99   1900924358   288pp   £13.99

Animal Tracks: The Story of The Animals
by Sean Egan £12.99   1900924188   256pp   £12.99

Like a Bullet of Light: The Films of Bob Dylan
by CP Lee   1900924064   224pp   £12.99

Rock's Wild Things: The Troggs Files
by Alan Clayson and J Ryan   1900924196   224pp   £12.99

Dylan's Daemon Lover
by Clinton Heylin   1900924153   192pp   £12.00

Get Back: The Beatles' Let It Be Disaster
by Sulpy & Schweighardt   1900924129   320pp   £12.99

XTC: Song Stories
by XTC and Neville Farmer   190092403X   352pp   £12.99

Born in the USA: Bruce Springsteen
by Jim Cullen   1900924056   320pp   £9.99

Bob Dylan
by Anthony Scaduto   1900924234   320pp   £10.99

Firefly Publishing: An Association between Helter Skelter and SAF

The Nirvana Recording Sessions
by Rob Jovanovic   £20.00
Drawing on years of research, and interviews with many who worked with the band, the author has documented details of every Nirvana recording, from early rehearsals, to the *In Utero* sessions. A fascinating account of the creative process of one of the great bands.

The Music of George Harrison: While My Guitar Gently Weeps
by Simon Leng   £20.00
Often in Lennon and McCartney's shadow, Harrison's music can stand on its own merits. Santana biographer Leng takes a studied, track by track, look at both Harrison's contribution to The Beatles, and the solo work that started with the release in 1970 of his epic masterpiece *All Things Must Pass*. "Here Comes The Sun", "Something" – which Sinatra covered and saw as the perfect love song – "All Things Must Pass" and "While My Guitar Gently Weeps" are just a few of Harrison's classic songs.

Originally planned as a celebration of Harrison's music, this is now sadly a commemoration.

The Pretty Things: Growing Old Disgracefully
by Alan Lakey   £20
First biography of one of rock's most influential and enduring combos. Trashed hotel rooms, infighting, rip-offs, sex, drugs and some of the most remarkable rock 'n' roll, including land mark albums like the first rock opera, SF Sorrow, and Rolling Stone's album of the year, 1970's *Parachute*.

"They invented everything, and were credited with nothing." Arthur Brown, "God of Hellfire"

The Sensational Alex Harvey
By John Neil Murno   £20
Part rock band, part vaudeville, 100% commitment, the SAHB were one of the greatest live bands of the era. But behind his showman exterior, Harvey was increasingly beset by alcoholism and tragedy. He succumbed to a heart attack on the way home from a gig in 1982, but he is fondly remembered as a unique entertainer by friends, musicians and legions of fans.

U2: The Complete Encyclopedia by Mark Chatterton   £14.99

Poison Heart: Surviving The Ramones by Dee Dee Ramone and Veronica Kofman   £9.99

Minstrels In The Gallery: A History Of Jethro Tull by David Rees   £12.99

DANCEMUSICSEXROMANCE: Prince – The First Decade by Per Nilsen   £12.99

To Hell and Back with Catatonia by Brian Wright   £12.99

Soul Sacrifice: The Santana Story by Simon Leng UK Price   £12.99

Opening The Musical Box: A Genesis Chronicle by Alan Hewitt
UK Price £12.99

Blowin' Free: Thirty Years Of Wishbone Ash by Gary Carter and Mark
Chatterton UK Price £12.99

www.helterskelterbooks.com

All Helter Skelter, Firefly and SAF titles are available by mail order from www.helterskelterbooks.com.

Email: info@helterskelterbooks.com